METAPHORS OF MIND
IN FICTION AND PSYCHOLOGY

Winner of the 1986
Midwest Modern Language Association
Book Award

METAPHORS OF MIND

IN FICTION AND PSYCHOLOGY

Michael S. Kearns

THE UNIVERSITY PRESS OF KENTUCKY

Scholarly publisher for the Commonwealth, serving Bellarmine College, Berea College, Centre College of Kentucky, Eastern Kentucky University, The Filson Club, Georgetown College, Kentucky Historical Society, Kentucky State University, Morehead State University, Murray State University, Northern Kentucky University, Transylvania University, University of Kentucky, University of Louisville, and Western Kentucky University.

Editorial and Sales Offices: Lexington, Kentucky 40506–0024

Library of Congress Cataloging-in-Publication Data

Kearns, Michael S., 1947–
Metaphors of mind in fiction and psychology.

Bibliography: p.
Includes index.
1. English fiction—19th century—History and criticism. 2. Psychology and literature. 3. Mind and body in literature. 4. Mind and body. I. Title.
PR868.P75K44 1987 820'.9'343 87-10620
ISBN 0-8131-1625-2

Portions of the following chapters have been published in earlier forms: chapter 2 in *Metaphor and Symbolic Activity* 2 (1987), by permission of Lawrence Erlbaum Associates, Inc.; chapter 4 in *The Victorian Newsletter* no. 67 (Spring 1985), by permission of the *Newsletter*; and chapter 5 in *Dickens Studies Annual: Essays on Victorian Fiction* 15 (1986), by permission of AMS Press, Inc., New York.

CONTENTS

ACKNOWLEDGMENTS

Metaphors of Mind has been seven years in the making. More people than I can now remember have contributed to my understanding of this chapter in the history of ideas and the representation of ideas. To those many individuals, I want to say that although you are not acknowledged here by name, you know who you are and you know that your support was invaluable.

It's a bit easier to identify the various institutions without whose help the project would still consist of a file cabinet of notes and a large box of index cards. The National Endowment for the Humanities funded a summer seminar on Charles Dickens, during which I was able to refine my conception of the relationship between Dickens and the psychology of his time. A year spent at the Johannes Gutenberg University, in Mainz, West Germany, as a Fulbright professor, gave me time to write the first several drafts of *Metaphors of Mind.* I have not only Gutenberg University and the Fulbright Commission to thank, but also the students in my advanced Melville seminar, whose critical attention to my assertions about how we can use historical psychology to better understand the spirit of an era forced me to be much more careful about such assertions.

Closer to home, I am grateful to Ohio Wesleyan University, whose generous sabbatical policy allowed me a semester to do the essential final revisions of *Metaphors of Mind.*

Finally, I want to extend a special word of thanks to the Midwest Modern Language Association and the University Press of Kentucky for instituting and underwriting the competition into which I entered my manuscript. The Association and the Press are serving scholarship in a very important way with this competition.

Although I cannot thank all individuals, I must mention two. The task of copyediting my manuscript fell to Murdoch Matthew, who did an outstanding job of simplifying my sometimes knotty syntax. He seemed to enter fully into the spirit of the argument I was advancing, to such an extent that his suggested revisions occasionally clarified points of that argument for me. To my wife, Ulrike Kalt, fell the task of helping me talk through my confusions about the material I was struggling with, and of helping me preserve some mental stability while I was trying to keep psychologists from Hobbes to William James, novelists from Defoe to Henry James, balanced in my mind. (The metaphor is intended.) Thank you. Thank you all.

METAPHORS OF MIND
IN FICTION AND PSYCHOLOGY

I
THE PROBLEM OF METAPHORS OF MIND

Early in the nineteenth century, Samuel Coleridge compiled an entertaining list of the dominant metaphors of mind used by psychological philosophers of the eighteenth century. Coleridge starts by applauding Aristotle's position on the association principle, a position he praises as entirely "unmixed with fiction" in contrast to those descriptions offered by later writers. According to Coleridge, Aristotle spoke of "no successive particles propagating motion like billiard balls (as Hobbes;) nor of nervous or animal spirits, where inanimate and irrational solids are thawed down, and distilled, or filtrated by ascension, into living and intelligent fluids, that etch and re-etch engravings on the brain, (as the followers of Des Cartes, and the humoral pathologists in general;) nor of an oscillating ether which was to effect the same service for the nerves of the brain considered as solid fibers, as the animal spirits performed for them under the notion of hollow tubes (as Hartley teaches)—nor finally, (with yet more recent dreamers) of chemical compositions by elective affinity, or of an electric light at once the immediate object and the ultimate organ of inward vision, which rises to the brain like an Aurora Borealis, and there disporting in various shapes (as the balance of plus and minus, or negative and positive, is destroyed or re-established) images out both past and present" (101). Coleridge praises Aristotle for delivering "a just *theory* without pretending to an *hypothesis*" and for excluding "place and motion from all the operations of thought, whether representations or volitions, as attributes utterly and absurdly heterogeneous" (101-2). The hypotheses of particles, spirits, ether, and so forth simply interfere with a clear presentation of the principle of association.

Coleridge, his editors note, was wrong about the metaphors used by Hobbes and Hartley (Coleridge 101 nn 2, 3). Nevertheless, the general problem of metaphorical speech applied to the human mind was significant and of long standing. Most of the psychological philosophers of the eighteenth and early nineteenth centuries addressed the problem explicitly. Most urged exactly what Coleridge praises Aristotle for: excluding "place and motion" from the list of terms appropriate for describing the human mind. Most held that the philosophy of mind should deal purely with the phenomena of the mind, unadorned by metaphorical language. Especially to be avoided was metaphorical language derived from the workings of the human body or from Newtonian physics.

The curious fact, and the starting point of my investigation, is that despite this wide agreement, these philosophers—as well as novelists, physiologists, authors of school texts on mental science—all persisted in using such metaphors as Coleridge describes. How these metaphors were used and revised, and why, is a topic that scholars have dealt with only superficially, although they have used the phrase "metaphor of mind" frequently. There has been no extensive survey across several genres and several centuries to explore the function, development, and adequacy of the metaphors. In offering that survey I am well aware that the territory is terribly broad for one book, that my historical scope is limited, and that treating only English-language works reduces the opportunities for illuminating comparisons. Nevertheless, the period and works I discuss allow me to demonstrate one significant change in metaphors of mind and how they were used. The metaphor "mind-as-entity," which was shared by all writers on the mind, gave way to the metaphor "sentience-as-life," which was advocated by psychologists after the middle of the nineteenth century, was implemented by the novelists at the same time, and finally began to be integrated into the language of psychological texts at the end of the century. My survey is thus a study of the search for a language of the mind in the midst of changing concepts of the mind.

This discrepancy between the resolve to avoid metaphors and the reliance on them in practice manifests itself in the writings of Thomas Reid, an early and vigorous proponent of the psychological language praised by Coleridge. In his first major book, *An Inquiry into the Human Mind* (1764), Reid praises Descartes for applying the method of reflection to the operations of the mind and for attempting to maintain the language of the mind when talking about the mind. Reid feels that this is a significant advance over what he terms the "medieval" method of drawing analogies from sources other than the mind (259-60). Nevertheless, there was a problem in Descartes's method: he believed that although other faculties of his mind might deceive him, "his consciousness could not," and this belief tended to "spiritualize the body, and its qualities." The Cartesian does not take the existence of the body as a first principle but holds that the body and things external to the body can only be known through sensations (260-61). Descartes's new method of reflection led to such extreme positions as that of Berkeley, who held that not only the secondary qualities of matter but also the primary qualities (for example extension and form) were "mere sensations of the mind." In Reid's view, the result of "reasoning upon the Cartesian principles" is that "matter was stripped of all its qualities; the new system, by a kind of metaphysical sublimation, converted all the qualities of matter into sensations, and spiritualized body, as the old had materialized spirit" (261).

Reid proposes a middle way between the two extremes: "to take our notions of the qualities of body, from the testimony of our senses . . . and our notions of our sensations, from the testimony of consciousness" (261). This proposal, especially the point that we take "our notions of our sensations, from the testimony of consciousness," persists as a theme throughout the period I am considering; every psychological philosopher and every psychologist believed that such testimony exists and that it is trustworthy. Owen J. Flanagan calls this proposal the "*Thesis of the Autonomy of Psychological Explanation (Autonomy Thesis,* for short), the thesis that the science of the mind should proceed to frame its laws and principles in terms of its own specialized vocabulary without trying to force translations into the vocabulary of any already existing natural science" (60). Flanagan's term is a useful label for this major tenet of eighteenth-and nineteenth-century psychology and psychological philosophy.

The autonomy thesis in its early form may be regarded as the first attempt to specify a unique subject matter and methodology for the study of the mind. It was a forerunner of the attempt by nineteenth-century psychologists to establish psychology as a unique and scientific discipline. The metaphorical language used to talk about the mind was regarded as necessarily primitive; it had originated early in the linguistic history of humankind and had not developed. Reid could refer to a number of credible expressions of this belief. Locke, for example, traced the language of these "ideas that come not under the cognizance of our senses" to the same source as all other words which stand for intangibles:

> I doubt not, but if we could trace [these ideas] to their sources, we should find in all languages, the names, which stand for Things that fall not under our Senses, to have had their first rise from sensible *Ideas*. . . . to give Names, that might make known to others any Operations they felt in themselves, or any other *Ideas*, that came not under their Senses, ["the first Beginners of Language"] were fain to borrow Words from ordinary known *ideas* of Sensation, by that means to make others the more easily to conceive those Operations they experimented [sic] in themselves, which made no outward sensible appearances . . . [403]

Locke went on to remind his readers that there exist "no Ideas at all, but what originally come either from sensible Objects without, or *what we feel within ourselves, from the inward Workings of our own Spirits, which we are conscious to our selves of within*" (404, emphasis added). Although the words used to describe "the originals and principles" of human knowledge have been suggested by nature, the concepts themselves come from within.

This historical account was congenial to Locke's sensationalist epistemology, but Reid finds it lacking. Insofar as nature is a good teacher, the analogy between tangible things and intangible concepts should pose no problems. But as he states, nature contributes more to the formation of the mind than to formation of knowledge about the mind. "*The way of reflection*," which Reid calls the "only way that leads to truth," is exceedingly difficult to carry out because we usually attend to external objects (*Inquiry* 252). Since few people are capable of or practiced in "attentive reflection" on mental operations, "the way of analogy" becomes an easy but inadequate substitute (254). Reflection is difficult, and thinking in terms of externals comes naturally; thus it is not surprising that the mind has usually been conceived of as "some subtile matter" and that the "objects of thought are said to be *in the mind*, to be *apprehended*, *comprehended*, *conceived*, *imagined*, *retained*, *weighed*, *ruminated*" (255).

The main problem, Reid insists, is not using metaphorical or analogical language but elevating the analogical method above the method of reflection. Metaphors cannot be avoided. In his *Essays on the Intellectual Powers of Man*, first published in 1785, Reid notes once again that it is strictly impossible to "explain by a logical definition" the powers and operations of the mind (4); the sole arbiter must therefore be the way words are used, since usage will reflect the common-sense understanding of our intellectual powers and will also reflect what nature has taught us concerning these powers. Because of common sense we "attribute to one internal principle" all activities such as seeing, deliberating, loving (5). It is equally a matter of common sense to distinguish between "things in the mind, and things external." But here usage must be carefully controlled. Reid points out that the distinction "is not meant to signify the place of the things we speak of, but their subject" (8). Perhaps the most important factor in our understanding of our minds, as reflected in language, is the analogy between sentence structure and mental structure: "the operations of the mind, which are expressed by active verbs, the mind itself, which is the nominative to those verbs, and the object" which the verbs govern (14). This structure is common to all languages, Reid believes, hence it must be regarded as very likely having a "foundation in nature" (14). Reid's juxtaposition of the study of language and the study of mind is typical of his era, and the analogy can be found back into the seventeenth century (Aarsleff, Cohen). But Reid warns that even such an obvious and compelling analogy as that between mind and language should not be accepted uncritically but should be tested. For instance, we tend to assume that when we think of something our minds contain an image of it, an image that either is being or has earlier been *impressed*; we do this because in every moment of our waking lives our experience is that bodies affect one another "only by contact and pressure" (51). Reflection, however, will show us the absurdity of this assumption. We simply cannot find such physical images in our minds. Reid ends his discussion of analogy with a caution: we must be careful not to "be imposed upon by those analogical terms and phrases, by which the operations of the mind are expressed in all languages," especially those "drawn from some supposed similitude of body to mind" (52). Or, more succinctly, our explanations of mental phenomena must preserve the autonomy thesis.

Nevertheless, in spite of these cautions, in spite of his decades-long elaboration of the problems that can result from analogies of mind based on physics or biology, Reid frequently resorts to just such terms and phrases. His solution to the Cartesian split, for example, runs directly counter to the autonomy thesis. Reid claims that "the testimony of common sense" leads him to believe that his "mind is a substance, that is, a permanent subject of thought," and his reason holds that this substance is "unextended and indivisible" and hence cannot contain anything resembling extension (*Inquiry* 270). Why would a philosopher so concerned with accurate language take the curious step of defining mind as "substance" and then denying that term the qualities associated with it by ordinary usage—extension and divisibility? One reason is that Reid's goal here is to refute the Berkeleian position as he understands it, that the qualities of matter are inaccessible to mind. Reid postulates an unextended and indivisible mental substance to explain how we can think about physical entities, without having tangible images of them in the mind, just as well as we can think about spirits (271). A mental substance as Reid describes it can contain *intangible* images of physical bodies. As I will show in Chapter 3, the implicit assumption here, that a mind must contain some representation of external reality, is a subtle but important result of the influence of the mind-as-entity metaphor.

The attractiveness, in fact the inescapability, of the mind-as-entity metaphor is especially visible in Reid's discussion of mental processes, for example from *Essays on the Intellectual Powers of Man*, essay 4, chapter 4, "Of the Train of Thought in the Mind." He begins, "Every man is conscious of a succession of thoughts which pass in his mind while he is awake, even when they are not excited by external objects"; this succession is a function of "the constitution of the mind itself," which generates "a constant ebullition of thought, a constant intestine motion" (436). The succession, Reid notes, has been called many things but is most often called "the *train of ideas*," of which there are two types: those that "flow spontaneously, like water from a fountain," and those that "are regulated and directed by an active effort of the mind, with some view and intention" (437). The language here is perfectly in keeping with the assumed relationship between mind, thought, and external world: the mind has both active and passive modes, and in the active mode it can either direct the flow of thoughts, the train of ideas, or let them "flow spontaneously." Although the autonomy thesis calls into question the common usage "train of ideas," Reid uncritically adopts it as a full and accurate description of what is to be found in the mind.

When Reid describes some of these trains in detail, the language of the mind-as-entity metaphor becomes even more prevalent and questionable. He suggests for instance that the mind is divided into two separate areas, the heart and the imagination: "Whatever possesses the heart makes occasional excursions into the imagination, and acts such scenes upon that theatre as are agreeable to the prevailing passion" (443). He suggests that both the mind and its thoughts are tangible, as in his description of the progress of a child's mind: "As children grow up, they are delighted with tales. . . . every thing of this kind stores the fancy with a new regular train of thought, which becomes familiar by repetition, so that one part draws the whole after it in the imagination. [The child's exercise of invention] gives rise to innumerable new associations, and regular trains of thought, which make the deeper impression upon the mind, as they are its exclusive property" (447-48). Just like a piece of clay, the child's mind can take impressions; thoughts are the *impressing* agents. The same is true of the adult's mind. When a mature adult is speaking extemporaneously and fluently, Reid says, the thoughts must be running "in a beaten track. There is a mould in his mind . . . [and] his discourse falls into this mould with ease, and takes its form from it" (452).

The figurative language of these passages directly contradicts the autonomy thesis and seems also to contradict Reid's description of the mind as an unextended and indivisible substance. The language presents the mind as an *extended* substance, capable of being filled (that is, having dimensions) and as divisible into segments, areas, or compartments. Although Reid's caution about the problem of "analogical terms and phrases" is several hundred pages earlier in the book, readers might reasonably expect him to abide by it here. At the very least we might expect Reid to use similes rather than metaphors to illustrate mental processes, so as not to imply that the mind really is an extended, divisible substance. We must suspect that for Reid the metaphor represents and constitutes the actuality, that mind can literally be described as having tracks or moulds. Reid's stated position, as elucidated by Peter Heath, is close to our modern position: "that the mind has dispositions and capacities, which extend, among other things, to the learning, use and manipulation of general words, and that our possession of general conceptions consists, therefore, simply in the exercise of these capacities, not in the discovery, acquisition, and storage of mental or transcendental furniture" (228). But his metaphorical statements indicate that Reid's own habits of thought about mental processes assume a material mind.

The contradiction between Reid's formulation of the structure of the mind as an *indivisible* and *unextended substance*, on the one hand, and his unselfconscious use of figurative language connoting a divisible and extended mind, on the other, is typical of the English empirical tradition during the eighteenth and nineteenth centuries.

A century before Reid, Thomas Hobbes in his *Leviathan* described the main use of speech as "to transferre our Mentall Discourse, into Verbal; or the Trayne of our Thoughts, into a Trayne of words." Yet in the same passage his metaphor "Trayne of our Thoughts," Hobbes observes that a common abuse of language is to use "words metaphorically: that is, in other senses than that they are ordained for; and thereby deceive others" (101-2). He goes on to say that such metaphorical speech, like any other use of language which departs from the actual "ordained" nature of things, "can never be true grounds for any ratiocination" (109-10). Clearly, for Hobbes as for Reid, "trains of thought" are important components of the human mind, autonomy thesis or no. In fact Hobbes is the source of a definitive illustration of the use of "trains of thought" to analyze apparently random mental leaps. He writes that in a particular conversation, one man's sudden question of the value of a Roman denarius puzzled him until he realized that "the original subject of discourse naturally introduced the history of the king, and of the treachery of those who surrendered his person to his enemies; this again introduced the treachery of Judas Iscariot, and the sum of money which he received for his reward," hence the question of the value of that reward. (This illustration is related by Dugald Stewart, *Elements* 2:121, and quoted as late as 1890 by William James, *Principles* 540.)

Half a century after Reid, Thomas Brown declared that the language of the mind was inadequate because the prevalent physicalistic metaphors drew attention not to mental phenomena, as would be proper, but to mental faculties. In his *Sketch of a System of the Philosophy of the Human Mind* (1820), Brown proposes to look directly at "the simple sequences of the Phenomena of the Mind, the relations of which to each other or to certain bodily changes, are all which those words, can be justly employed to denote" (x). He suggests that all mental phenomena be regarded "simply as *states of the mind*," which is the most reasonable approach because "from the beginning of life to its close the mind has existed, and is known to us only as thus existing, in various states of changeful feeling" (xi).

Thus, he insists, "it is in our power to philosophize on these changes of mental state, as we philosophize on any of the changeful phenomena of the material world which they indirectly indicate to us" (xii). Applying the autonomy thesis in this way—looking strictly at states of mind—will result in the science Brown calls "mental physiology"; this is where analogy enters his system. He begins the first chapter of his *Sketch* by asserting, "There is a PHYSIOLOGY OF THE MIND, then as there is a *physiology of the body*,—a science, which examines the phenomena of our spiritual part simply as phenomena, and, from the order of their succession, or other circumstances of analogy, arranges them in classes under certain general names" (2). In Brown's opinion, the mind can be studied with the same methods used in the study of the phenomena of the material world, especially close observation and classification, guided by that fundamental concept "change of state." As Brown points out, the "mental physiologist" is to be guided by what he calls "circumstances of analogy." In thus describing his program, Brown rigorously preserves a mentalistic view. But like Reid and Hobbes, he uses language that implies the mind to be a relatively passive and simply structured entity, and he allows the "circumstances of analogy" to be determined by the physicalistic view.

The resulting violation of the autonomy thesis can be seen in lecture 10, "On the Laws of Physical Inquiry in Relation to the Study of Mind," in his *Lectures on the Philosophy of the Human Mind* (1820). Brown insists that the method of analysis—breaking down a complex phenomenon into parts—is the only way to make discoveries in the science of the mind (100). The subject of this analysis is not parts of "affections," since the mind's affections "must be always *simple* and *indivisible*," but the various states of mind that have led up to the affections being analyzed. For Brown, this kind of inquiry is a fundamental human activity: it is the "very nature" of the inquiring mind to "decompose" affections that seem to result from combinations of previous states (101). For the mental scientist, analysis "is founded wholly on the feeling of relation which one state of mind seems to us to bear to other states of mind, as comprehensive of them; but while this seeming complexity is felt, it is the same thing to our analysis, as if the complexity, instead of being virtual and relative only, were absolute and real" (102).

Brown goes on to point out that there can be no terms to describe these processes other than those derived from the material world; we feel as if our mental affections "could be actually divided into the separate elements which appear to us thus virtually or relatively to be comprehended in them" even though we know at the same time they are indivisible, simple states of the mental entity (102). It is in this sense that Brown speaks of a "*chemistry* of the *mind*." Like a chemical compound, a mental affection may seem to have radically different properties from each of its constituents, and it can be traced to these constituents only through careful reflection (103).

By explaining his program so clearly in language that is explicitly physicalistic, Brown at first appears to meet the metaphorical problem squarely. He does not ask us, as does Reid, to strip a common term of its connotations—to conceive of mind as an insubstantial substance. Rather, he would have us adopt the method of physiology or chemistry while keeping always aware that the complexity of the phenomenon being investigated is only "virtual and relative." The problem with this kind of approach, as Robert Cummins points out in his study of psychological explanation, is that it can at best be termed *morphological* analysis (126): the approach is self-consistent but has little connection with actual mental events. Brown's approach depends on the concept "mental state," but as Coleridge tellingly observes, "What is a thought? What are its circumscriptions, what the interspaces between it and another? When does it begin? Where end?" Coleridge continues, "How opposite to nature and the fact to talk of the 'one moment' of Hume, of our whole being an aggregate of successive single sensations! Who ever felt a single sensation? . . . And what is a moment? Succession with interspace? Absurdity! It is evidently only the *licht-punct* in the indivisible undivided duration" (in Richards, *Coleridge* 68). Coleridge's point is clear. *If* the mind were an entity of the kind implied by the figurative language of these psychological philosophers, mental physiology could make methodological sense. But they insist it is not such an entity.

The twentieth-century reader may wonder why these writers create the problem for themselves of using physicalistic metaphors while condemning such use. One explanation has to do with the role played by the mind-as-entity metaphor, as I will explain in Chapters 2 and 3. A second explanation is that the study of mind especially before the middle of the nineteenth century was an intensely moral endeavor, its primary goal being to understand human nature in order to further moral behavior. If Reid or Brown had been forced to choose between defending the study of mind as a science (or a proto-science) and defending it as a moral discipline, he would have chosen the latter. While the physicalistic approach serves the scientific cause, an anti-metaphor stance serves the moral cause. These philosophers believed that using metaphors can actually lead to amorality. In treating the mind as functioning in the same way physical entities function, the moral scientist is separated from reality: he believes he is dealing with realities when he is actually dealing only with abstract ideas to which he has given names.

This methodological error can have a moral as well as a theoretical result. As Berkeley points out in his *Treatise Concerning the Principles of Human Knowledge* (1710), to think of the mind as a "ball in motion" and of the will as "the *motion* of the soul" leads to the erroneous moral position of viewing mind as having to go where it is struck (236). Such a position denies free will. In keeping with his desire to defend the mind's freedom, Berkeley uses language in which the human mind is active in perception and reflection. The mind can "consider," "observe," "single out," "make" and "frame" ideas: "This perceiving, active being is what I call *mind*, *spirit*, *soul*, or *myself*. By which words I do not denote any one of my ideas, but a thing entirely distinct from them, *wherein they exist*, or, which is the same thing, whereby they are perceived; for the existence of an idea consists in being perceived" (178). Yet Berkeley's moral program does not preserve him from elsewhere figuring forth the mind as a passive entity. He accepts the common view that the senses are *imprinted* with sensations, which then exist "*in* a mind perceiving them" (179). Berkeley denies the existence of matter as defined by philosophers (that which has extension and substance and exists independently of our perception of it), but the language he uses when discussing the human mind connotes just these qualities—substance (because the mind can be imprinted) and extension (because ideas exist within it).

This is not to say that the mind-as-entity concept implied by Berkeley's language represents a problem for him. Quite the contrary: his is a universe which contains only minds, the minds of human beings and then the mind of the supreme being who has established a set of laws or procedures by which the ideas of external nature are imprinted on human minds. Those ideas imprinted by Him are "real things or ideas," and all others are "chimeras" (189-90). Extension and substance can exist nowhere but in the human mind or in the mind of God; in fact one of the essential differences between the human and the divine conditions is that "the supreme spirit, which excites those ideas in our minds, is not marked out and limited to our view *by any particular collection of sensible ideas*, as human agents are by their size, complexion, limbs, and motions" (199).

As Daniel Robinson points out, Berkeley is not properly labeled a "subjective idealist." His system has a specific "court of last recourse," the "Spirit wherein all reality" resides. It is a coherent, self-consistent system which places all philosophical problems, especially epistemology, within a psychological context (Robinson, *Intellectual History* 219-21). Berkeley does believe that a certain kind of knowledge is available to human beings: knowledge of one's mental operations. The thoughtful person can defend himself from "*being imposed on by words*" by seeking "to obtain a clear view of the ideas he would consider," ideas which can be regarded in a "naked, undisguised" state (176-77). In the words of another eminent historian of psychology, Berkeley is as much of an empiricist as Locke: "In the empiricism of Berkeley, mind generates matter. We must substitute for a theory of knowledge about objects a psychological description of objects; and it is plain that these objective ideas are formed through experience" (Boring 184). Even with mind generating matter, the mind-as-entity metaphor remains the predominant element in Berkeley's language. Human minds are the only *things* in the world, the only entities of which we have first-hand knowledge; these *things*, as that term is commonly understood, have the only extension and substance we can know anything about.

I show in later chapters that even the empiricists who most strenuously attempt to be objective, such as Brown and, later, the physiological psychologists Carpenter and Bain, share this stance with Berkeley. All of these writers agree that although we dispute the boundary or interconnection between the mind and the material world, and although we can scarcely obtain unambiguous knowledge about existence outside the mind, we can in principle view the mind dispassionately with some hope of understanding it. This agreement extends beyond the theoretical statements to the figurative language. The metaphor mind-as-entity is equally common in those writers traditionally labeled *idealists* and those labeled *empiricists*.

According to one of the most often read and recommended "mental scientists" of the first half of the nineteenth century, Dugald Stewart, understanding the mind depends on directly confronting the problem of metaphorical language applied to the mind. The system of analogical language used to talk about mind is complicated because the actual "communication between Mind and Matter" is incomprehensible (*Elements* 2: 91). Hypotheses of perception themselves, according to Stewart, have been characterized by a contradiction: casting the hypotheses and phenomena in "general maxims of philosophizing, borrowed from physics" while asserting the idea of the soul's immateriality: "To the former of these circumstances is to be ascribed the general principle upon which all the known theories of perception proceed; that, in order to explain the intercourse between the mind and distant objects, it is necessary to suppose the existence of something intermediate, by which its perceptions are produced; to the latter, the various metaphorical expressions of *ideas*, *species*, *forms*, *shadows*, *phantasms*, *images*, which, while they amused the fancy with some remote analogies to the objects of our senses, did not directly revolt our reason, by presenting to us any of the tangible qualities of body" (2:93).

Analogical language cannot be avoided in such a situation. What the mental scientist can do, Stewart says, is to vary his metaphors and thus "accustom himself to view the phenomena of thought in that naked and undisguised state in which they unveil themselves to the powers of consciousness and reflection" (3:315-16). The suggestion that one should consciously manipulate one's metaphors shows an unusual sensitivity to the role played by metaphor in forming concepts; the variation can function as a powerful exploratory heuristic. But the claim that the variation allows one to view one's mental phenomena in their "naked and undisguised state" appears naive. Does Stewart really mean that metaphorical language can be transcended even when it cannot be discarded? Probably he does; his language implies that elements of thought, including metaphors, are limited and discrete and hence can be objectively scrutinized by the mind's eye. Stewart's solution draws directly on the mind-as-entity metaphor.

The problem then in Reid, Berkeley, Locke, Brown, and Stewart is that they intrude the metaphor of mind-as-entity even into warnings about such language. The problem extends beyond these eighteenth-and early nineteenth-century philosophers, and beyond mind-as-entity as well. In general, the problem results from a tension between the drive to develop a non-metaphorical language of the mind and the intrinsically metaphorical nature of all such language. Such a problem is clearly insoluble, and once identified it does not require much additional explication. The autonomy thesis may be unrealizable in practice. The more interesting phenomenon, the one I focus on for most of this book, is the emergence of new metaphors as other kinds of mental experience came under scrutiny and became more important.

Literary historians have long agreed that throughout the eighteenth and nineteenth centuries interest in character increased and that psychological validity became more important, as for example in the Gothic writers. (See Hart.) Nineteenth-century novelists were more concerned than their predecessors with "verisimilitude of feeling" and less with "verisimilitude of action" (Gose 17); they wished to depict how the external world "impinged with its specific gravity, its full concreteness, on consciousness" (Alter 87). These phenomena have been fully studied, albeit more impressionistically than empirically. The fictional exploration of personality and identity has been the subject of perceptive studies (as for example those of Chase and Langbaum). The use of the language of the new experimental sciences and of association psychology by individual literary figures has also been treated at book length. (See for example Wimsatt's admirable study of Samuel Johnson, *Philosophic Words*, and Caldwell's of Keats.) Coleridge as a representative Romantic has been the object of a case study of the metaphorical uses of "inner senses" (Lyon). This list could be multiplied tenfold. Nevertheless, some essential work remains to be done. Literary historians (and for that matter historians of psychology) have yet to analyze how the actual language used to talk about mind changed during these two centuries and how the changes correlate with changes in the concept of mind. This is the gap I am working to fill.

One of my findings is that the language did not develop at the same rate in fiction and in psychology; new metaphors are quite visible in novels by the middle of the nineteenth century but do not emerge in psychological works until later. A further important conclusion is that while the concept of mind may seem to have changed dramatically, the new metaphors still relied on comparisons with aspects of the physical world. They more adequately answered Reid's call for a mentalistic language of the mind but did not—in fact, could not—entirely replace the physicalistic approach.

In the following chapters I describe my conclusions. Chapter 2 explains how I use current theories of metaphor and defines several terms that are useful in analyzing the various relationships between metaphors and the concepts that the metaphors are intended to represent. I show that metaphors of mind are of particular interest precisely because it is impossible to arrive at a language of the mind of the sort desired by Reid and Brown. I go on to illustrate the prevalence of mind-as-entity during the eighteenth and into the nineteenth centuries (Chapter 3), the continuing use by nineteenth-century psychology of the mind-as-entity metaphor despite theoretical developments that should have made the metaphor less tenable (Chapter 4), the attempts of Charles Dickens and Charlotte Brontë to extend the mind-as-entity metaphor (Chapter 5), and the specific techniques developed by Henry James and George Eliot to represent mental experiences that had not been of great interest earlier (Chapter 6). I conclude with a brief comparison of the metaphorical language of William James' *Principles of Psychology* (1890) with the metaphors from these earlier writers. I show that the later psychologists and novelists wanted to represent the life of the mind in functional interaction with the surrounding web of impressions and relationships, that this desire departed significantly from the practice of the novelists and psychologists whose primary concept was of the mind as an entity, and that the later novelists were more successful than the psychologists in implementing the newer goal.

Let me say a word about my own position with respect to metaphors and mind. Writing this book has led me to three fundamental points. First, as I. A. Richards pointed out half a century ago, "we cannot get through three sentences of ordinary fluid discourse" without metaphor (*Philosophy of Rhetoric* 92). I agree. I have tried to keep my own metaphors to a minimum, but where striving for relatively non-metaphorical expressions would have involved me in impossible linguistic contortions, I have used metaphors without apology. Second, I have remained as skeptical as possible about the actual existence of such a thing as "the mind." Whenever I use "the mind," "a thought," and similar locutions, I do not mean to imply that I believe there really are existents attached to the words. This skepticism goes hand in hand with my contention in Chapter 2 that no literal representation of the human mind *as experienced* is possible. I say skepticism;

I do not mean to go as far as Gilbert Ryle (and others who follow his lead) and hold that the "official doctrine" of two separate substances, Mind and Body, enshrines a glaringly obvious "category mistake." Since "a person's thinking, feeling, and purposive doing cannot be described solely in the idioms of physics, chemistry and physiology, therefore they must be described in counterpart idioms," the result being, according to Ryle, a theory of a (mental) "ghost in the (bodily) machine" (18). Ryle's position is theoretically solid but of limited practical use, because we nevertheless continue to behave, verbally, as if most representations of mental activity are literally true. This third point I also deal with in Chapter 2.

There is a term that I must mention because it is not appropriate to my work. I fear that most people, when they see the words "literature" and "psychology" together in a title, will think of "literary psychology." I ask them not to. Leon Edel defines this term in his collection *Stuff of Sleep and Dreams*. For Edel, literary psychology relies on the basic postulates of psychoanalysis: that an unconscious exists, that it contains "certain suppressed feelings and states of being," and that the literary psychologist can detect these feelings and states, as they influence "deeper intentions and meanings" in the work, by studying the author's choices (33). I avoid the large body of literary-psychological analysis for two reasons. First, my skepticism about the existence of "the mind" extends to such constructs as "the unconscious." Second, pre-Freudian psychology will never be well understood in either its theoretical manifestations (psychology texts) or its literary manifestations until it is approached without Freudian conceptual and terminological baggage. Indeed, the common term "the unconscious" has a totally different meaning for major psychologists of the nineteenth century like Bain and Lewes.

If a descriptive term were needed, Hugh Richmond's "historical psychology" would be more appropriate. I have aimed at a "comprehensive humanistic study" whose goal is to illustrate the "inevitable interaction between art and society"; I study the "evolution of human sensibility and mental processes in ways also analogous to and largely including such more selective disciplines as the History of Science, or even the History of Ideas" (209). But a label such as "historical psychology" is not necessary for my study, and I have tried to keep terminology to a minimum and give as much space as possible to discussing metaphorical passages. The terms I use to describe how metaphors function are defined as they occur, mostly in Chapter 2.

Two more terms deserve comment here: "metaphor" and "psychology." The best definition of "metaphor" I know is from Janet Soskice, whose *Metaphor and Religious Language* has helped me clarify my own goals, methods, and scope; we both deal with metaphorical representations of that which most people agree cannot be expressed literally. Soskice defines metaphor as "that figure of speech whereby we speak about one thing in terms which are seen to be suggestive of another" (15); this definition leads to the conclusion that "the minimal unit in which a metaphor is established is semantic rather than syntactic" (23). When I use "metaphor" I mean it in this sense; occasionally I further specify, for example "theory-constitutive metaphor" and "generative metaphor" (both defined in Chapter 2). I also use Richards' terms "tenor," "vehicle," and "ground," with the meanings he gave them: "tenor" is "the underlying idea or principle subject which the vehicle or figure means," and "ground" comprises "the common characteristics" shared by the tenor and the vehicle (*Philosophy* 96, 117). Theorists of metaphor have serious doubts about these terms, especially the word "means" in the definition of "tenor," but the terms remain useful if we keep in mind Richards' own qualifications. He pointed out that we often cannot specify the "ground" of a metaphor and that "the relative positions of tenor and vehicle" may shift back and forth in an extended metaphor (117, 121); not all of his critics give him credit for this and other subtleties.

Although in this opening chapter I have used the term "psychological philosopher," I will now drop this awkward locution and simply use "psychologist" and "psychology." The eighteenth and nineteenth centuries had a variety of terms for the study of the human mind and behavior: "moral philosophy," "mental philosophy," "mental science," and of course Brown's "mental physiology," to name a few. All of these dealt with the same subject matter, shared many of the same illustrative examples, referred to the same predecessors, criticized the same errors. The books with these terms in their titles served the same purposes as our century's "Freudianism," "behavioral psychology," and the like; they constituted the psychology of the time. William Carpenter is generally known as a nineteenth-century physiologist, David Hume as an eighteenth-century philosopher. But when either was writing about knowledge, behavior, perception, or beliefs, he was writing *psychology*. As with these two, so with the rest of the non-fiction writers I discuss: in the context of a study of metaphors of the mind, they are properly referred to as *psychologists*.

II
METAPHOR THEORY AND METAPHORS OF MIND

Metaphor theory has been a scene of extensive activity in the past two decades. Today we can say that the field not only has been discovered but finally is being properly explored; in Wayne Booth's apt metaphor, "students of metaphor have positively pullulated" (49). After centuries of neglect, regarded at best as ornamental to the main business of conveying information about tangible realities, metaphor is now recognized as one of the most challenging aspects of language. In particular, "the problem of metaphor" comprises a number of questions. Max Black has listed the most central of them:

1. How do we recognize a case of metaphor?
2. Are there any criteria for the detection of metaphors?
3. Can metaphors be translated into literal expressions?
4. Is metaphor properly regarded as a decoration upon "plain sense"?
5. What are the relations between metaphor and simile?
6. In what sense, if any, is a metaphor "creative"?
7. What is the point of using a metaphor?

[*Models and Metaphors* 25]

The problem of "metaphors of mind" is fortunately not so complex because, except for facts about the structure and function of the nervous system and the sensory apparatus, nothing having to do with the mind can be described literally.

Paul Churchland contends that this state of affairs is not unchangeable, that "the genuine arrival of a materialist kinematics and dynamics for psychological states and cognitive processes will constitute . . . a dawning in which" our "inner life" is finally revealed in its intricacy, "even, if we apply ourselves, in self-conscious introspection" (160). At present, however, the physical foundation of mental events can barely be described and understood by neurophysiologists. All but Black's first, second, and final questions vanish, and these can be answered thus: we can never use anything but metaphor to talk about mind, and we automatically treat all descriptions of mental processes as metaphorical. In this chapter I consider the implications of these statements in light of recent trends in the theory of metaphor, showing, first, that the deviance theory of metaphor is not tenable, and second, that written descriptions of mental processes constitute a genre that calls up particular expectations in readers. I then briefly discuss several possible relationships between metaphors of mind, concepts of mind, and the formation of psychological theory, and outline the various roles played by the metaphor mind-as-entity during the eighteenth and nineteenth centuries.

The Contextual Approach in Current Metaphor Theory

In response to the first statement, it might seem more appropriate to say that the language of mind is literal, since this language consists almost solely of dead metaphors, which presumably have lost their metaphorical vitality. Usage has established that in an expression like "my thoughts were all in a whirl," thoughts can be caught in a vortex as easily as can dust particles in a whirlwind; a literal reading of the expression might therefore seem more reasonable than a metaphorical reading. This position receives some support from Donald Davidson. Discussing the dead metaphor "mouth of a bottle," he writes: "Once one has the present use of the word [mouth], with literal application to bottles, there is nothing left to notice. There is no similarity to seek ["between animal and bottle openings"] because it consists simply in being referred to by the same word" (37). That is, the one-time metaphorical expression has become literal by becoming established usage. Davidson's argument, however, does not take into account the longevity of dead metaphors. John Searle, in suitably metaphorical language, stresses this fact: "Dead metaphors have lived on. They have become dead through continued use, but their continual use is a clue that they satisfy some semantic need" (255). Given a "semantic need" to designate the place where a river empties into another body of water, it is possible to find relatively non-metaphorical expressions to do the job, for example "the place where a river empties into another body of water" rather than "river's mouth," another of Davidson's examples.

The problem arises in attempting to extend this argument to metaphors of the mind. There is no equivalently non-metaphorical or minimally metaphorical expression for "my thoughts were all in a whirl," and there would be a semantic gap if this expression were stricken from our language. Further, any such gap in our psychological language would be significant, because describing the mind and explaining its processes has been regarded as one of the most important human endeavors during the past several centuries. As shown by Michael Smith, Howard Pollio, and Marian Pitts, who surveyed works written in American English from 1675 to 1975, novel metaphors most frequently occurred in discussions of psychological processes (922-23). Further, "psychological processes" was the least often used metaphorical vehicle, indicating that, unlike the often used categories of "body" and "nature," this area of human experience was not well enough understood to use to explain other areas (928). Thus Smith, Pollio, and Pitts interpret their results as supporting Sperber's Law, that an era's dominant concerns are reflected in its metaphors, the concerns becoming, in Sperber's words, "centers of metaphoric attraction" (912-13).

Smith, Pollio, and Pitts look only at novel metaphors in well-known texts. Their conclusions apply equally well to putatively dead metaphors used in discourse about the mind. Such metaphors are actually not dead, as can be seen by trying to give an adequate literal paraphrase. For example, "My thoughts were in a whirl" is not simply another way of saying "I was confused."

The sentence expresses an extreme state of confusion characterized by a too-rapid procession of thoughts. Nor is it simply another way of saying "I was extremely confused; it was as if my thoughts were following one another too rapidly." An "as if" statement differs noticeably from an identity statement. Moreover, even this purported literal statement contains a metaphor, thoughts "following one another." We might then try a further refinement to replace that metaphor, perhaps "rapid succession of mental states." But what is a mental state, and who can say when one ends and another begins, a discrimination necessary if we really intend to talk about "states"?

The point is that each attempt at a literal paraphrase moves further from the subjective assertion embodied briefly and vividly in the original expression: "my thoughts were in a whirl." Thus even this seemingly dead, literal expression has to be regarded as a metaphor. It exhibits all of the characteristics we generally attribute to a metaphor, characteristics summarized by Andrew Ortony: "(1) the inexpressibility thesis—metaphors express what is literally inexpressible; (2) the compactness thesis—metaphors express complex relationships compactly; (3) the vividness thesis—metaphors are more vivid than their literal equivalents" ("Psychological Aspects" 77-78). Davidson may be generally correct about dead metaphors functioning as literal expressions. After all, it would be difficult to make a case for the metaphoricity of "the mouth of a river" like the one I have made for "thoughts in a whirl"; the expression is certainly compact, but it does not express what is literally inexpressible, and its vividness has been lost through centuries of use. This is all the more reason to regard the language of the mind, with its figurative expressions, as a special case in which even so-called dead metaphors are qualitatively different from dead metaphors in other areas of language use.

For the study of metaphors of mind, the most pertinent of Ortony's theses is inexpressibility. Most psychological treatises of the eighteenth and nineteenth centuries began with the point that mental phenomena had not been adequately described, and most then went on to express a version of the autonomy thesis, calling for a description of the mind in the language of the mind. Such a description, they felt, would be not only adequate but accurate—not figurative. Yet like Reid, Brown, and the others discussed in Chapter 1, sooner or later all fell into language either explicitly or (more usually) implicitly metaphorical. Mental phenomena were (and still are) literally inexpressible, nor is it possible to *literally* represent the *experiencing* of mental phenomena. There is no objective language that will allow two people to communicate about their inner lives with any certainty that each is evoking an exactly matching "train of ideas," emotion, or "mental state" in the other.

As my example of thoughts being in a whirl illustrates, the more we attempt to specify in literal language something that is literally inexpressible, the longer the expression becomes, with no gain in the clarity of what is being communicated. This is why vividness and compactness belong in Ortony's list. Metaphors of mind fulfill these theses well, expressing mental phenomena in images that do justice to their complexity. Locke's blank slate, as vigorously as it was criticized during the two hundred years following the publication of his *Essay Concerning the Understanding*, remained compelling as a description of the process and mechanism of human learning because of his metaphors—not that anyone believed in the existence of an actual slate somewhere in the cranium, but the dominant theory of sensations and memory required some mechanism for recording sensation-impressions from the external world.

Ortony also insists quite rightly on the importance of context in determining what is and is not metaphorical, a point essential in understanding why and *how* we automatically treat all descriptions of mental phenomena as metaphorical. According to Ortony, metaphors do not exist in isolation as linguistic expressions but rather are linguistic expressions used in a particular way; some kind of metaphor-intention either had to be present before the utterance was voiced or must be inferred retrospectively ("Psychological Aspects" 73-75). This is in keeping with the recent movement away from viewing metaphors as semantically deviant expressions and toward a contextual or cognitivist view (Miall, "Introduction" xii-xiii).

One example of how complex the latter is can be seen in Ina Loewenberg's list of the conditions necessary for a performance of a "metaphorical proposal," viewed as a "speech-act" (*P*), (I am paraphrasing here):

1. Speaker believes that *P* as an assertion is false.
2. Speaker believes that hearer believes that *P* as an assertion is false.
3. Hearer believes that *P* as an assertion is false.
4. Hearer believes that speaker believes that *P* as an assertion is false.
5. Speaker believes that "to consider the referents of the constituent terms of *P* according to *P* has heuristic value."
6. Speaker believes that "his hearer does not already consider the referents of the constituent terms of *P* according to *P*."
7. Speaker intends hearer to take *P* as a proposal to consider the referents in the way proposed.
8. "The hearer takes the utterance of *P* to be such a proposal because he believes the speaker intends him to." [175-6]

This list and others like it, however, leave crucial cognitive or linguistic moves unexplained. How does the listener determine that the speaker believes that *P* as an expression is false? What does the term "believe" actually mean in the first six conditions? In the case of metaphors of mind, as I will show, "believes that *P* as an assertion is false" would have to mean something like "behaves (linguistically) as if *P* is true but would deny its literal truth if and only if asked to agree that it is literally true."

The contextual approach, although incomplete, is still superior to the approach through "semantic deviance." One advocate of the latter approach, Searle, believes that metaphor is to be understood through "the principles which relate literal sentence meaning to metaphorical utterance meaning"; readers utilize a "strategy" of first seeking the literal meaning of a metaphorical sentence before recognizing that it is metaphorical (250, 274). Proponents of this view suggest that a metaphor viewed strictly as a linguistic expression would be "deviant" if read "literally":

it would not make sense. One of the most often used examples is "Juliet is the sun," where Juliet is clearly not a hot gaseous body ninety-three million miles from our planet. Nevertheless, as this example should make clear, some of what Black calls the "system of associated commonplaces" ("Metaphor" 40) of the metaphor's vehicle (here, "the sun") are appropriate to a determination of the metaphor's vehicle: if Juliet is not hot she nevertheless is a life-giving power, provides warmth and light to one's spirit or heart, and so forth.

Starting with such observations about the possible range of meanings of a word and the limitations imposed on that range by a given metaphor, the approach through semantic deviance attempts to explain how the recipient of the metaphor deems certain semantic features or selection restrictions appropriate. For instance, Tanya Reinhart identifies two distinct ways to interpret metaphor: the "focus-interpretation" and the "vehicle-interpretation." Focus-interpretation relies on a comparison between the metaphor and a syntactically similar literal expression to provide an understanding of the "basic (cognitive) content of the metaphor." Vehicle-interpretation latter provides rather for an understanding of the metaphor's figurative content, and it may only be available to a privileged few language users, poets in particular. For example, in T. S. Eliot's "the yellow fog that rubs its back upon the window-panes," the vehicle-interpretation "has to do with establishing a relationship between the two concepts involved—the fog and the cat." The focus-interpretation, on the other hand, will just tell us basically what the metaphor is "about"—fog touching a window. Only the vehicle-interpretation yields "a full understanding of the metaphor."

Reinhart's discussion lacks just one item, but it is an essential item: How does the cat enter the picture? The poem's words tell most astute readers to select "cat" from among all animate entities that might engage in such rubbing, that have muzzles and tongues, that seem to "curl once about" a place before falling asleep. But how do the words do this?

Timothy Crusius and W. Ross Winterowd take a similar approach to a type of metaphor they call "open," which has for its tenor the semantic feature [-concrete] and for its vehicle "something from the natural, non-symbolic world" (32). The authors focus on open metaphors that "'enspirit' language," for example "the Word made flesh." They suggest that in apprehending not only these but all metaphors, there is a "flash," a brief moment in which the metaphor is perceived as literal and hence irrational—it violates the selection restrictions associated with the semantic feature [-concrete] of the tenor. In this moment metaphor is "language at its most creative and elusive" because it is disrupting our compartmentalization of reality (30). This clear and persuasive description leaves out one key detail: how that "flash" is generated. The only possibility here, as with Reinhart's description, is that some sort of "black box" processes the input—the semantic features of a given utterance—and generates the output—the recognition that the utterance is metaphorical.

Shifting the focus of analysis to *context* as Ortony suggests and away from the actual linguistic expression may seem like simply moving the black box, but it has two distinct advantages. First, it conforms to recent experiments suggesting that processing "anomalous expressions" takes no longer than processing "literal expressions." As summarized by Walter Kintsch and Teun van Dijk, this new evidence contradicts "the classical processing theory," that "metaphors are first rejected as semantically anomalous, and then reinterpreted on the basis of some special strategy to yield appropriate interpretations" (312). For Reinhart's reader to substitute a word into the metaphor in order to make some literal sense and then to compare that sense to the anomalous expression, or for Crusius and Winterowd's reader to experience momentary confusion in the form of a flash, would demand a longer processing time than readers in controlled experimental settings actually take. These hypothesized processes, however, may be used in apprehending some novel metaphors. As Kintsch and van Dijk note, such metaphors probably require "more extensive problem-solving activities," hence more time to apprehend, than do "conventionalized or semiconventionalized metaphors" (313). Nevertheless, the processes are not likely to be used in apprehending novel metaphors *of the mind*, for the simple reason that no literal description of a mental phenomenon is possible: any processing strategy requiring a comparison between the given expression and a literal description will not hold for this special class of metaphors.

The view of metaphor as determined by context offers the further advantage of tallying with what Kenneth Goodman and others have been insisting and demonstrating for the past twenty years, that reading is a whole-to-part process. (See for example Goodman's famous "Reading: A Psycholinguistic Guessing Game.") The processing of a metaphor is governed at least as much by what a reader expects before encountering the metaphor as by the metaphor's actual words and syntax, as shown by the studies of the time required for apprehension (Tourangeau 21). According to Merrie Bergmann, an expression counts as a metaphor "when it has been given a metaphorical interpretation" (214-15).

Bergmann specifically does not want to say that "the underlying grammatical structure has the form of a simile which may be literally interpreted"; rather, we interpret an utterance as a metaphor because the context suggests non-literal meanings (219). That is, a reader will already be keyed into the necessary processing strategy for metaphor before reaching the metaphor. Bergmann specifies three roles that context can play: (1) it can "signal that an expression *is* to be interpreted metaphorically"; (2) it can indicate or activate "associated commonplaces and connotations . . . as well as relevant knowledge about the author's beliefs and purposes"; (3) it can "signal *which* connections and commonplaces are relevant, as well as which parts of terms' literal contents are to be dropped in the metaphorical interpretation" (223). She refers to the "broadening function in metaphorical interpretation," by which she means a dropping of some of the selection restrictions of the vehicle. In processing "Juliet is the sun," for example, "we drop part or all of the literal content of 'sun' when interpreting the word in the metaphorical context," and we do this more or less automatically because of signals previously given us by the context (220).

Such an approach to metaphor requires identifying what kinds of signals the context may provide. A step in this direction is taken by Dorothy Mack, who identifies three categories of signaling devices: genres, "cultural preconceptions" and formulas, and precoded language processes (249-50). For the first, "metaphoring occurs unmarked WITHIN such genres, since genre-markers, such as *once upon a time* . . . cue hearers not to expect literalness." For the second category, she cites as examples allusion, epithet, emblem, and cliche. The third category involves personification and similar processes.

This is at best a short step, however. Neither Bergmann nor Mack does more than express in a complicated way a point made earlier by Derek Bickerton, that "our linguistic expectations adjust themselves to the mode of discourse we are reading" (37). Bickerton continues: "If, in reading a poem, we encounter lexemes such as *moon*, *rose*, or *autumn*, we are likely (indeed, without explicit indications to the contrary, highly likely) to give them values such as 'unattainable beauty,' 'perfect beauty,' and 'ripeness and/or decay,' rather than 'satellite of earth,' 'species of flower,' and 'third season of the year.' But we would in no circumstances do this while reading an almanac or horticultural catalog" (37). Bickerton's example is equally valid whether the readers are teachers of English or students in Introduction to Literature. Awareness of the mode of discourse on the level Bickerton is describing seems to be so thoroughly instilled during secondary education (at least in the United States) that by the age of seventeen students have trouble applying the more pedestrian, non-symbolic, non-metaphoric meanings to words in a poem, however appropriate those meanings might be.

For a mode of discourse in which descriptions of mental processes are likely, the adjustment Bickerton speaks of is complex. When the reader encounters such a description—which is necessarily metaphorical—the reader accepts the literal content for its heuristic or esthetic value but withholds belief. All talk of the mind (except for descriptions of experimental studies) constitutes a kind of genre or mode of discourse which carries with it two injunctions: "*Read this literally* for its heuristic or esthetic value, but *do not* take the literal reading so far that it runs counter to our belief in the immateriality and uniqueness of each individual mind." In Bergmann's terms, "broadening" occurs in discussions of mental operations; we seldom if ever *interpret* statements about the mind literally. However, up to a point we do behave as if a literal reading is appropriate—in conversation we can exchange statements that represent the mind as a physical entity, for instance, because such statements are useful. In this situation our responses will be guided within certain channels by the selection restrictions pertaining to the metaphor's vehicle. The selection restrictions also enter the picture when we are asked or forced to attend to the metaphor, to interpret it. In this circumstance a reader will never overtly impute to the mind characteristics suggested by a literal reading of the metaphor.

As long as the context is one in which statements about the mind are expected, the reader does not first process such statements as literal, recognize anomalies (violations of our beliefs about the mind), and then reinterpret the statements as metaphors. The set of possible responses to a metaphor of mind is therefore quite complicated. The reader may not recognize the metaphor as such and yet respond in metaphorical language that shares the same selection restrictions, may accept the metaphor as literally valid up to a point (that is, may accept some of the vehicle's selection restrictions), or may deny the appropriateness of the vehicle's selection restrictions and thus refuse to accept the metaphor. Further, a reader's response may pass through different modes, for example accepting as heuristically valuable the first several sentences of an extended metaphor, then deciding that the vehicle is after all inappropriate. Fortunately, all of these possible responses can be understood by means of Paul Grice's "cooperative principle," which applies to all metaphorical utterances: readers agree to acknowledge writers' intentions, and writers expect such cooperation (45-47). In the case of metaphors of mind, cooperation involves the injunction "Do not take this literally" and the commonplace beliefs in mind's immateriality and uniqueness. Should the writer either intentionally or unwittingly signal that a literal reading of the depiction is appropriate or desirable, the reader must then decide whether or not to cooperate. The same thing will happen if the depiction diverges too much from the commonplaces and the concept of mind they embody.

The Contextual Approach in Historical Metaphors of Mind

For pre-twentieth-century metaphors of mind, the commonplaces were based on a fundamental belief in the divinity of the mind or that part of the mind termed "the soul." That is, cooperation was blocked by hints that the mind was material in nature. A comparison will make this point clear. David Hartley's *Observations on Man, His Frame, His Duty, and His Expectations* (1794) was frequently attacked during the first quarter of the nineteenth century as advocating a materialistic view of mind. His theory of association was adopted in some form or other by every major mental philosopher to follow him, but his "vibrations hypothesis" earned him the contempt or pity of these same philosophers. The problem in Hartley's system was, in the words of one critic, that "the chain of causation [vibrations from the external world transmitted to the mind via the sensory nerves] need not be broken at any point, and the explanation of consciousness either drops out altogether or we are to assume that vibrations are equivalent to consciousness of vibrations" (Peters 439). The strength and breadth of the reaction against Hartley may be difficult to understand today. His theory did not need the vibrations hypothesis, and in any case his expression of that hypothesis was limited to the first few pages of his book. But opening pages are crucial for establishing cooperation between writer and reader. Hartley's error was not theoretical but rhetorical: he did not lead his readers slowly enough to the proposition that he intended only hypothetically and metaphorically, that the mind has a material component which can sense vibrations in matter.

William Godwin's novel *The Adventures of Caleb Williams* (1794) generated no antagonism among the same readers who condemned Hartley's materialism, although the novel frequently draws on metaphors implying an extended and tangible mind. An example is Godwin's rendering of Caleb's discovery that his master and mentor, Falkland, is a murderer and, more heinous yet, has allowed an innocent man to be executed for the crime. Once the possibility occurred to Caleb that Falkland might be guilty, the idea became "fixed" in his mind, so that his "thoughts fluctuated from conjecture to conjecture, but this was the centre about which they revolved" (107). When his suspicion was validated by evidence he regarded as undeniable, Caleb's spinning thoughts generated tremendous pressure: "My mind was full almost to bursting. . . . my thoughts forced their way spontaneously to my tongue." And again, to underline the existence of this internal pressure: "I . . . gave vent to the tumult of my thoughts in involuntary exclamations" (129).

Caleb's description is exactly the kind of situation in which Bergmann's "broadening function" applies. The reader of this passage is guided by both the genre (novel) and the local context (a moment of introspection) to ignore most of the semantic features pertinent to the literal concept "mind as container" which informs these sentences. What the sentences literally say is that the mind is of limited size and so can be "filled almost to bursting"; it seems to have a shape such that thoughts can revolve within it; thoughts themselves are like molecules of a gas when heated, becoming more and more excited and finally bursting out through the container's weakest point. Literally the mind is no more like a container than Juliet is like a hot, gaseous body, but Godwin never allows his first-person narrator to express the results of his internal scrutiny in a way that requires the metaphors to be taken literally. Unlike Hartley, Godwin never violates the cooperative principle, so his readers take the sentences as a valid but not literal representation of several physiological facts and subjective sensations: the tendency to flush when excited, the resulting sensation of a head full of blood, and the sensation of ideas being all in a whirl.

Godwin's novel represents the normal case, in which metaphors of mind excite no special notice. Most of the metaphors I discuss in the subsequent chapters belong to this category. These are metaphors for which the cooperative principle operates and which observe the constraints of the genre "discourse about mind," calling on a reader to accept a literal reading of metaphors of mind as heuristically or esthetically valuable but not requiring this reading to violate our culture's belief that each mind is immaterial and unique. In the chapters that follow these conditions are assumed.

To better define these conditions, I will briefly consider several metaphors that do excite notice either intentionally or accidentally. There are three cases in which metaphoricity may be remarked on and may either interfere with or enhance the cooperation between writer and reader: apparent inaptness, apparent aptness, and ironical inversion. The late eighteenth-century and nineteenth-century reaction to Hartley is an example of the first case: Hartley offended his readers' sense that the mind cannot be referred to as a tangible physical object *in fact*. His metaphor was inapt—unsuitable—so that his readers could not ignore the literal content of the utterance. This is the situation warned against by handbooks of prose style when they point out that dead metaphors have a habit of coming to life when carelessly handled. Inaptness also has an historical and cultural aspect. For example, in beginning Hobbes' *Leviathan* we read that "Sense" (sensation) is caused by external objects "which presseth the organ proper to each Sense . . . which pressure, by the mediation of Nerves, and other strings, and membranes of the body, [is] continued inwards to the Brain, and Heart, causing there a resistance or counter-pressure." The modern reader may be put off with this image of the brain and heart being literally impressed with sights, sounds, and the like from outside. But readers of the seventeenth and eighteenth centuries thought of perception as consisting of a passive mind being impressed by stimuli from the external world. An informed reader of Hobbes' psychology or that of any other historically distant writer will have to recognize some metaphors as apt in their time, however inapt they seem now. Once the reader makes this adjustment, the metaphor can become a window into the set of commonplaces that constitute the psychology of the era. The reader who fails to adjust will not be able to make sense of such images.

The second case occurs when the reader remarks on the aptness of the metaphor. In this situation, the reader cooperates by taking notice of the figurative language rather than passing over it as an accurate but unremarkable representation of a mental state or phenomenon. A metaphor is especially apt when it seems to have been selected or devised for a given situation, when it shows some artfulness rather than seeming to be what came most readily to the author's pen. A writer not often praised for either psychological interest or artful language provides an example of an especially apt metaphor. Daniel Defoe's Moll Flanders, describing her perplexity in choosing between two lovers, notes that "These things oppressed my mind so much that, in short, the agonies of my mind threw me into a high fever, and long it was that none of the family expected my life" (41). What Moll does not say is as significant as what she does. Had Defoe had her write, "My mental anguish caused a life-threatening fever," he would have lost quite a bit in vividness. Such an utterance, furthermore, would seem less true to her character, less *apt*, both because of its diction and because it does not convey the same focus on discrete agents and actions that is a large part of how she sees the world. She is always either a victimizer or a victim, in this case as much a victim of her mind's anguish as of the machinations of her first lover. An apt metaphor fulfills at least one of Ortony's theses of vividness and compactness especially well.

In the third case, the literal content of a normally dead metaphor is emphasized for ironical effects which occur because the literal content is incongruous in the context. As in the second situation, the reader is led to react with "Aha," although here the metaphor's use may constitute a criticism of the view of mind on which the metaphor is based. Thomas Reid, while no more able to avoid metaphors than his contemporaries, nevertheless seized every opportunity to illustrate the problems caused by metaphorical language used to talk about the mind. Two of his favorite targets were Locke's view of the mind as occupying a "presence room" and hypothetical physiologies such as Hartley's. Reid implicitly criticized both when he wrote that the optic nerves consist of empty tubes which transmit light rays from the retina to "the very seat of the soul, until they flash in her face" (*Inquiry*

199). Reid's readers would have seen as absurd the suggestion of empty tubes, would *not* have automatically passed over the statement as an accurate but unremarkable representation of the process of perception, and thus would have joined Reid in rejecting the concept of the soul occupying an actual chamber in the head and having eyes that might even be temporarily blinded.

This range, of possible responses by readers to metaphors of the mind and of degrees of cooperation between reader and text, is worth emphasizing, because it indicates that such metaphors may constrain but do not control how we conceive of the mind. While there are certain expressions and formulas that come more easily and quickly when we describe a mental process, we are also free to create new figures. This freedom must be kept in mind when considering the relationship between metaphors of mind, concepts of mind, and psychological theory. The metaphors from Godwin, Hobbes, Defoe, and Reid all bear a family resemblance to what George Lakoff and Mark Johnson refer to in *Metaphors We Live By* as "MIND-AS-ENTITY," a metaphor which characterizes the mind as tangible, localized, and discrete (27). Moll Flanders' mind, like a living being, can suffer agonies and fever. Not only is Caleb's mind like a container, his thoughts are like molecules of gas, exerting more pressure as they become heated by his increasing suspicion and final discovery of his master's crime. Reid took Locke to task for representing the soul as having a seat within the mind.

The term "mind as entity" will be extremely important for this study; it succinctly characterizes the set of "commonplaces and connotations" associated with representations of mental phenomena during this period. But I do not want to grant it the power to shape perceptions and conceptions, as Lakoff and Johnson do when they define mind-as-entity as an "ontological metaphor" (27). By this they mean that our mental metaphors "are so natural and so pervasive in our thought that they are usually taken as self-evident, direct descriptions of mental phenomena. The fact that they are metaphorical never occurs to most of us" (28). Such metaphors are "lived by" to the extent that they are "reflections of systematic metaphorical concepts that structure our actions and thoughts. They are 'alive' in the most fundamental sense" (55). The weakness in this position is the connection drawn by Lakoff and Johnson between the surface aspects of language (for example, various expressions such as "I'm going to pieces" and "His mind snapped") and a type of metaphor (here an ontological metaphor) that is said to *structure* both how we act and how we conceive of what we do when we act. When the authors note that, in referring to a concept being structured by a metaphor, they mean "partially structured" (13), they only call attention to the slippery character of that verb "structure."

As a skeptical reader, I am impressed by Lakoff and Johnson's data and the metaphors they infer from the data, but I remain unpersuaded that the metaphors always control how we actually *conceive of* the particular aspect of experience. That the metaphors can control conceptions I accept, but not that they must. The term "ontological metaphor" does not allow for changes in the relationships between metaphors of the mind and concepts of the mind from one era to another, from one author to another, even within one author's career. If a special term were needed, "root metaphor" would be more flexible and useful. A root can be botanical or etymological; it can constitute a starting point, a limiting factor, an anchor, a source or conduit for nourishment. (It can also carry a much broader meaning, that given it by Stephen Pepper in his *World Hypotheses*.) However, I prefer to do without the adjective; in my discussion I have tried to make clear through context when I am using "metaphor" to mean a specific utterance and when I am using it to mean the more general concept that served all of the "root" functions during the eighteenth and nineteenth centuries. Mind-as-entity was not strictly lived by and was not the exclusive structuring principle within the psychology of these two centuries. Precisely because it was not an ontological metaphor, there was room for other metaphors to be introduced and elaborated as interest developed in less well understood psychological phenomena. The most important of these new metaphors, as I show in Chapter 6, were web-of-relations and mind-in-landscape. Both have more to do with the increasingly prominent concept mind-as-a-living-being, which by the end of the nineteenth century achieved an acceptance approaching that of mind-as-entity.

Within the domain of psychological theory, metaphor may play a more sharply defined role. It has been suggested that metaphors serve three functions for psychological theory: communication, generation and elaboration, and analysis (Nash 337). A more accurate arrangement would place analysis and elaboration under one head, and generation under another. In both elaboration and analysis, the metaphor serves to explain or extend something that is already more or less known, whereas generation entails creation or exploration. A metaphor that serves the function of elaboration is what Richard Boyd calls a "theory-constitutive metaphor." Such metaphors, according to Boyd, "provide a way to introduce terminology for features of the world whose existence seems probable, but many of whose fundamental properties have yet to be discovered. Theory-constitutive metaphors, in other words, represent one strategy for the accommodation of language to as yet undiscovered causal features of the world" (364).

Boyd also says that such metaphors are one of many strategies by which the scientific community arranges language "so that our linguistic categories 'cut the world at its joints'" (358). These metaphors further articulate an existing theory or view of the world and thus are a component of what Thomas Kuhn describes as "normal science": "research firmly based upon one or more past scientific achievements, achievements that some particular scientific community acknowledges for a time as supplying the foundation for its further practice" (10).

Generation is a different process. It is possible that in attempting to arrange language, by means of metaphor, so that language corresponds with the existing theory, scientists will discover new phenomena and will be forced toward a conceptual revolution. But the new theory that emerges is not likely to be *constituted by* the earlier metaphor. More likely, a new metaphor will be discovered during the pre-revolutionary ferment, will gain adherents during the revolution, and will then help generate the new theory. A metaphor that participates in this process is what Donald Schön labels "generative metaphor." He explains this term not with metaphorical language but with a story. Some researchers were attempting to better understand how a paintbrush picks up and distributes paint. The breakthrough came with the insight that a paintbrush is like a pump; following this discovery, the researchers arrived at "new perceptions, explanations, and inventions," all of which were generated by the metaphor and by the exploration of the similarity implied by the metaphor. Schön insists that a generative metaphor does not result from the perception of specific similarities between the pump and the paintbrush, that is, between the tenor and the vehicle. Rather, it results from the attempt to account for the "pre-analytic detection of similarity"—the scientist recognizes that the two objects or phenomena are similar but cannot yet say exactly how, and in attempting to specify how, the scientist is generating a theory.

In short, a generative metaphor is the bridge between a hunch and a new theory, whereas a theory-constitutive metaphor is applied according to the dictates of an existing theory. A theory-constitutive metaphor is a tool for surveying a territory whose boundaries are known; a generative metaphor is a means for orienting oneself during a new exploration. This distinction could have so many exceptions and grey areas as to be nearly useless for a general theory of metaphor and theory change, but it is quite useful in understanding the changes in the depiction of mental events during the eighteenth and nineteenth centuries. As I show in the following chapters, the metaphor mind-as-entity often performs a theory-constitutive function in both fictional and psychological writings during the eighteenth century: writers were limited in what mental phenomena they could represent and how they could represent them. The new metaphors used by some nineteenth-century novelists, however, suggest the presence of another "root" metaphor, sentience-as-life, which was serving a generative function. In Schön's terms the "pre-analytic detection of similarity" between life and the mind had begun to result in "new perceptions, explanations, and inventions"—and also in new metaphors that effectively began to express the new emphasis on mind as something other than a relatively static, impressible entity.

Janet Soskice offers a useful insight into the relationship between metaphors and models in disciplines that are not as well defined as the hard sciences but that nevertheless rely on metaphor's theory-constitutive and generative functions. Writing on metaphors and religious language, she defines a theory-constitutive metaphor as one that proposes a model; it is to be distinguished from "metaphorically constituted theory terms," by which she means the "metaphors which are the linguistic projections of such a model" (102). Soskice emphasizes the role of models in processing metaphors: a reader will construe an odd expression as metaphorical if he is able to "see it as suggesting a model or models which enable him to go on extending the significance of what he has read or heard" (51). More precisely, "an originally vital metaphor calls to mind, directly or indirectly, a model or models," but "as the metaphor becomes commonplace [or dead], its initial web of implications becomes, if not entirely lost, then difficult to recall" (73). Soskice's key phrase is "go on extending the significance," because it indicates that model and extended metaphor are two components of a single process serving to elaborate and communicate concepts. To regard extended metaphors and models as related in this way is more helpful in the study of pre-twentieth-century psychology than to adopt Black's distinction between metaphors and models, a distinction most applicable to twentieth-century hard sciences but often carried over uncritically by metaphor theorists to other areas.

Nevertheless, Black has something to contribute to the study of metaphors of mind. His five "conditions for the use of a theoretical model" can be extended beyond modern science. The conditions are these:

1. In an "original field of investigation" there exist "*some* facts and regularities."
2. "A need is felt for further scientific mastery of the original domain."

3. Some aspect of a "relatively unproblematic, more familiar, or better-organized domain" is described.
4. There must exist "explicit or implicit rules of correlation" allowing translations of statements about the secondary field into statements about the original field.
5. "Inferences from the assumptions made in the secondary field are translated by means of the rules of correlation and then independently checked against known or predictable data in the primary domain." [*Models and Metaphors* 230-31]

"The key to understanding the entire transaction," Black continues, "is the identity of structure that in favorable cases permits assertions made about the secondary domain to yield insight into the original field of interest." Metaphor-making and model-making differ in that "a metaphor operates largely with *commonplace* implications. You need only proverbial knowledge, as it were, to have your metaphor understood; but the maker of a scientific model must have prior control of a well-knit scientific theory" (239).

Black's conditions are appropriate for describing pre-twentieth-century endeavors, if they are applied cautiously. In particular, the concepts of scientific mastery and independent verification must be understood in the context of the divine organization of the universe that was accepted as a self-evident fact. Within this context, discovery and elaboration of analogical relationships among various domains would be considered scientific as soon as the initial connection was made, as long as some identity of structure was present. Independent verification was provided simply by God's having organized the universe in a logical way and having designed the human perceptual and cognitive apparatus to be able to discover this logic. Because of the relative inaccessibility of mental phenomena, model-making was essential to pre-twentieth-century psychology. (I do not mean to imply that it is any less essential in the twentieth century, but that would be another book.)

To help preserve the integrity of the term "model," I will refer to "extended metaphors" in the history of psychology, but I intend that such metaphors be understood as functioning very much like Black's models. Hence within the "original field" of pre-twentieth-century psychology there existed many "facts and regularities," chief among them being the principle of association and the tendency of mental operations to fall into certain classes; these classes suggested distinct "faculties" of the mind, although the mind itself was held to be an indivisible entity. Psychologists agreed that these regularities in themselves could not account for the complexity of mental phenomena. There were two well-understood secondary domains, Newtonian physics and biology, with physics being especially influential on psychological theories (Lowry 15-21). Psychologists agreed that between the internal and external realms (the mental and the physical) there existed an "identity of structure." Thus Hartley could feel perfectly safe in applying Newtonian mechanics to the assumed vibrations in sensory nerves in order to explain sensation; his problem was that he applied the "rules of correlation" too explicitly and seemed to equate human consciousness with mechanical vibrations. Likewise, Reid could call for an "anatomy of the mind" as a substitute for the impossible-to-obtain "natural history" of the mind (*Inquiry* 5, 8). Both Hartley and Reid believed that the mind was fairly well understood, that "further scientific mastery" was nevertheless possible and desirable, and that such mastery would result from making the study of mind more like the study of physics and biology, which were "relatively unproblematic" and "better organized." Reid commented that only with Newton did natural philosophy gain maturity, "and it need not appear surprising, if the philosophy of the human mind should be a century or two later in being brought to maturity" (*Intellectual Powers* 62).

It is true that these psychologists were operating primarily with proverbial knowledge about both the primary and secondary domains, and neither rigorously applied the methods of the secondary domain. For Hartley, it was enough to know the principle of inertia; no calculus enters into his psychology. For Reid, mental anatomy meant introspection into the mature male mind in repose, with neither functional nor comparative analysis forming more than an aside. Nevertheless, despite the reliance on commonplace implications and proverbial knowledge, these psychologists' metaphors are similar in function to models in the harder sciences.

I do not intend the terms "extended metaphor," "theory-constitutive metaphor," and "generative metaphor" to neatly divide up the linguistic space they encompass; the meanings do overlap. For example, a theory-constitutive metaphor is probably present in the language used by a psychologist to develop an extended metaphor, such as Thomas Brown's attempt to regard the "science of mind" as "*mental physiology*," analogous to that other science "relating to the structure and offices of our corporeal frame" (*Lectures* 12). A generative metaphor could not be presented as an extended metaphor, since by definition it first occurs as an intuition, before there is any question of constructing "rules of correlation" between the two domains. When such rules are constructed, the metaphor becomes extended. A generative metaphor may become theory-constitutive, as happens at the end of the nineteenth century when functionalism came to dominate American psychology through the work of William James. In their surface manifestations, however, all three types will always fulfill Ortony's three theses of inexpressibility, compactness, and vividness. This is the condition of their being metaphors: they are figuring forth the phenomena of thought, which by common consent cannot be described literally.

One further domain must be mentioned: physiology. The inexpressibility thesis applies as well to most physiologists' writings on the mind at least until the middle of the nineteenth century. While physiology in principle can be described empirically, hence literally, almost all neural physiology before the nineteenth century and a good deal of it even into the middle of that century drew on the metaphor mind-as-entity and was hypothetical. Until enough concrete data about nerve impulses and the structure of the brain was collected, verified, and analyzed, all physiology was metaphorical according to Ortony's inexpressibility thesis—figuring forth what could not be described literally. Such physiological writings are thus within my scope. Nevertheless, I do not discuss how these hypothetical, metaphorically constituted theories were replaced with theories based on data gathered by scientific means acceptable to twentieth-century researchers and theorists. Bringing in this additional topic would add only details, no major points, to my picture of the changes in metaphors of mind.

III
CORPUSCULAR THOUGHTS, TANGIBLE MINDS: EIGHTEENTH-CENTURY PSYCHOLOGY AND FICTION

Although there are no clear demarcations between historical periods in the understanding of the mind, there is a stretch of time, from the beginning of the eighteenth century through the first third of the nineteenth, when the language and the concepts used for talking about the mind remained relatively unchanged. For convenience in discussion I refer loosely to this period as the eighteenth century, to indicate that the dominant metaphor of mind and the primary psychological theories remained constant. Psychology from the beginning of the eighteenth century, whether the explicit psychology described in textbooks, the implicit psychology dramatized in novels, or the psychology on which empiricists based their philosophical works, was a well-defined endeavor. There was a general goal: discover the laws of thought and thereby improve human life; a standard methodology: introspection, analogy, and classification; and a set of explanatory procedures: especially associationism and faculty psychology. Most discussions of the human mind during this period were carried on within the constraints established by Descartes and Locke and dwelt at length on the problems and strengths of their two systems, just as philosophy in general centered on "criticisms of the Galilean-Cartesian-Newtonian world-view" (Morris 28).

The most important feature of psychological systems during this period was the metaphor mind-as-entity, which attributed to the mind the traits of tangibility, passivity, impressibility, simplicity of structure, and specificity of location. Caleb Williams' mind is presented as a container for thoughts; as such, it is of limited size, occupies a definite area of space, and seems unable to exercise will power to control the thoughts it contains. The thoughts themselves are imaged as atoms. The mind of Moll Flanders is "oppressed" by external conditions and causes in her a fever; she speaks of her mind as she might speak of her liver. Even the criticisms of metaphorical language used to discuss the mind convey the impression of mind-as-entity, as in Brown's desire to institute a "physiology of the mind."

The language associated with this metaphor remained viable until nearly the middle of the nineteenth century. Poe's *Narrative of Arthur Gordon Pym* (1838), for example, is not emphatically psychological, but the psychology it does contain conforms to the period. *Pym* seems to have been composed as Poe claimed to have composed "The Raven," to affect readers' emotions in a particular way. The narrator, Pym, is caught up in a series of nautical adventures each one more harrowing and fantastic than the last: he stows away on a ship that is taken over and terrorized by mutineers, later witnesses the massacre of another shipload of compatriots by a primitive tribe, and finds himself on a small boat being drawn toward the South Pole and a wall of white mist out of which a tremendous figure looms. Such adventures and their effects on the mental states of the characters concerned were the lifeblood, so to speak, of the Gothic tales Poe was in part emulating. Where Pym describes mental events he focuses on sensations, portraying his mind as passive and impressible. The following examples are representative:

> I experienced a sudden rush of blood to my temples—a giddy and overpowering sense of deliverance and reanimation. [25]
>
> [The note's full meaning could not] have imbued my mind with one

tithe of the harrowing and yet indefinable horror with which I was inspired by the fragmentary warning thus received. [34]

I shall never forget the ecstatic joy which thrilled through every particle of my frame. [88]

And now I found these fancies creating their own realities, and all imagined horrors crowding upon me in fact. [185]

These four examples are typical of the period in their correlation between idea and physiological sensation ("rush of blood" accompanying "sense of deliverance"), the powerful and precise effect of external stimuli (the fragmentary note imbuing Pym's mind with horror), the specificity of physiological description (joy thrilling through every particle of Pym's body), and the ability of ideas of the imagination to tangibly impress the mind. There is nothing in these examples that would have been out of place in *Moll Flanders* or *Caleb Williams*.

Unlike those other first-person works, however, *Pym* contains relatively few such utterances. Poe was clearly aiming for a certain effect by drawing on the same psycho-physiology of fright used by Godwin; the mind-as-entity metaphor is fundamental to the technique. But his relatively minimal attention to mental events suggests that he was aware of the limitations either of the language or of the concept of mind the language embodied. Pym literally rushes through his adventures (the novel is quite short); descriptions concentrate on what he does rather than on what he thinks and feels. The passivity of Pym's mind, as implied by the figurative language, is unimportant to the story compared to his physical activity. At the end of Pym's narrative, when he seems to be entering a supernatural realm, the novel records only what the hero sees, when readers might expect a great deal of attention to his mental impressions. Perhaps no language would have been fully adequate to the job. Poe's silences about certain mental events, like those of Austen I discuss at the end of this chapter, can be read as an indication that the set of concepts and terms based on the mind-as-entity metaphor could not encompass mental events like Pym's; as these events moved from the fringes of psychological interest toward the center, the writer either had to remain silent about them or find new metaphors.

In order to understand how the figurative language of psychology developed to accommodate this shift, however, it is essential to understand how well the mind-as-entity metaphor worked when such mental events were not of much interest, that is, through the first third of the nineteenth century. In this chapter I discuss the metaphor's theory-constitutive function in the psychological explanations and fictional representations of two central phenomena: the formation of ideas and the development of the mind. The phenomena themselves cannot be separated, but treating them as separate topics helps illustrate an important element in psychology during this period: the mind, although a unity, was held to have two rather distinct aspects. The passive, impressible, tangible aspect is seen most clearly in references to the formation of ideas; the more active aspect is seen in references to the mind's development.

Psychologists on the Formation of Ideas

During the period from the end of the seventeenth century until the second third of the nineteenth, the theory of the formation of ideas was based on relatively mechanical and automatic processes. Locke was regarded as essentially correct in tracing all ideas to sensations and therefore all knowledge ultimately to combinations of sense impressions, although his discussion of the formation of ideas was seen to present problems. Locke's language was usually agreed to be, in Sir William Hamilton's words, "the most figurative, ambiguous, vascillating, various, and even contradictory" of any philosopher (*Philosophy of Sir William Hamilton* 212). The following list is representative of Locke's metaphors in the *Essay*:

Mind is "white Paper, void of all Characters" [104].

Our senses "convey into the Mind" perceptions [105].

The brain is "the mind's Presence-room" [121].

Knowledge begins by the mind "laying in, and storing up those *Ideas*, out of which is to be framed all the knowledge it is capable of," and "the *Understanding* is not much unlike a Closet wholly shut from light, with only some little openings left, to let in external visible Resemblances, or *Ideas* of things without." [162-63]

These figures of speech illustrate the aptness of Hamilton's criticism. How could the mind be like both white paper and a monarch? How could it both possess a presence-room and be a closet? If we follow Hamilton's lead and read the sentences simply as revealing a capricious use of language, we have to wonder how Locke manages to seem for most of the length of the *Essay* so reasonable and analytical. If Locke had had a steady and clear view of the human understanding, surely he would not have attributed to the mind mutually exclusive analogues. But the figures also show that the mind, for Locke, was relatively passive, was capable of receiving and sometimes forced to receive impressions from the external world through the agency of the senses, and received these impressions in an organ akin to a monarch's presence-room. These more general features are not mutually contradictory or ambiguous. They are manifestations of mind-as-entity, and the fact that Locke's actual figures all share the same features shows the metaphor functioning in a theory-constitutive fashion: Locke was not really free to explore totally new ways of representing perception, the acquisition of knowledge, and memory. The superficial contradictions and ambiguities of his figures are those inherent in any attempt to express the inexpressible, and their shared features imply a common source: the mind-as-entity metaphor.

David Hartley took the Lockean system a step farther, attempting to ground it on physiology. The opening sections of his *Observations on Man* draw on the concept of mind as a relatively passive, impressible entity. Hartley agrees with Locke that while the mind has some ideas which "appear to spring up" on their own accord, the truth is that "*ideas of sensation* are the elements of which all the rest [of a person's ideas] are compounded" (ii). Hartley says that he took his theory of perception "from the hintes concerning the performance of sensations and motion" at the end of Newton's *Principia* (5); the hints result in his first four propositions (8-11). First, "the white medullary substance of the brain, spinal marrow, and the nerves proceeding from them, is the immediate instrument of sensation and motion." Second, "the white medullary substance of the brain is also the immediate instrument, by which ideas are presented to the mind: or, in other words, whatever changes are made in this substance, corresponding changes are made in our ideas, and *vice versa*." Third, "the sensations remain in the mind for a short time after the sensible objects are removed." Fourth, "external objects impressed upon the senses occasion, first in the nerves on which they are impressed, and then in the brain, vibrations of the finall, and, as one may say, infinitesimal, medullary particles."

As I pointed out in Chapter 2, the causal connection from the object of sensation to the mental image of the object is continuous in Hartley's system. A person might perceive, for example, a red block of wood. The qualities of redness and squareness in the block itself are transmitted to the eye, where they occasion vibrations of particular frequencies in the nerves leading from the eye to the white medullary substance of the brain; vibrations in the medullary particles cause the ideas of redness and squareness to be presented to the mind. This causal chain is possible only if the mind is an entity, yet the mental entity in this case need not be material, as proposition 2 makes clear: "whatever changes are made in this substance, corresponding changes are made in our ideas." An immaterial as well as a material entity can be changed; the only requirement is that it have enough points of impression to preserve the one-to-one correspondence from the external impressions, through the organs of sense, and then through the white medullary substance. Because that substance itself is the immediate instrument of sensation, it must be able to present to the percipient principle a series of stimuli corresponding exactly to the original impressions in number, intensity, succession, and so forth, and the percipient principle must be able to receive each stimulus. If the correspondences are to hold, that principle must be an entity, although Hartley's system may be more progressive than Locke's in that he does not immediately turn to physicalistic metaphors to represent the mental events.

This relatively mechanical process did not stop with the mind's reception of impressions; it continued with the formation of ideas within the mind. The two basic steps in the formation of ideas depend on the mind-as-entity metaphor: *perception* occurs by means of the impressions of sense data on a passive mind, and *association of perceptions into ideas* occurs according to categories determined by the external world.

Karl Figlio has described eighteenth-century theories of perception as built on a "simple model," which "incorporated the passive impression notions of the mind in relation to its environment and created the sensorium as a 'natural object'" (200). This model was developed by analogy with the theory of the impression of external objects upon nerves; it "did not emerge from the study of the nervous system, but was a presupposition" of such study (200). What Figlio calls a "model" I call an "extended metaphor." The "passive impression notions" were part of the mind-as-entity metaphor and contributed to its theory-constitutive function, helping psychologists account for the formation of ideas. According to the psychology of the eighteenth century, impressions were organized into ideas by the mechanism of association. The descriptions of this mechanism are of special interest because they relate the shape of ideas either to physical processes in the nerves and brain or to the structuring of events in the external world.

The autonomy thesis as a theoretical principle was not strong enough to offset the mind-as-entity metaphor and inspire a way of explaining the formation of ideas that did not depend on analogies with the physical world. Hume's explanation of how the association mechanism works illustrates this point. He begins his *Treatise* in the standard fashion, like Locke and Hartley dividing "the perceptions of the human mind" into two kinds, impressions and ideas, which differ "in the degrees of force and liveliness, with which they strike upon the mind, and make their way into our thought or consciousness," impressions being the more forceful. In this category Hume includes "all our sensations, passions and emotions, as they make their first appearance in the soul." Ideas are "the faint images of these [impressions] in thinking and reasoning" (1).

Thus far his description embodies the passive-impression theory, and he continues in the same vein when he describes how an impression can be derived from an idea. "An impression," he writes, "first strikes upon the senses. . . . Of this impression there is a copy taken by the mind, which remains after the impression ceases; and this we call an idea." This copy can give rise to other impressions, for instance those of "desire and aversion"; these impressions too are copied, and may "in their turn give rise to other impressions and ideas" (7-8). The phenomenon of the association of ideas results from the same kind of mechanistic operation of the mind, and in fact Hume asserts that one of the three main kinds of association, contiguity in time or place, is created by the operation of the senses: "as the senses, in changing their objects, are necessitated to change them regularly, and take them as they lie *contiguous* to each other, the imagination must by long custom acquire the same method of thinking, and run along the parts of space and time in conceiving its objects" (11). This is a radical suggestion, that the operation of the senses creates not only the mind's ideas (its contents) but also its structure—the preference for linking ideas contiguous in space and in time.

Yet the suggestion is perfectly in keeping with the conceptual limitations imposed by the mind-as-entity metaphor functioning in a theory-constitutive manner. Neither the passive-impression theory nor the principle of association logically requires the mind to be conceived of as an entity that takes copies of impressions. It is possible to imagine other means than those described by Hume to account for the ability of ideas to give rise to other ideas. Likewise, there is no compelling reason why the imagination "*must* run along the parts of space and time in conceiving its objects." The assumption that memories of the external world are stored so as to replicate that world underlies this statement, but the assumption lacks proof or logical necessity. However, it does conform to the metaphor: an entity (in the everyday sense of the term) has extension in both space and time, and since the mental entity has these features they may well be used for organizing impressions. The metaphor does not provide Hume with proof for his "must run," but it makes the suggestion more plausible and reduces the need to seek additional explanations.

This is not to say that a concept of the mind as an entity is part of Hume's theoretical understanding of the mind. Indeed he makes clear in the *Treatise* that any attempt to describe "the substance of the soul" (by which he here means "mind") cannot be understood: "All our perceptions are not susceptible of a local union, either with what is extended or unextended; there being some of the one kind, and some of the other: And as the constant conjunction of objects constitutes the very essence of cause and effect, matter and motion may often be regarded as the causes of thought, as far as we have any notion of that relation" (250). He continues, in discussing the question of personal identity, to assert that human beings "are nothing but a bundle or collection of different perceptions, which succeed each other with an inconceivable rapidity, and are in a perpetual flux and movement" (252). Thus it is absurd to insist that the human mind has any sort of *simplicity* or *identity* (253). And earlier, he defines "a *mind*" as "nothing but a heap or collection of different perceptions, united together by certain relations, and suppos'd, tho' falsely, to be endowed with perfect simplicity and identity" (207).

Clearly, Hume's theoretical predisposition is to deny the mind any separate status—it certainly cannot be described as an extended substance, nor can perceptions be localized in the physical frame. Yet Hume's language for describing mental phenomena is solidly rooted in the mind-as-entity metaphor. This is the same kind of contradiction that I described in Chapter 1 between assertions of the autonomy thesis and expressions relating the mind to various physical operations. The writer's theory and practice contradict each other; the theory advocates the autonomy thesis and draws on the concept of substance defined metaphysically, while the practice relies on physicalistic language derived from everyday senses of "substance" and "entity." It has been suggested that Hume was not able to follow up on his own suggestions toward a so-called "relational theory of mind . . . because of an inconsistent retention of the very categories which he ostensibly opposed"—the categories of substance and cause (Morris 103).

Hume's retention of these categories is implicit in his language; in fact, the language of the mind-as-entity metaphor made such retention inescapable. For example, the creation of the sensorium as a "natural object," in Figlio's apt phrase, follows directly from that metaphor: in order for ideas to be formed at all, there has to exist a specific, tangible place where spirit and matter can meet. These qualities can be seen in definitions such as that given in Rees's *Cyclopaedia*: mind is the sensorium plus a conscious or percipient principle, the sensorium being "that organized substance, which, without any farther medium, furnishes to the conscious or percipient principle the objects of consciousness or percipiency" ("Philosophy, Mental" n.p.). Rees probably means "substance" in what Morris calls the "metaphysical sense" as traditionally applied to the mind: "an immaterial 'that,' capable of continued and independent existence, and analyzable into qualities and a substratum which has relations and supports these qualities, without itself being a relation or quality or sum of qualities" (8). Rees would reject any attempt to read "organized substance" in its everyday sense, which would connote tangibility (having substance), extension, and thus a specific location. The everyday sense implies that with the right instruments one could actually investigate the sensorium in operation as one would investigate any other "natural object." The "metaphysical sense" runs counter to that implication, on the reasonable grounds that no material instruments but only the mind can perceive what the sensorium is doing. Unfortunately, the same kind of argument can be made against the existence of a sensorium defined as Rees defines it. How can a "substance" in the everyday sense provide "ideas" to the "conscious or percipient principle," and how can "substance" in the metaphysical sense receive sense impressions from tangible external objects?

This problem does go beyond terminology; it also derives from an insurmountable discrepancy between an individual's subjective experience and what can be demonstrated objectively about perception and knowledge. But the theory-constitutive function of the mind-as-entity metaphor is also an important cause. This function results from the inability of human beings to limit their discourse to "metaphysical" meanings of terms. "Everyday" connotations will slip in and will shape our predispositions: the mind-as-entity metaphor predisposes us to conceive of the entire mind as an entity and not just as a "substance" in the metaphysical sense defined by Morris. Rees explicitly divides the mind into a thing and a principle, but if the principle is not to remain an abstraction, it must take on the attributes of the thing. When this happens, it becomes difficult to explore further the ideal nature of that "conscious or percipient principle" as well as the principle's active nature. Rees probably intends "the conscious or percipient principle" to be regarded as active and to be taken as the more significant component of the mental system. However, most readers will more easily imagine the sensorium (because it is defined as a substance), hence that component stands out in the definition and renders the whole system relatively passive. Most of the activity that does occur takes place when the sensorium transmits sensations to the percipient principle.

The theory-constitutive power of the mind-as-entity metaphor is striking in descriptions of the process by which ideas of the sublime are formed. According to Ernest Tuveson, the Lockean system was revolutionary in its insistence that "even the most abstract and sublime ideas . . . even the idea of God, are *composed of*—not refined from—discrete impressions" (*Imagination* 20-21). Psychologists after Locke were concerned to rescue these particular ideas from his system, yet the method they settled on still required a mental entity that could receive impressions and replicate external processes and states in an internal space.

Dugald Stewart, in his representative essay "On the Sublime," proceeds by identifying "a few of the natural associations attached to the idea of what is physically or literally Sublime" (394). In particular, he points out those associations "arising from the tendency which the religious sentiments of men, in every age and country, have had to carry their thoughts *upwards*, towards the objects of their worship" (394-95). The problem with this "poetical" usage is that, since we now know the earth to be spherical, "the *natural* association cannot fail to be more or less counteracted" in every mind familiar with the facts (397). But even this counteraction can have a positive effect: "the conclusions of modern science leave the imagination at equal liberty to shoot, in all directions, through the immensity of space; suggesting, to a philosophical mind, the most grand and magnificent of all conceptions" (398).

Stewart's language displays the typical problems of attempts to apply the autonomy thesis without scrutinizing every word of every sentence that purports to describe a mental process. On the one hand the upward tendency of thoughts is a "*natural* association," one which derives from and correlates to the actual structure of the external world. On the other hand it is a learned association, because it is "counteracted" by modern knowledge. Stewart reconciles this apparent contradiction by metaphorically representing the mind as containing a space shaped by all of a person's knowledge, that acquired through perception and that acquired through study and reflection. Within this space, thoughts move in directions determined by the metaphoric location of the percipient principle, either at the center of a solid celestial sphere or at the center of infinite space. In either case the actual movement of the thoughts creates in the mind the sublime sensation, and the movement itself is stimulated by an external source, either a tangible scene or the written word.

As an example of the movement and the resulting sense of sublimity, Stewart offers religious writing, which is "beautifully accommodated to the irresistable impressions of nature; availing itself of such popular and familiar words as *upwards* and *downwards*" (407). These writers have taken note of "the frailty of the human mind, governed so much by sense and imagination, and so little by the abstractions of philosophy. Hence the expression of *fallen* Angels, which, by recalling to us the eminence from which they fell, communicates, in a single word, a character of Sublimity to the bottomless abyss" (407). The writers, according to Stewart, recognized that because of its early and long-lasting reliance on sense data, the mind cannot help being "impressed"—shaped by the hierarchical structure of nature. It is a "natural bias of the imagination" to see natural phenomena as physically connected; we tend to "conceive the firmament to be something *solid*, in which the sun, moon, and stars are mechanically fixed." Modern readers familiar with such "abstractions of philosophy" as the laws of gravity and inertia also experience a "sentiment of Wonder" in addition to the emotion "excited" by perceiving the vastness of the sky (419); this sentiment enhances the sublime sensation stimulated by the movement of the thoughts within the mental entity. Fortunately for the natural philosopher, early impressions from sense data will always be stronger than knowledge about intangible concepts which the mind simply cannot encompass, such as infinity and action at a distance.

Stewart's description conveys an image of thoughts moving within a static mental space; the thoughts themselves are not created by the mind but are stimulated from without. Thomas Upham uses a more refined image to show how thoughts can represent processes outside the mind concurrently with those processes. This image occurs in Upham's description of the difference between the emotions of beauty and sublimity. He asks his reader to consider the person

> who is supposed to behold a river at its first rise in the mountains, and to follow it, as it winds and enlarges itself in the expanse of the ocean. For a time the feelings, which are excited within him, as he gazes on the prospect, are what are termed emotions of beauty. As the small stream, which had hitherto played in the uplands amid foliage, that almost hid it from his view, increases its waters, separates its banks to a great distance from each other, and becomes the majestic river; his feelings are of a more powerful kind. We often, by way of distinction, speak of the feelings existing under such circumstances, as emotions of grandeur. At last it expands and disappears in the immensity of the ocean; the vast illimitable world of billows flashes in his sight. Then the emotion, widening and strengthening with the magnitude and energy of the objects, which accompany it, becomes sublime. [*Intellectual Philosophy* 407]

This extended metaphor accurately represents what Upham and other psychologists of his time believed to be taking place in the mind of a perceiver. The flow of the feelings is directly proportional to the size of the river beheld by the perceiver. Even more specifically, the objects and processes perceived are reproduced within the mind, as the final sentence makes clear; it is this internal representation which actually generates the emotions.

Such exact parallelism between what is seen—the flow of the river—and what is felt—the flow of the emotions in a smooth increase from "beautiful" to "sublime"—can exist only if the mind contains a duplicate of the external scene, which means that the mental entity must have real dimensions both in space and in time, thus must have *substance* and *extension*. The extended metaphor does not state this in so many words, but over the full length of the description the implications accumulate that the writer's thoughts about the subject are being shaped by mind-as-entity operating as a theory-constitutive metaphor. Upham was surely aware that his extended metaphor violates the autonomy thesis so important to his mentors Reid and Stewart. On the other hand, it vividly and compactly expresses the otherwise inexpressible. This practical virtue was more important for Upham, especially for Upham the educator and writer of textbooks, than any theoretical defect.

Among modern writers on the theory of the sublime in the eighteenth century, Tuveson has noted this underlying current of implication in the language used by the theorists. In tracing the development of the concept of the imagination as a "means of reconciling man, with his spiritual needs and his desire to belong to a living universe of purpose and values, with a cosmos that begins to appear alien" (*Imagination* 97), Tuveson sees this concept as requiring that the mind's ability to expand or rise be "not entirely metaphorical." The language of writers on the sublime implies that the "contemplation of a physically vast object" increases "the physical extent of the mind." This "physical enlargement" corrects a problem of Lockean psychology, the restriction of the mind to a narrow chamber, a "cabinet," a restriction which, combined with Locke's elimination of the innate idea of God, seemed to leave no possibility of "grace" (101, 105).

Tuveson describes a revolutionary change from this view, which by the middle of the eighteenth century had become what he calls the "orthodox moral aesthetic," to a view which required neither a parallel physical process in the mind nor the actual existence in nature of qualities that the mind could respond to in a sublime way. Tuveson labels both Burke and Alison revolutionaries in this sense. Burke insisted that the imagination had no cause that human beings could understand and that the feelings of sublimity arose from the mechanical process of repetition rather than from an elevation or enlargement of the mind (166, 170). Alison's revolutionary work was his *Essays on the Principle of Taste*, which traced sublime emotions to associations between certain sensations and certain qualities, associations formed early in life; the emotion of sublimity is a response not to a natural existent but to a sign or symbol, and it is a response conditioned in youth (188). What Tuveson fails to remark is that these revolutionary theories preserve the metaphor of mind-as-entity. Burke's mental entity may not enlarge, but it still replicates the external phenomenon; Alison's mental entity responds as it does because of shapes impressed on it in youth. Near the end of his book Tuveson asks why there were so few technical innovations in the arts during this period. He suggests that "the teleological theory of imagination" kept interest focused on showing "the goodness of human nature" and likewise held back any impetus to study the mind "for its own sake" and to look at "the real problems of the personality" (178-79). I offer a second explanation. The continuing dominance of mind-as-entity contributed to the belief that the mind was pretty well understood and that not much was to be gained by studying the individual human being rather than "the mind" in general.

Novelists on the Formation of Ideas

It is well known that the novelists of the eighteenth century frequently refer to trains of association, the example most often cited being Laurence Sterne. Less well known are two important facts: the novelists were as interested as their philosopher contemporaries in the more general topic of the formation of ideas, and the key features of the mind-as-entity metaphor—passivity, impressibility, and extension—are as prevalent in the novels as in the psychological treatises. These features can be explored in three novels frequently mentioned as showing psychological interest and insight: Samuel Richardson's *Pamela* (1740-44), Charles Brockden Brown's *Wieland, or The Transformation* (1794), and Sterne's *The Life and Opinions of Tristram Shandy, Gentleman* (1760-67).

What makes *Pamela* psychological in the eyes of most readers is the moment-to-moment view into Pamela's thoughts, in particular her unintentional revelations of her attraction to Mr. B as that attraction grows into love. This is obviously the novel's strength. Its weakness is Pamela's almost complete inability to reflect and her correspondingly passive and superficial self-awareness. Both the weakness and the strength may result from the theory-constitutive role of mind-as-entity. By "theory-constitutive" here I don't mean that Richardson consciously applied theories of psychology when constructing his novels. But his explorations of Pamela's character do have the limits that are associated with mind-as-entity; the novel may be read as if Richardson consciously set out to apply the psychology of his time to a fictional case study of the mind of a young servant girl threatened with the loss of her virtue.

For such a reading, the first point is that while Pamela's letters are not devoid of reflections, those she presents consist almost entirely of simple comparisons between a present condition—not a state of mind—and a previous one. This kind of reflection conforms to the mind-as-entity metaphor in that it implies the formative connection between the mind and the external world. Richardson shows Pamela's life as a succession of conditions; her triumph is that she preserves her condition of chastity while adding the condition of honored, beloved, honest wife. Ian Watt gives Richardson "the central place in the development of the technique of narrative realism" (26), because he defined the "primary convention" of "formal realism": "that the novel is a full and authentic report of human experience" including "the individuality of the actors concerned, the particulars of the times and places of their actions" (32).

There is no question that Pamela's report is incredibly detailed, but it can be called psychologically authentic only within the context of the psychology of the eighteenth century. Watt correctly notes the belief of post-medieval philosophical realism that "truth can be discovered by the individual through his senses" (12); it is equally important that two important manifestations of this belief, the passive-impression theory of perception and the principle of the association of ideas, required the individual mind to be shaped ("impressed by") the external world through the agency of the senses. As a relatively passive entity, the mind will be unlikely to engage in reflections that do more than compare conditions. Thus Pamela's reflections are seldom very personal, seldom fully described, usually general and superficial: "I gave myself over to sad Reflections upon this strange and surprising discovery of John's"—that he had been showing Mr. B her letters to her parents—"for now I see, as he says, my Ruin has been so long a hatching" (111-12). Richardson effectively portrays Pamela's confusion at this new discovery by having her shift from proclaiming her own worthlessness in one sentence to wondering in the next why her master wants to ruin her if he really does love her. But the result of her reflection is nothing more than a stark contrast between virtue as she has been taught to understand it and the likely outcome of Mr. B's "devil's work."

The mental entity as imaged by Hartley, Hume, and Locke was a corpuscular system: each impression was discrete, each idea was a unit, and consciousness consisted of a string of ideas and impressions or a train of thoughts, coupled together but still separate. Pamela's mind is no different, hence her more detailed retrospects remain collections of specific impressions juxtaposed against her present impressions. Each succeeding situation is to be measured point for point against definite preceding situations. One of her more dramatically effective retrospects serves to acquaint both Mrs. Jewkes (who functions as her jailor) and the reader with some details of her past, in order to dramatize her present dilemma: "So I have lived above sixteen Years in Virtue and Reputation, and all at once . . . I must renounce all the Good . . . for a Pair of Diamond Ear-rings" and a few other treasures (174). We are pleased that the usually timid Pamela speaks so forcefully, but we should also notice that she sees the two conditions as simple contrasts; it seems as if for Pamela and for Richardson her virtue and the earrings are equally discrete and tangible.

She performs a similar measurement of dramatically contrasting conditions when she has finally accepted Mr. B's protestations of love and realizes that the marriage will really take place: "What a different Aspect every thing in and about this House bears now, to my thinking, to what it once had! The Garden, the Pond, the Alcove, the Elm-walk. But, O! my Prison is become my Palace!" (293) These examples show that Pamela's awareness of herself is literally superficial—limited to the surface of her mind and the tangible details of her existence. The awareness is also passive; it is not something she seeks but something that comes to her from the external world. The passive-impression theory even seems to apply to a feeling that can only have come from within her, her developing love for Mr. B: "I know not *how* it came, nor *when* it begun; but creep, creep it has, like a Thief upon me; and before I knew what was the Matter, it look'd like Love" (214). She may be using the pejorative simile because in this one case she does not have access to the discrete perceptions and associations which make up the feeling; she lacks the precise details of *how* and *when*. Without this knowledge she can only regard the feeling negatively, although at the same time she is powerfully influenced by it.

Richardson's strength and weakness as a psychologist in this novel are two sides of the same coin: he concentrates exclusively on his heroine's moment-to-moment conditions and treats them as discrete, each having a particular impact on Pamela's passive mind. That mind, after Mr. B asks her to remain just one fortnight longer, is "tortur'd with twenty different Thoughts in a

Minute," and her final decision, to deny his request, follows on this detail: "and the odious frightful Closet [where he had hidden himself] came into my Head" (84). In this passage her mind is simply a "presence-room" for recording the reversals of her opinion, simplistically signaled with a series of contrastive words and phrases ("but" and "but then" three times each, "well" and "well then" once each), and the final series of thoughts that leads to the decision, just as simplistically signaled with a series of *and*'s. My point is not to deny *Pamela* status as a psychological novel but to identify those aspects which are rightly called psychological. When we praise Richardson for recording the minute fluctuations of Pamela's thoughts and even more for creating the method he called "writing to the minute" which makes possible such recording in the first place, we need to understand that these thoughts are the reactions of a relatively passive mind to externally imposed or impressed stimuli, that Pamela's mind is as much a prisoner of the external world as she is a captive of Mr. B, that her concept of herself as virtuous has been totally shaped by her parents and her early religious training, and that as a result her mind has nothing which could properly be called its own life.

It is also necessary to understand that in choosing a young servant girl as his protagonist, Richardson could not avoid the limitations attributed by his era to a woman's ability to form ideas. The mind-as-entity metaphor required that all minds be somewhat passive, but within this general rule women were viewed as more open than men to external impressions, more likely to form casual, false associations, and less able to engage in fruitful reflections. Stewart presents this standard view in a section of his *Elements*, titled "The Sexes," in which he concentrates on women and mentions men only by contrast. His controlling assumption is that woman's "delicacy of frame" leaves her not just physically but mentally susceptible to external pressures. For this reason women's minds are "more open to the effects of casual impressions, and of such associations as regulate the train of thought in a mind which has no particular object in view" (4:240). Because women tend to be more driven by their passions than men, he continues, they are also inferior "in a power of steady and concentrated attention." Stewart voices the common belief of his period when he states that of all fields of action the one least accessible to women was "the philosophy of mind": "for as their early habits invite their attention constantly to sensible objects, their minds become singularly alive to things external, and of consequence more liable to those habits of inattention to the phenomena of the internal world, which, while they damp their curiosity with respect to these phenomena, prevent the cultivation of that power of *reflection*, without which it is impossible to study them with success" (4:242). This passage effectively summarizes the supposed natural limitations of the female mind. Where the woman is young, not well educated, and in a situation that constantly forces her to experience the strongest passions of fear, hope, and love, it is not surprising that her mental activity consists almost solely of recording the impressions of the moment and that her reflections consist of simple contrasts.

Brown's *Wieland* exhibits the same focus on details as *Pamela*, but where Richardson records minutia of time, place, and event, Brown stresses the sensations that arise from events and the ideas generated by the sensations. Brown wrote that "An accurate history . . . of the thoughts and feelings of any man, for one hour, is more valuable for some minds than a system of geography" (quoted by Pattee in his introduction to the novel, xxxviii). *Wieland* embodies this goal fairly successfully. Clara Wieland, the narrator, is exceedingly impressible, especialy when the stimulus has something about it of the sublime or mysterious. She gives the following description of her state of mind after an apparently "super-human" event occurs: "My heart was scarcely large enough to give admittance to so swelling a thought. An awe, the sweetest and most solemn that imagination can conceive, pervaded my whole frame. . . . An impulse was given to my spirits. . . . I was impressed with the belief of mysterious, but not of malignant agency" (51). This is an excellent example of the phenomenon that Hume described: an idea (Clara's "thought") giving rise to a whole series of sensations and ideas. And her reactions when she first hears Carwin's voice demonstrate how powerless she is to resist external impressions: "I cannot pretend to communicate the impression that was made upon me by these accents. . . . [The voice] imparted to me an emotion altogether involuntary and incontroulable [sic]" (59). When she sees the man's face, the same thing happens: "The impression that it made was vivid and indelible" (60); the face "continued for hours to occupy my fancy, to the exclusion of almost every other image" (61). This series of events, as Clara narrates it, reveals both the impressibility of her mind and her susceptibility to different kinds of stimuli, not only visual and aural but also the inner stimulus of a thought.

Clara's mind is not unusually passive in the context of the novel. Her descriptions of her brother's mental processes show that mental passivity is actually part of Brown's systematic psychology. We see this as early as her description of Wieland's reaction to the first strange voice (39-40). Clara's great fear was that he would respond to the event rather than remain indifferent, since any reaction would indicate "a diseased conditon of his frame." Her basis for this belief is that "the will is the tool of the understanding, which must fashion its conclusions on the notices of sense." If Wieland's senses were in some way "diseased," they would carry stronger than normal impressions from the event to his passive mind, adversely affecting his understanding and thus his will. This is exactly what happens, as subsequent events reveal—Wieland is strengthened in his conviction that he has been chosen by God for some great test of faith. This event also makes an impression on him because of his "ardent and melancholy" character: he tends to fasten on certain abstract ideas, which obtain "an immovable hold upon his mind" because through frequent repetition they have been "rendered familiar, and, in some sort, palpable to his intellect." His mind, like Clara's, is equally impressible by external phenomena and his own thoughts, so it is not surprising that her fears are realized. The event does have "a visible effect in augmenting his gravity." Clara remarks that "when we sifted his thoughts, they were generally found to have a relation more or less direct with this incident" (40).

Implicit in the attempt to "sift" someone's thoughts is the concept of thoughts themselves as discrete units which can be separated out according to size or weight, as if they are atoms or corpuscles. Thoughts are separable from the individual mind. They are the elements upon which the mental entity performs its operations; like the mind itself, they are entities. This concept accounts for such passages as the following: "Order could not readily be introduced into my thoughts. . . . I strove to give a slower motion to my thoughts . . . but my efforts were nugatory" (105). Even more significant than thoughts from external events having an independent existence is the implication that those generated by the mind also become independent—independent of the will. This phenomenon helps explain the subjective impression of the mind being divided against itself. Clara's moment of division comes when she is trying to decide whether or not to keep a suggested rendezvous with her tormentor: "What was it that swayed me? I felt myself divested of the power to will contrary to the motives that determined me to seek his presence. My mind seemed to be split into separate parts, and these parts to have entered into furious and implacable contention" (159).

It was a first principle of the psychology of this period that the mind was indivisible. Nevertheless, the psychologists could not deny the subjective reality Clara describes; even in the eighteenth century people experienced the sensation of a mind split into separate parts, contending against itself. In the nineteenth century, this sensation became one of the ingredients in portraying the life of the mind, but then in the nineteenth century the link between the mind of man and the mind of God was weakened or done away with altogether. The eighteenth century accounted for the sensation by granting thoughts the same separate-entity status as mind. Each thought could exert a separate influence on the mind, one thought impelling the will in one direction, the next thought impelling the emotions or the intellect in another. As Hume had explained, the copies of impressions taken by the mind can give rise to other impressions and ideas, and each idea generated will be linked by association to the generating idea or impression. As Clara's thoughts whirl through her mind, each one will call up a different set of associations, including associated emotions, while the "I" is buffeted like a small boat in a tempest.

Yet the impressibility of the human mind, as dictated by the mind-as-entity metaphor, helps Clara return to health after the havoc wreaked by her brother. The destruction of her house breaks "the monotonous and gloomy series" of her thoughts; "A new train of images," she relates, "disconnected with the fate of family, forced itself on my attention" (266). Thus she accedes to her uncle's request to accompany him to Montpellier and finally does find a fulfiling life. Her sick mind could be impressed with new sensations, which would result in new associations and ideally a whole new cast of character. This kind of regeneration may not be possible for minds in which deluded ideas have become "palpable," such as Wieland's, because these minds have no way to distinguish between the deluded ideas and impressions from the external world.

Unlike Richardson and Brown, Laurence Sterne seems to have been aware that the concept of mind-as-entity held problems as an explanation of the formation of ideas. He took both the passive-impression theory and the principle of associaton to logical and comical extremes. Yet his critical ploy is consistent with mind-as-entity in its theory-constitutive role: the metaphor will be explored and its limits defined, but it will not generate any new concepts. Sterne's criticisms did not lead him to new understanding of the formation of ideas; no less than the minds of Pamela and Clara Wieland, Tristram Shandy's mind is shaped by the external world.

It is clear from the presentation of Walter Shandy's hypothesis concerning the best manner of birth that Sterne was dissatisfied with the passive-impression theory's view of the mind as a physical entity. The hypothesis was based on Walter's post-Cartesian decision that the seat of the soul is not the pineal gland. Rather, "the chief sensorium, or headquarters of the soul, and to which place all intelligences were referred, and from whence all her mandates were issued,—was in, or near, the cerebellum." He was also convinced that "the subtlety and fineness of the soul depended upon the . . . finer net-work and texture in the cerebellum itself," which means that Caesarean section was the preferred method of birth, and failing that, then feet first rather than head first. Of normal birth, Father Shandy remarked, "what havoc and destruction must this [pressure on the head during the process of birth, which he estimates at 470 psi] make in the infinitely fine and tender texture of the cerebellum" (163-64). Walter found it even more alarming that "this force, acting upon the very vertex of the head, not only injured the brain itself or cerebrum,—but that it necessarily squeezed and propelled the cerebrum towards the cerebellum, which was the immediate seat of the understanding!" (164). For Walter this amply explained why "so many of our best heads are no better than a puzzled skein of silk,—all perplexity—all confusion within-side" (165).

Each sentence in this discussion, taken alone, seems relatively reasonable. Walter Shandy is certainly correct in discarding Descartes' hypothesis about the pineal gland, but he does not question the principle that "the chief sensorium" has a specific location. Does Sterne question it? Sterne certainly makes fun of Walter's pseudo-exact location of the sensorium—"in, or near, the cerebellum"—but he says nothing against specifying some location. Walter is not unreasonable in believing that the deformation of the skull during birth may deform the brain, but Sterne implies that it is something else again to hold that the "fine and tender *texture* of the cerebellum" can be damaged by the pressure and that squeezing together the cerebrum and cerebellum during birth may cause confusion in the adult. What Sterne seems to be criticizing here is not the assumption that the mind is a tangible entity or that it is marked by vibrations from the external world transmitted through the senses, but the hubris of those who would specify its location within the cranium and regard it as directly impressible by gross physical forces.

The basic components of the metaphor—passivity, impressibility, and extension—remain intact; Tristram's moral character is formed by the action of external events transmitted through vibrations to his mind and imprinted there. One of the most important of these events is Uncle Toby's freeing of the fly when the boy was ten years old. Tristram describes the result thus: "The lesson of universal good-will then taught and imprinted by my uncle Toby, has never since been worn out of my mind" (131). The incident found "a passage" to Tristram's "heart" as a result of his nerves setting his "whole frame into one vibration of most pleasurable sensation," which tells us that the process was a mechanical one, like that described by Hartley, but also that Tristram was already so formed as to find the vibration pleasing. Not only was the lesson "imprinted" on his mind but the impression endured through the wearing-down actions of everyday life. This description contains none of the comical exaggeration of his father's hypothesis about the sensorium; it seems to represent Sterne's view of the formation of fundamental ideas that make up an individual's character.

Tristram's attempt to draw his uncle Toby's character is in keeping with this view of mind and character being shaped by individual events. And here too Sterne illustrates the problems without offering an alternative view. Tristram's narrative method in general, as he describes it, is digressive and progressive "at the same time," allowing him to introduce and reconcile "two contrary motions." He has "constructed the main work and the adventitious parts of it with such intersections, and has so complicated and involved the digressive and progressive movements, one wheel within another, that the whole machine, in general, has been kept a-going" rather than proceeding haltingly, as do the stories of many less fortunate authors, first a bit of the "main work" and then a digression (95). The two wheels of Tristram's portrait of his uncle are Toby's modesty and his hobbyhorse. The relationship between the wheels is complicated, in that there is no point-for-point connection between Toby's mental furniture and the significant events of his life, yet simple in that his modesty and his hobbyhorse together provide the motive force of the "machine": the hobbyhorse, a model of the siege of Namur, is intended to relieve Toby of the difficulty of explaining verbally (especially to the opposite sex) how he received his groin injury.

The digressive method is how Tristram (and Sterne) attempt to reflect the complexity not only of such seemingly simple situations and characters but also of the actual attempt to illustrate accurately and literally. A structure of wheels within wheels, of intertwining progressions and digressions, is a promising way to capture the non-linear, non-corpuscular nature of experience. The structure itself could be a metaphor in that it gives us (in Dr. Johnson's phrase) two ideas for one, the tenor being that literally inexpressible aspect of mental experience. In this particular instance there are no clear signals to tell a reader to adopt such a perspective, yet that very lack could be regarded as part of the structural metaphor. But a problem arises with this reading. In attempting to get at the essence of Toby through the wheels that move him, Tristram resembles the scientists of Schön's paintbrush-as-pump story, with one important difference: the pump metaphor did help the scientists generate a new description of how a paintbrush works to pick up paint, whereas Tristram's/Sterne's structural metaphor remains constrained by the old metaphor of mind-as-entity. The wheels-within-wheels metaphor allows him to tell the story so that it embodies the confusion within Toby's mind, but it does not lead him to a better grasp of how Toby is moved. It is like an attempt to modify the crystal spheres model of the heavens, or like Hartley's adoption of Newton's concepts without the attendant calculus—important details remain inexpressible both literally and metaphorically.

One of the novel's pleasures (and difficulties) is trying to follow Tristram as he tries to trace various lines of reasoning to explain Uncle Toby. Indeterminacy is the rule, as we see in Tristram's association of Uncle Toby's modesty with his reticence in using words. Early in his story Tristram first connects one of Toby's character traits to a physical event: his modesty, which was almost equal to that of a woman, "if such a thing could be" (90), is shown to be a result of the groin injury he suffered during the seige of Namur. The injury took four years to heal, in part because Toby became so perplexed in attempting to explain the history of his wound and the history of his part of the battle that his cure was retarded and his life endangered (101). The problem was that "when he could not retreat out of the ravelin without getting into the half-moon, or get out of the covered way without falling down the counterscarp, nor cross the dyke without danger of slipping in," his mind became fretted, which led to "sharp paroxysms and exacerbations of his wound" (104-5). Tristram then exhibits the same problem. Having gone this far with one of the main wheels, he launches into a digression by asking if his imagined critic has read Locke's *Essay Concerning the Understanding*, his purpose being to describe three causes of "obscurity and confusion, in the mind of man." Like Walter's belief about the best method of birth, the three causes are all based on a conception of the human mind as a physical system: "dull organs," "slight and transient impressions," and "a memory like unto a sieve, not able to retain what it has received" (106-7). There follows a digressive analogy relating one Dolly, her thimble, and her sealing wax to impressions made or not so well made on the memory. But the only purpose of this analogy and the reference to Locke, Tristram finally announces, is, "after the manner of the great physiologists," to show the world what Uncle Toby's confusion was *not* caused by (108). The cause was words, especially "the unsteady uses" of the words relating to Toby's hobbyhorse.

Tristram's own attempt at explanation seems exceedingly unsteady until he comes to this point about the power of words to impress Toby's mind. Here the digression ends, as Tristram begs his "gentle critic" to "drop a tear of pity upon his scarp and counterscarp;—his glacis and his covered way;—his ravelin and his half-moon: 'Twas not by ideas,—by heaven! his life was put in jeopardy by words" (108). Yet the first mention of the scarp, the glacis, and so forth made explicit the point that whether the mental excitement derives from words or ideas, the result is physiological—"exacerbations of his wound." While the digression effectively satirizes "the great physiologists" in their attempt to explain mental processes by strictly physical means, Toby clearly believes that the problems of explanation were harming his health: although he "could not philosophize upon it;—'twas enough he felt it was so" (105). Tristram, and through him Sterne, betrays no doubt that the mental entities of "covered way" and "half-moon" were having an adverse effect, or that Trim's suggestion of actually modeling the battlefield caused Toby's bowling green to be instantly "painted" upon the "retina" of his "fancy" and thus brought the hobbyhorse into being at one stroke.

The overall effect of these wheels within wheels should be that we understand how a physical event (Toby's injury) affected his mind, led to the externalization of his memories in the form of a model, and contributes to his verbal difficulties with the widow Wadman. We understand this interaction just as we understand how Toby's modesty is revealed during the story of Aunt Dinah and the coachman—not with "great contours" but with "some familiar strokes and faint designations" (94). That is, we remark Toby's gentleness and modesty in his expressions, expostulations, and whistling of "Lillabullero" while his brother narrates the elopement.

Sterne was well aware that, as Locke, Reid, and others had said, it was impossible to obtain a record of all that had passed within a given mind since birth. The best that could be achieved was a general understanding of the processes by which ideas were formed, and a record of the contents of a few individuals' minds for an hour or so. For these ends, the passive-impression theory of perception and the association theory of the formation of ideas were sufficient. With the story of Walter's hypothesis, Tristram and Sterne show that it is not valid to apply the theory in a coarse way, and with the story of the origin of Toby's hobbyhorse they show allegiance to mind-as-entity by recording the momentary fluctuations of Tristram's ideas and the formative effect of discrete external events on his and Toby's characters.

Such a reading of Sterne's approach to the topic of the formation of ideas helps resolve a major critical-historical question: the extent to which he is Lockean or anti-Lockean. On a strictly verbal level, notes W. G. Day, Sterne borrows from over sixty authors, uses the language of Locke's *Essay* eight times, and by these direct borrowings to some degree satirizes Locke. Day concludes that Locke should not be taken as *the* key to the novel. Looking more at concepts, Howard Anderson concludes that *Tristram Shandy* constitutes a significant criticism of Locke's view of associationism as an "unnatural" process. Anderson believes that associationism leads us to an understanding of the passions and principles that dominate Tristram's mind (104). To be sure these are "non-rational connections," and Locke did identify them as aberrant, but in the context of the novel they are comprehensible and above all natural: "they are the common associations of the human mind," although given a unique cast by being part of Tristram's mind (103-6).

Given the preponderance of these non-rational connections in the novel, Arnold Davidson suggests that not Locke but Hume is the psychologist whose thought "pervades the novel" (18). Tuveson just as cogently holds that Sterne uses "association of ideas" in the Lockean sense ("the combinations which by chance form outside the reflective activity of the understanding") but intends no serious criticism of that theory ("Locke and Sterne" 268). Neither Locke nor Sterne conceive of mental activity as "the mere setting up of connections in a neural machine" (261). Marco Loverso agrees, finding Locke and Sterne aligned in their approach to consciousness and self-knowledge through the concept of the train of ideas. Much earlier, Kenneth MacLean called Sterne "the most industrious of all Locke's literary apostles" (17). The most convincing proponent of this position is Helene Moglen, who sees Locke's epistemology and theory of language as fundamental to the characterization of Tristram, to the structure of *Tristram Shandy*, and finally to the psychology implicit in the novel. But it is Locke creatively interpreted, Moglen correctly insists: "Tristram, in his search for identity, attempts to rise above the mechanism of his responses by ordering his impressions—attempting to trace them to their source, discovering in memory the unifying self that is the sum of its experiences. That Tristram is hindered at every point by the conditioning forces that propel him, even at the moment of his seeking to become master over them, is the tragi-comic paradox of the human dilemma. But the affirmation is posited in the attempt" (17). And in her concluding chapter, Moglen sees Sterne's interpretation of Locke as prophetic of the "contemporary vision," looking forward to Bergson, William James, Joyce, and the absurdists.

There are several explanations for these different readings of the Locke-Sterne question, chief among them being the difficulty of pinning either author down to a single position. With Sterne the possibility of irony is ever present, and with both authors what they say on one page may be directly or implicitly contradicted on the next. While we cannot easily determine their likemindedness either by looking strictly at Sterne's direct borrowings or by attempting to interpret the psychology of each, we can notice the significant similarity in their figurative language. This approach reveals that Sterne is aware of the problems inherent in the mind-as-entity metaphor but does not improve on that metaphor. His reference to an image being painted on Toby's fancy is not qualitatively different from the Lockean school's sieves and impressions. This is a perfect instance of the metaphor operating in a theory-constitutive way. The experiential problem that Sterne is dealing with (language's impact on mind *and* body), his structure of wheels within wheels, and his willingness to experiment with language and narrative structure could lead to a conceptual revolution or at least to a new generative metaphor. Instead he carries on with normal science, as it were, adding to the existing theory of how ideas are formed (by substantive externals and by the mind itself) another component: ideas painted by words. As James Swearingen observes, "Locke does not realize the full promise of his initial insight [into the formation of ideas] because he studies the mind as an empirical object" and thereby "misses the richly complex processes of consciousness available to a reflective method" (35-36). Sterne succeeds, "albeit in a tentative and philosophically unsystematic way," where Locke fails: he creates a narrator who "engages in the reflective explication of his own consciousness as rooted in a particular time and place" instead of trying to construct a consciousness on the basis of a few limited principles.

Development of Ideas and the Active Mind

The developmental psychology of the eighteenth century combines a view of the mind as a relatively passive entity with a view of the mind as active in its own formation. These two views are balanced differently by different writers, but the general outlines are clear. Ideas are formed by the laws of association operating on perceptions impressed by the external world and on perceptions and ideas generated by the mind itself. As the mind matures, it becomes able to select among experiences which will yield impressions, and it becomes able to reflect on its own operations. If the mind develops in the normal way it will achieve a healthy balance between reliance on and independence from external impressions. Normal development requires that the young mind be well stocked with the right kind of impressions—those from the natural and human realms—and that mental exercise be suited to age: younger minds should not engage in speculation and reflection.

A mind shaped according to these principles would necessarily be impressed with accurate ideas about the external world and about its own relationship to that world; such a mind could then take an active role in its own further development. Failure to understand this possibility has led literary historians to oversimplify all of pre-twentieth-century psychology as built on a strictly passive, impressible mind. (See for example, Ryan.) True, the mental entity was most likely to be represented as passive in discussions of the early formation of ideas, but when the psychologists considered, as they sometimes did, the development of the mental entity itself, they attributed to it a certain amount of active power.

It was a fundamental tenet of the psychology of the period that the relationship between the mind and the external world was not accidental but had been designed by God to serve His ends. As Upham describes the relationship, "We have seen the mind placed in the position of a necessary connexion with the material world through the medium of the senses, and in this way awakened into life, activity, and power. Inanimate matter seems to have been designed and appointed by Providence as the handmaid and nurse of the mind in the days of its infancy; . . . Material eyes were given to the soul . . . that it might see . . . and material hands, that it might handle. . . . By means of these and other senses we become acquainted with whatever is visible and tangible, and has outline and form" (*Mental Philosophy* 119).

One of the more curious aspects of this passage is that a mind can be talked about without referring to the person to whom it belongs. This concept is conveyed by the presence of the mind or the soul as the subject of nearly every clause and nearly every proposition implied by the embedded sentence elements. Only one clause uses the personal pronoun: "we become acquainted with whatever is visible and tangible." A second curious aspect is Upham's easy shift from "mind" to "soul," a shift that suggests equivalence. Upham seems equally comfortable with suggesting that the *soul* was awakened into life, activity, and power by the material world. The mind can exist in relation to the external world independently of a person, so it seems, and the soul has an infancy and can be awakened. Both points reveal the theory-constitutive pressure of the mind-as-entity metaphor. Even this divinely designed process must conform to the model of the mind as an entity, albeit in this case not the passive entity implied by the simple model of perception and the association principle.

The point could also be expressed from the perspective of the natural sciences. Sampson Reed's goal is to show how "the natural sciences, the actual condition of society, and the Word of God, are necessary to the development of all minds" (81-82). In other words, "the natural sciences are the basis of all useful knowledge" (35). To develop this point Reed relies on an explicit simile, mind as a physical system: "The actual cohesion of the human mind is, as it were, the solid substance, in which the laws of moral and intellectual philosophy and political economy (whatever may be their quality) exist embodied, as the natural sciences do in the material world. A knowledge of those laws . . . is the natural consequence of the development of the affections by which a child is connected with those that surround him" (54). If the mind is brought by careful stages to an encounter with something like one of the abstract sciences, it can become like "an active solvent" of the subject, which then falls to pieces and *recrystallizes* (the term is Reed's) in "an arrangement agreeable to that of the mind itself" (68).

Implicit in Reed's and Upham's descriptions is the responsibility of individuals and society in general to provide conditions in which impressions accurately represent the external world and thus contribute to the formation of healthy minds. Stewart considers this relationship several times in his *Elements*. He identifies education's first priority as making sure that "the understanding is well stored with particular facts," for example those from chemistry, physics, and history; only then can one profit from introspection and examination of one's own mental faculties (2:421). Education should attempt to "impress truth on the mind in early infancy," because we see on a daily basis "how susceptible the tender mind is of deep impressions" (2:73-74). The most valuable task of education is to associate an infant's first conceptions of the Deity with "the early impressions produced on the heart by the beauties of nature" (2:74-75). The almost certain result of such association will be to make the mature individual sensible of the "innumerable proofs" of the universe's "harmony of design." This harmony "forces itself irresistably on the thoughts of all who are familiarly conversant with the phenomena either of the material or of the moral world" (3:289).

The language of this program carries its own justification in the form of the concept of an impressible mind. It was simply not open to question that the external world could be accurately represented or that invisible moral realities were as tangible as the visible physical realities. According to Stewart, the unquestionable presumption of every thoughtful individual had to be that "there is one great *moral system*, corresponding to the *material system*; and that the connexions which we at present trace" among the objects composing the material system intimate "some vast scheme, comprehending all the intelligent beings who compose the other" (3:296). Although the youthful mind is naturally passive, structured to take whatever impressions are presented to it, maturity brings the ability to exercise some control over the impressions to be received. The mind never outgrows its essentially passive nature but rather develops a complementary "active power."

The passive-active relationship is expressed by Wordsworth in the following familiar lines from "Expostulation and Reply," which can be regarded as a mind-as-entity paradigm:

> The eye—it cannot choose but see;
> We cannot bid the ear be still;
> Our bodies feel, where'er they be,
> Against or with our will.
> Nor less I dream that there are Powers
> Which of themselves our minds impress;
> That we can feed this mind of ours
> In a wise passiveness.

As Wordsworth expresses the concept, it is paradoxical: How can the mind be fed by passiveness, and how can a person feed a mind when the mind is the person? Yet Wordsworth's point is exactly that the mind as an entity can relax itself and admit impressions from the "powers." For the psychology of this period, a person's development is fundamentally complete when the mind can exercise significant control over its impressions. Thus Stewart on "good sense in the conduct of life": "that temper of mind which enables its possessor to view . . . with perfect coolness and accuracy, all the various circumstances of his situation; so that each of them may produce its due impression on him, without any exaggeration arising from his own peculiar habits" (*Elements* 2:459-60). Wordsworth and Stewart are making the same point as shown by their figurative language, and it is a point common to all theorists of the mind contemporaneous with them: once a person has reached that high stage of development, the feelings and emotions should be held in check so that the mind can take impressions. To understand that the mind *will* take impressions is to achieve maturity; once the impressions have been taken, they can then be calmly viewed in the mind's presence-room or sensorium and can be acted on in accordance with the principles of good sense. This intrinsic activity of the mind is part of the development of every normal human being and is an essential component of the psychology of the period, an aspect which is too often overlooked by historians who see the passive-impression theory as a full and complete description of pre-modern psychology. Such oversight has the effect of creating sharp historical discontinuities, as Robert Langbaum does when he oversimplifies post-Lockean associationism in order to dramatize the "new certainty about self and the self's perceptions" established by Wordsworth and the other "romanticists" (46).

An excellent example of the novelistic presentation of mental development as governed by the mind-as-entity metaphor is found in Brown's *Wieland.* The narrator specifically notes that the elder Wieland's character was formed as a young man, when he "spent all his time pent up in a gloomy apartment, or traversing narrow and crowded streets." The result was that "His heart gradually contracted a habit of morose and gloomy reflection" which only became stronger as he progressed through life to his dramatically mysterious ending—spontaneous combustion (8). Likewise, his son's temper, characterized by "a sort of thrilling melancholy," has been solidified by the active efforts of his intellect: "All his actions and practical sentiments are linked with long and abstruse deductions" (25, 39). The characters of both men were warped because their education was exactly the opposite of that recommended by Stewart. Both entered on reflection and introspection before their minds were strong enough for those arduous tasks. As a result, each was particularly susceptible to "exaggeration [of impressions] arising from his own peculiar habits." Despite the mal-formative influences of their youth, both father and son developed minds of extraordinary active power. Both minds are powerful enough to create hallucinations, and the father's possibly generates a self-consuming fire. Their active powers take these particular forms, the language makes clear, because their youthful experiences "contracted" their "life, activity, and power"; their environments were their handmaids and nurses, but indifferent ones.

Wieland is also typical of the novels of the eighteenth century in treating the characters' early years with relative brevity. The novelists were not particularly interested in the development of the mind as such. They considered that no complete history was possible—they could not record every impression. It was possible either to record or to infer the impressions that combined to form a given idea; it was also possible to record the hue of the impressions taken by a young mind, to relate them to a particular cast of character, and to show how this cast brought about a particular state of mind in a mature individual. Richardson was not interested in the formation of Pamela's mind but wanted to show how her moment-to-moment experiences impressed themselves on her mind. Similarly, Sterne did not try to trace the growth of Tristram's mind but concentrated on showing that mind's moment-to-moment ebullitions. Tristram's description of the processes in Dr. Slop's mind is a perfect model of Sterne's conception of his task with respect to Tristram's mind: "The thought [of Mrs. Shandy lying in bed about to give birth] floated only in Dr. Slop's mind, without wail or ballast to it, as a simple proposition; millions of which, as your worship knows, are everyday swimming quietly in the middle of the thin juice of a man's understanding, without being carried backwards or forwards, till some little gusts of passion or interest drive them to one side" (179). For Slop, the gust is provided by a noise overhead, near Mrs. Shandy's bed, and he is reminded of a task more important than simply getting his medical bag opened.

The novelist can proceed quite effectively by noting the direction taken by the mind in response to any given gust of passion or interest. It is neither possible nor necessary to describe how each of those millions of simple propositions came to exist in the mind: one need only describe the tendency imparted to the mind by a particular stimulus, in the same way that one need not know the behavior of each molecule in a gas-filled chamber in order to know how the pressure in the chamber will change as the temperature is changed. Once the general shape of the youthful mind has been sketched by indicating the tone and timbre of early impressions, the novelist is free to assume that shape as a given in depicting the character's later life.

The mind-as-entity metaphor continued to influence the fictional portrayal of mental development well into the nineteenth century, although the changing view of the balance between the mind's passivity and activity was creating some tension in the language. We can see this tension develop in three novels of Jane Austen: *Northanger Abbey* (written in 1797, published in 1818), *Emma* (1816), and *Persuasion* (written in 1817, published in 1818). Austen's two final novels are striking because they lack much of the language associated with mind-as-entity although they dwell on events whose significance lies totally in the minds of the characters concerned, that is, on events that invite and even seem to require the use of the language. Her first is as much at ease with this metaphor as the final two are not.

Austen's sparing use of sensationalist language in *Emma* indicates her awareness of how much the mind-as-entity metaphor does not account for. She presents Emma going through changes and being defined in the context of characters around her. Emma makes errors of interpretation and then learns from each error, her greatest error being her failure to see that Mr. Knightley is her destined husband. The references to Emma's mind assume the mind-as-entity metaphor, for example when she discovers that Mr. Elton is wooing her and not Harriet Smith: "her mind had never been in such perturbation, and it needed a very strong effort to appear attentive and cheerful till the usual hour of separating allowed her the relief of quiet reflection" (133). This description is different only in degree from those in *Wieland* and *Pamela*; Emma's thoughts, like those of Clara and Pamela, are in a turmoil, and the pressure can be relieved only by reflection.

But that difference in degree is important. Austen does not attempt to show her heroine's mind as a series of changes of state caused by impressions and associations; she does not engage in the kind of anslysis characteristic of the earlier writers. When Mr. Elton declares his love for Emma, Austen writes, "It would be impossible to say what Emma felt, on hearing this—which of all her unpleasant sensations was uppermost. She was too completely overpowered to be immediately able to reply" (131). "Uppermost" and "overpowered" are typical of the psychological language of the time, indicating the physical nature of the mental event: the sensations are occupying space in her mind (hence one must be uppermost, although she cannot say which) and have a force of their own independent of her will.

But whereas Richardson or Brown would have continued in this vein, Austen regards it as impossible to present the chaos of Emma's emotions and sensations. Of less interest to her than the chaos are the actions which follow this momentary state: what Mr. Elton says and how Emma responds. Nor does Austen delve into Emma's mind when the heroine is alone and able to indulge in the relief of quiet reflection. She presents Emma's thoughts fully, alternating between having Emma speak her thoughts aloud and describing those thoughts with the same dispassionate narrative voice she used to describe Emma's actions. There is no description of the physiological impact of these thoughts; there are no references to Emma's heart, brain, or blood, to vibrations, upwellings, effusions, and so forth. We might say that these references are lacking because of the type of person Emma is—she is restrained, phlegmatic, definitely not as susceptible as Clara Wieland to rushes of wild feeling. However, to account for the differences in this way is not particularly compelling. We can know characters only through the language with which they are presented to us; we can base our judgment that Emma is restrained rather than passionate only on the terms used to describe her. It is at least as plausible that the differences between Austen's language and that of Brown or Richardson, for example, result from the inability of the mind-as-entity metaphor to represent the mental phenomena that were becoming interesting in Austen's era.

The existence of an inner chaos, the ease with which a supposedly mature mind could deceive itself—these facts of mental life could be referred to in general, as Austen does, but the psychophysiological language of the earlier writers was not adequate to her goal. This goal can be described as the presentation of an individual who develops in a smooth, continuous manner—who is slowly molded by events that might cause discontinuities or cracks in the mental clay of an earlier author's character. The difference is analogous to the difference between "ebullitions" and "the relief of quiet reflection": both connote mind as an extended substance, but the latter conveys an impression of continuity in contrast to the former's impression of discontinuity. Austen in fact concludes her presentation of this period of Emma's perturbation with an ordinary statement of the relationship between a young person's spirits and the cycle of day and night: "To youth and natural cheerfulness like Emma's, though under temporary gloom at night, the return of day will hardly fail to bring return of spirits. The youth and cheerfulness of morning are in happy analogy, and of powerful operation; and if the distress be not poignant enough to keep the eyes unclosed, they will be sure to open to sensations of softened pain and brighter hope" (137-38). The message here is clear: Emma's is a daylight personality, thus any gloom is a relatively insignificant aberration, an ebullition.

Emma's conversations with herself always sound rational and dispassionate. Her mind is definitely active, perhaps even overactive from Austen's perspective, since her penchant for matchmaking is one of the objects of the novel's irony. Still, it is a limited activity, not comprising significant reflection on or exploration of those impossible-to-represent tumults but evincing the powerful operation of her naturally cheerful disposition. Most important to Austen is the continuity of Emma's character. Emma's mind and physical organization do undergo perturbations in response to impressions and ideas, but despite her youth her mind is rather more active and less susceptible to the pressures of the external world than the minds of the other characters I have discussed so far. Thus *Emma* represents one possible modification of the earlier focus on mind-as-entity; that metaphor is still present in the novel but is less dominant than the consideration of the whole human being. Emma is a discrete entity herself; Clara Wieland in comparison is a collection of impressions and reactions.

Austen had not always focused on continuity rather than ebullitions, as her first novel, *Northanger Abbey*, shows. One of Austen's distinctive attributes, her concern with precise language, is already easily visible in this work. The hero, Henry Tilney, serves as her mouthpiece when he criticizes Catherine Morland for referring to a book as "very nice"; his point is that the adjective "nice" has come to be used in "every commendation on every subject," with the result that no precise meaning remains attached to the word (108). Austen practices the desirable precision in her own descriptions, for example writing of General Tilney that he was "past the bloom, but not past the vigour of life" (80); without attributing to him a specific age, she places him precisely in a time of life. She pays similarly careful attention to states of mind: "Catherine's feelings, as she got into the carriage, were in a very unsettled state; divided between regret for the loss of one great pleasure, and the hope of soon enjoying another, almost its equal in degree, however unlike in kind" (86). The pleasure she has lost is that of walking with the Tilney family; the one she will gain is a visit to a castle that has been represented to her as delightfully Gothic. Austen is clearly criticizing Catherine for her willingness to accept the second pleasure, whose *kind*, having been shaped by the Gothic tales Catherine loves to read, is inferior to the pleasure to be derived from social intercourse.

This passage is noteworthy for its suggestion that Catherine's feelings are as easily described, discriminated among, and categorized as the "times of life" of her main characters. Other passages convey the same confidence in describing mental states: "Catherine's understanding began to awake; an idea of the truth suddenly darted into her mind" (117); and this: "Northanger Abbey!—These were thrilling words, and wound up Catherine's feelings to the highest point of extasy [sic]. Her grateful and gratified heart could hardly restrain its expressions within the language of tolerable calmness" (140). Austen's language implies that it is also relatively easy to correlate external influences with ideas and predispositions. Catherine comes to the painful awareness that the attitude she carried to Northanger Abbey "might be traced to the influence of that sort of reading" she had "indulged" in while at Bath. The result of the reading had been to create a "delusion." More specifically, her "imagination" had determined to view "each trifling circumstance" with alarm, and her "mind," which had been "craving to be frightened," had bent all impressions "to one purpose" (199-200). Except for points of style, these descriptions could have come from Defoe, Godwin, or for that matter Hume or Thomas Brown; they conform to the terms and concepts of the eighteenth century.

Austen became much less certain about how to describe mental operations during her later years, a development that correlates with her tendency in her late works to look at "a region of character that is not really expressible in social or moral terms," a region that is "asocial" and includes the "qualities of responsiveness, openness to being moved" (Bodenheimer 622). *Persuasion*, her final novel, carries the hesitation of *Emma* even farther. On the one hand, Austen focuses almost exclusively on the thoughts and emotions of her heroine, Anne Elliott, and on those events that cause her strong sensations. On the other hand, the mental states are frankly confused and confusing—confusing for Anne, and presented as confused: "It was agitation, pain, pleasure, a something between delight and misery" (185). This typical sentence stands in striking contrast to the self-assured "past the bloom, but not past the vigour of life"; the best Austen can do is call the sensation "a something" and indicate what it is not. The limitations of the usual language of the mind may also be the reason for one of Austen's infrequent lengthy syntactic metaphors, when Anne meets her former lover after a separation of eight years:

> Her eye half met Captain Wentworth's; a bow, a curtsey passed; she heard his voice—he talked to Mary, said all that was right; said something to the Miss Musgroves, enough to mark an easy footing: the room seemed full—full of persons and voices—but a few minutes ended it. Charles shewed himself at the window, all was ready, their visitor had bowed and was gone; the Miss Musgroves were gone too, suddenly resolving to walk to the end of the village with the sportsmen: the room was cleared, and Anne might finish her breakfast as she could. [84-85]

This choppy string of clauses and verb phrases suggests that everything happens too quickly for Anne to do more than register impressions. It is not as if Austen cannot render a two-minute event in controlled, detailed, syntactically ordinary sentences and paragraphs; such is her usual practice when she feels she can adequately represent the feelings associated with impressions. Here she apparently feels she that language cannot represent the irrational quality of Anne's mental events. As Anne realizes after the visit, "with all her reasonings, she found, that to retentive feelings eight years may be little more than nothing"—reasoning is not able to control these feelings. Austen may also be doubting the method of analysis of sensations on which the psychology of her time was based: in such a charged and complex situation the method can scarcely identify the components of the mental event, let alone explain why they combine to produce the given sensation.

Anne's observation about her mind's relative independence from the passage of time and its shaping pressures correlates with a mental phenomenon that was receiving increasing attention from psychologists in the first third of the nineteenth century—the felt impression that the mind has sufficient power of its own and resources within itself to develop far beyond the shaping influence of the external world. The passage from Thomas Upham quoted a few pages earlier continues as follows: "but there are also inward powers of perception, hidden fountains of knowledge. . . . In other words, the soul finds knowledge in itself which neither sight, nor touch . . . nor any outward forms of matter, could give" (*Mental Philosophy* 119). Anne Elliott discovers that her love for Captain Wentworth has scarcely aged a day, and this is very much a discovery of inner knowledge, not imparted to her but only activated by an external event.

Nevertheless, the language of Austen and Upham remains within the limits of the metaphor mind-as-entity. For the soul to be able to find knowledge within itself, it must have both a searching faculty and something that is to be sought—both "inward powers of perception" and "hidden fountains" which those powers discover and from which they imbibe knowledge. The image suggests that the interior of the mind is no longer the simple space presented by Hume and Hartley but a textured place with localized features within which a percipient principle can experience certain impressions unavailable from the external world. It had always been agreed that "the mind begins very early to thirst after principles which may direct it in the exertion of its powers" (Reid, *Inquiry* 40). But this activity was not regarded as valid evidence about the nature of the mind itself, for the reason Berkeley gave: ideas are "passive and inert" and thus "cannot represent unto us by likeness or image that which acts" (272). During the eighteenth century, the mind was generally regarded as a "thinking, intelligent, active being" (Reid, *Intellectual Powers* 473), a "perceiving, active being" or "thing" (Berkeley 258). Upham preserves this view: he suggests a specific principle of development that places more value on the mind's activity, but he phrases the principle in metaphorical language that still allows the mind the qualities of extension and impressibility. He still represents the mind as localized, hence extended, although here it is living, active, and willful rather than passive.

Upham's metaphorical description fulfills Ortony's three theses: it expresses the literally inexpressible, is vivid, and is compact. It brings to life and makes tangible the abstract definitions of Reid and Berkeley. It is an excellent instance of the theory-constitutive role played by the mind-as-entity metaphor. Austen may have been aware of the problems and limitations of that metaphor; Upham, as a philosopher, was certainly aware of them. The problems had been well known for a century. Neither the novelist nor the psychologist solved them. Both writers foreshadow developments in psychological concepts and language that take place later in the century, Austen hinting at the mysteries of the mind (these will come to play a much greater role in fiction) and Upham creating an early instance of the mindscape metaphor. These developments and others that I discuss in subsequent chapters radically revise the concept of mind as a "perceiving, active being" and point toward the creation of "mind-as-a-living-being" as a generative metaphor. Such a revision was impelled and informed by the increasing influence of developmental psychology, aberrant psychology, neurophysiology, and the like in nineteenth-century thought.

IV
MIND AS ENTITY IN NINETEENTH-CENTURY PSYCHOLOGY

Most psychological works during the first two-thirds of the nineteenth century continued to draw on the mind-as-entity metaphor and to display the limitations of that metaphor in its theory-constitutive function. The novelists of the same time span, discussed in the following chapter, were seeking a means of representing the life of the mind, that is, mind as a living being identical with the character in whose brain it exists, whereas the psychologists, despite some general theoretical pronouncements in this direction, continued to treat the mind as a separable entity—localizable and discrete although "in substance" immaterial. They continued in this vein despite major changes both within psychology and across the culture—the theological connection became less important, and the physiological and what we now call functional and behavioral connections became more important.

In this chapter I illustrate the continuing dominance of scientific psychology by the mind-as-entity metaphor, first in two practical applications and then in scientific and academic psychology. I show that whether the genre is handbooks of what we now call psychiatry, school texts, psychological treatises with an avowedly physiological orientation or those with a more overtly introspective and analytical approach, the mind-as-entity metaphor is a notable feature of the language. I also show that one of the philosophical psychologists, George Henry Lewes, identified and developed a metaphor that could have helped him achieve a dramatic new understanding of the mind if he had not held so strongly to language that presented the mind as a physical system.

The first approach, physiological psychology, has been described as "an almost forgotten chapter in the history of psychology" (Danziger 119), but it has received at least tangential attention in Robert M. Young's *Mind, Brain, and Adaptation* as well as in studies of the history of mesmerism and phrenology. The second approach, which I call *philosophical*, has been even more neglected because it had no easily demonstrated impact on the major developments of twentieth-century psychology. When the philosophers are considered it is in light of their contributions to or (more usually) their inhibitions of the development of twentieth-century concepts. For example, Herbert Spencer is studied almost solely as a forerunner of the evolutionary component of modern psychology and not as a psychologist with a system thoroughly grounded in the major philosophical questions of his age.

This presentist approach, especially in its lack of interest in the philosophical psychology, does not do justice to the historical reality. David Leary has clearly demonstrated this point in the case of German-language psychology from the time of Wilhelm Wundt: "There was no necessary conflict between science and philosophy, particularly as regards psychology" (233). Leary goes on to say that Wundt held psychology to be the "*fundamental* science supporting the natural sciences, the social sciences, and philosophy"; he notes Wundt's fondness for pointing out that "all the natural sciences abstract their subject matter from immediate psychological experience" (234-35). The same points can be made for Wundt's English-speaking contemporaries. They shared the conception of psychology as the fundamental discipline or science, the one that gave meaning to all others. One of the most erudite historians of psychology observes that Alexander Bain was typical of his age in this regard: "Though he did not declare psychology to be the one foundation of philosophy, in practice he gave it that position," since his *Logic*, his *English Grammar*, his ethics and his metaphysics "were all suffused with the colour of his psychology" (Peters 465). It was a psychology that continued to regard the mind as an object of study no less suitable (and isolable) than a chemical reaction or a problem in classical mechanics.

Mind-as-Entity in Psychiatry and School Texts

The mind-as-entity metaphor remained dominant until well into the nineteenth century because it was useful. It contributed to a relatively enlightened approach to psychiatry (then referred to with such locutions as "mental hygiene") and relatively comprehensible presentations of mental science in texts designed for schools and colleges; these were areas in which a vivid, compact, and expressive metaphor could make a difference in the conception and presentation of problems. Ruth Caplan points out that early nineteenth-century American psychiatrists justified their "moral treatment" of the insane by citing the "malleability of the brain surface": their treatment consisted of trying to erase pathological conditions in the brain's surface (9). The same generalizations hold for British psychiatry. The psychiatrists did not deny the immaterial nature of the soul, according to Caplan; most of them "posited a dualism between brain and intellect. . . . The intellect was a spiritual potential, which became act through the medium of the limbs. If the brain were diseased, the intellect would be denied its avenue to act. . . . The intellect, however, could never be diseased, because . . . like the soul of which it is part, [it] is immortal and hence immutable" (6). For those individuals who were "mental aliens," who suffered from "alienated minds," cure was to be sought by "education and the imposition of regular habits of life and work, appropriate mental stimulation, orderly thinking, and correct values"; these treatments would reconstruct "damaged brain tissue" and thus make the organ of mind once again able to perform its duties (26). Caplan notes that after mid-century there was increasing belief in the primacy of purely physical causes and methods of cure, a shift related to the trend away from "natural philosophy" and toward "natural science" as well as to "clinical experiences that cast doubt on the universal applicability of moral treatment theory" (126). Despite this shift, mind retained its status as an entity, only becoming somewhat more physical and less immaterial. The picture had a less happy side, as Andrew Scull has shown. The continuing insistence by asylum directors and doctors in England on the "lesion" theory, despite absence of evidence that such lesions had anything to do with most mental illnesses, was an economic and political phenomenon. These medical persons were interested in preserving their share of the "growing market or trade in lunacy." If there really were such lesions, these professionals argued, then inhouse care was necessary (Scull 43, 167-68).

A leading figure in American psychiatry was Isaac Ray, whose book *Mental Hygiene* (1863) elaborates the theories of moral psychiatry in language reflecting the mind-as-entity metaphor. Ray's "general principle" of mental hygiene is that "whatever improves the physical qualities of the brain also improves, in some way or other, the qualities of the mind; and that judicious exercise of the mind is followed by the same result" (121). Anything that brings fresh blood or a "fresh impulse of the nervous current" can be helpful for the brain, as long as the stimulation is carefully applied (120). On the other hand, "whether excited or depressed, the mind is strongly exercised by the strange thoughts and emotions that possess it" in the early stages of mental illness; "it needs rest, repose, withdrawal from excitement" (135). The ill mind is so susceptible to impressions from the physical world that mentally ill people need to be kept away from their ordinary routines and previous associations in order for cure to be effective. This is one of the observations frequently made in asylums, Ray states. For instance, "the sight of a bundle of old clothes from home is sufficient to reproduce all the original excitement and agitation in many a patient, calm, quiet, and apparently convalescing" (140). This is why hospitalization of the insane is so important: only in the institution can the mentally ill person be protected from "circumstances that maintain the morbid activity of his mind and strengthen his aberrations" (145).

However inadequate it may have been as a basis for theory, the metaphor of mind-as-entity at least supported humane treatment of the mentally ill as necessary to reshape their minds. It does not account for the onset of aberrant behaviors in the mentally ill—why, for example, Dr. Manette in Dickens' *Tale of Two Cities* became fixated on shoe-making. But it provides a way of talking about how mental illness can worsen—when Manette receives a powerful emotional shock, he immediately reverts to his cobbler's bench and shuts out all external stimuli.

Mind-as-entity also provided a clear framework for carrying out the important work of training the mind. The principles as enunciated by leading psychologists during the eighteenth and early nineteenth centuries—the mind receives and is shaped by impressions, associations form pathways in the mind, the mind's operations are grouped into faculties or powers—formed the basis of school and university courses during the nineteenth century as well as the texts which often grew out of these courses. An excellent example is Dr. John Abercrombie's *Inquiries Concerning the Intellectual Powers, and the Investigation of Truth* (1833), as abridged by Jacob Abbott of Harvard, for use by schools and academies. In his introduction Abbott notes that the work's "useful tendency is most decided, both in making the pupil acquainted with his powers, and in guiding him to the most efficient and successful use of them" (4). The book's aim is "to exercise and strengthen the thinking and reasoning powers,—to enable the mind to grasp abstruse and perplexing subjects,—to think clearly and to reason correctly" (11). The mind-as-entity metaphor provides both the rationale and the method for this approach: the rationale, because as an entity it can, like a muscle, be strengthened and shaped, and the method, because if the mind is really an entity it will respond not only to exercise but also to the impression of "true relations" among facts of the external world (264).

Joseph Haven, like Abbott an important educator, published

his *Mental Philosophy* in 1857, a text based on lectures on psychology he had given at Amherst for years. This book is noteworthy for its systematic application of the mind-as-entity metaphor to the three main faculties of the mind: intellect, sensibilities, and the will. Haven consistently focuses on the mind's faculties and operations, the mind's perception of impressions, and the meaning of consciousness (the state when "the mind is aware of its own operations," 39). Haven's method is introspective: "In psychology, the observer has within himself the essential elements of the science which he explores; the data which he seeks, are the data of his own consciousness; the science which he constructs is the science of himself" (19). Characteristic of Haven's use of mind-as-entity are his statements that the mind can focus the "mental eye" and that it has a "mental canvas" (48, 114). The mind that can do such focusing and painting is an active entity; compared with most writers of the period, Haven attributes rather more active power to the mind. His imagery, however, also suggests limitations on the mind which seem a direct result of mind-as-entity, for instance spatial limits. In describing why human beings cannot perceive infinity, Haven writes that thought normally "passes around" the object thought of "with its measuring line. . . . But the infinite, the unconditioned, the absolute, in their very nature unlimited, cannot be shut up thus within the narrow lines of human thought": they may be true and real, but we can't "properly conceive them" (54). In other words we can't get within our heads the concept of something infinite because the space within our heads is finite. Yet Haven also insists that no physiological theory can explain how memory actually happens. He quotes Malebranche's theory of memory as depending on impressions made on brain fibers and then discusses various "metaphors" used to describe the process of memory, such as "type imprinted on the soul, impression made on it as of a seal on wax, image, picture, copy," and he grants the possibility that sensation may result from a physical effect produced on the sensorium. Nevertheless, no physiological theory, Haven writes, can explain how the phenomenon of memory actually comes about (136).

As these examples show, Haven was giving his students at Amherst the portrait of a mental entity that on the one hand was more than the sum of its physiological operations and on the other was limited like any finite system. This portrait was an accurate rendering of the period's beliefs about the mind; the apparent inconsistency within this portrait can be directly related to the differences between metaphysical and everyday senses of the term "mental substance." Haven's is a noteworthy attempt to balance physiological and psychological knowledge about the mind; it shows that the conceptual edifice built on the mind-as-entity metaphor lasted well into the nineteenth century.

Haven was typical; the more physiologically oriented psychologists did not exclude "moral" knowledge, and those with a more philosophical orientation did not exclude physiological knowledge. They were held to this center ground by the theory-constitutive operation of the metaphor. The physiologists were continually reminded that they were after all dealing with *mind* as it had been traditionally conceived since the eighteenth century—the attribute of the human being that makes spiritual life possible. The philosophers were reminded that they were dealing with something that apparently could not exist independently of the brain, spinal cord, and nerves, despite its lack of substance and extension.

The Mind as a Physiological Entity: Carpenter and Bain

Although in 1820 Thomas Brown called for a "physiology of the mind" analogous to the physiology of the body, he did not depart from the standard introspective approach to the mind's functions and components. Brown was trained in medicine, but little was then known of neural physiology; we might expect later psychological writers with more special training in physiology to better adapt their language to the developing emphasis on that area. That this did not happen can be seen in how William B. Carpenter and Alexander Bain deal with the most nagging problem of psychology, the interaction between mind and the physical world.

The various editions of Carpenter's *Principles of Human Physiology*, first published in 1842, were "the standard works in medical education in the mid-nineteenth century" (Jacyna 112). His main psychological treatise, *Principles of Mental Physiology*, was first published in 1874 but was based on ideas Carpenter had put forth at least since the fourth and fifth editions (1852 and 1855) of his *Human Physiology*, in the section titled "Of the Mind, and Its Operations." This section sets out to correct two fallacies, which Carpenter identifies as materialism and spiritualism, each of which relies on an incomplete set of data about mental phenomena. According to Carpenter, materialism is supported by the obvious connections between thoughts and the brain but runs against the universal conviction that humans possess "*a self-determining power*" which is partially able to "mould external circumstances to its own requirements, instead of being completely subjugated by them" (*Human Physiology* 538-39). The spiritualist, however, ignores inescapable physiological facts, for instance that the mind's actions can be disordered by corporeal conditions (540). The correct view, rather, is that mind and matter interact by means of "nerve-force": "the power of the Will can develope [sic] Nervous activity," just as "Nerve-force can develope Mental activity" (542). Carpenter preserves the most important spiritualist concept, that human beings do have an innate sense of something greater than themselves, by extending this relation between mind and body to "the relation of the Mind of the Deity to that Universe, whose phenomena, rightly interpreted, are but a continual revelation of His ceaseless and universal presence" (544).

Carpenter's assertion that the mind's two sets of properties, the spiritual and the material, are equally important might suggest that he has a clear and relatively complete understanding of both sets. But such is not the case. Consider Figure 1, a diagram from *Mental Physiology* (125).

This diagram shows that there is an ordinary "*upward* course" from impressions to intellectual operations and a corresponding downward course of influence from the Will to motor impulses. About the upward course Carpenter is explicit. If the upward

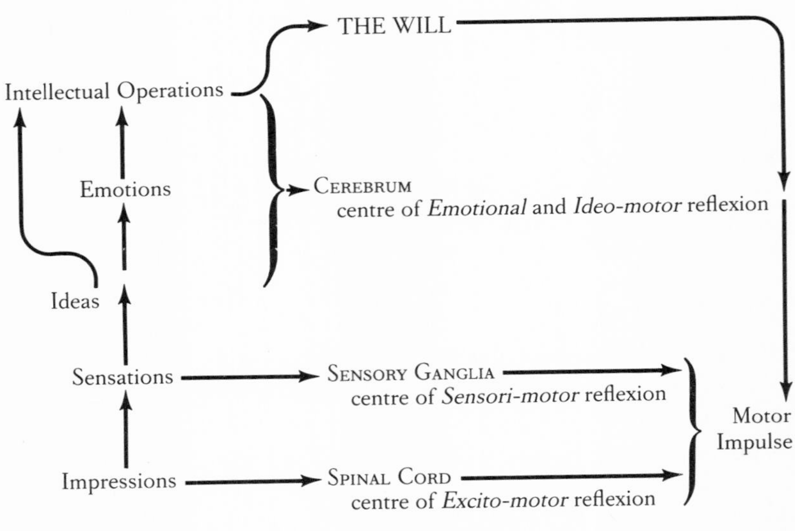

Figure 1. Carpenter's Diagram of the Flow of Impulse

course is interrupted, "the impression will then exert its power in a *transverse* direction, and a reflex action will be the result; the nature of this being dependent upon the part of the Cerebro-spinal axis at which the ascent had been checked" (124).

This degree of detail itself raises problems, as Lewes notes in commenting on such diagrams and discussions. Lewes begins by observing that "the assignment of even Thinking to the cerebral hemispheres is purely hypothetical" ("Mind as a Function of the Organism" 65). He continues:

> This may seem incredible to some readers, accustomed to expositions which do not suggest a doubt—expositions where the course of an impression is described from the sensitive surface along the sensory nerve to its ganglion, from thence to a particular spot in the Optic Thalamus (where the impression is said to become a sensation), from that spot to cells in the upper layer of the cerebral convolutions (where the sensation becomes an idea), from thence downwards to a lower

layer of cells (where the idea is changed into a volitional impulse), and from thence to the motor-ganglia in the spinal cord, where it is reflected on the motor-nerves and muscles.

Nothing is wanting to the *precision* of this description. Everything is wanting to its *proof*. . . . not a single step of this involved process has ever been observed; the description is imaginary from beginning to end. [66]

Lewes does not deny the possibility that there is some truth to such descriptions and models, but he insists that the evidence is not yet sufficient to identify which functions are played by the various parts of the central nervous mass.

An even more revealing problem in Carpenter's diagram is the difference in the amount of detail between the two courses. The left and center columns summarize the prevailing assumptions about how ideas develop and how reflex actions occur, based on knowledge of the various levels of the nervous system and the types of actions (reflex and willed). But how does the "downward course" operate? What happens when a willed act is blocked? Where does the force go? Are there various levels or possible outlets? At what physiological level is the will's power actually transformed into nerve-force? Carpenter does not ask these questions, and the diagram does not develop into something more detailed and potentially revolutionary. Instead, Carpenter's impelling metaphor seems theory-constitutive rather than generative; despite his ostensible emphasis on nerve-force, his concept of the mind continues to be informed by the mind-as-entity metaphor. The model serves the attempt of Carpenter and other Victorian physiologists to "naturalize" the mind, as Jacyna explains, to integrate mind into nature and thus repudiate the "conventional metaphysical and theological view which regarded the human, and by implication the divine mind, as *super*-natural"; at the same time the model allows Carpenter to preserve something of the mind's transcendent spirituality (Jacyna 110-11). If the model itself were the product of a generative metaphor, it would not just present common knowledge but would raise questions about the two courses.

Jacyna's point of course is that conceptual revolution is not Carpenter's goal. The mind-as-entity metaphor is perfect for the task of naturalizing the mind while preserving its spirituality. Everyday connotations associated with the metaphor easily allow for the naturalization of the entity, and the aspect of transcendence is preserved by placing the will figuratively over the cerebral hemispheres, assigning it the ability to stimulate the hemispheres, and thus giving it power over motor impulses. The diagram accurately represents the will's ascendancy, as Carpenter conceives it. It is assigned a definite article and printed in uppercase letters, and it is shown as a faculty in the singular whereas the other items on the subjective side of the diagram are either products (sensations, emotions) or processes (intellectual operations). Clearly, the will is part of mind, but a superior part. Although the "Correlation between Mind-force and Nerve-force is shown to be complete *both ways*, each being able to excite the other" (*Mental Physiology* 14), the will's force appears to be separate from either one. The *mind* is an entity; as such, it receives nerve-force and generates mind-force. "Force" is here the connection between substance and mind that makes perception possible: human beings can only experience force, and both mind and force are "essentially active" in Carpenter's system (11-12). The will is something else again. Carpenter stresses "the great fact of Consciousness," that "*we have within us a self-determining Power which we call Will*"; this fact plus the "intimate relation between Mental activity and Physical changes in the Brain" may lead the investigator to believe that "the phenomena of the Material Universe are the expressions of an Infinite Mind and will, of which Man's is the finite representative" (28). Carpenter further insists that the Will is able to shape the "physiological mechanism" by the way it habitually exercises that mechanism; hence "not only its *automatic* but even its *unconscious* action comes to be indirectly modified by the controlling power of the Will" (15). A final point indicating the qualitative superiority of the will is that it is only influenced by intellectual operations. Carpenter's diagram does not allow any of the lower products to have a direct influence on the will; all must be processed through the intellect. The diagram correlates perfectly with Carpenter's identification of the will as "a self-determining Power."

As Jacyna explains, Carpenter was always concerned to "qualify his physiological naturalism . . . the cerebral hemispheres were not *only* ganglia acting reflexively: they were also the agents by which an immaterial principle exerted its will in the world" (113). For this reason, according to Jacyna, Carpenter also "insisted upon a hierarchy of faculties. While the lower functions were performed reflexively, the highest were the result of the determination of an immaterial principle" (124-25). The mind-as-entity metaphor was flexible enough to accomodate attempts to preserve such a principle in the system. However, it was not sufficiently flexible to allow for the development by psychologists of a wholly new concept that would take immateriality and agency as first principles while still accommodating the advances in neurology.

Alexander Bain's work was broader than Carpenter's. Bain concerned himself more fully with the traditional problems of psychology and incorporated physiology into his solutions. In Young's words, "Bain's analysis of motor phenomena was the first union of the new physiology with a detailed association psychology in the English tradition and he thereby laid the psychological foundations of a thoroughgoing sensory-motor physiology" (*Mind, Brain* 114). Bain was also highly influential as a teacher in the new protoscience of psychology, with his two volumes *Senses and the Intellect* and *Emotions and the Will* serving as "the major texts in the English-speaking world until James's *Principles*" (Robinson, *The Mind Unfolded* 86). To one of the traditional problems, that of the interaction between the mind and the body, Bain devoted an entire book, *Mind and Body* (1875). This extended treatment displays the same limitations as does Carpenter's *Mental Physiology*: it combines a detailed and coherent *metaphorical* description of the physiology of the mind with vague, admittedly paradoxical descriptions of the mental components of the mind-body unity. In Bain even more than in Carpenter the problems of the mind-as-entity metaphor are manifest.

The question with which Bain opens his text seems to promise a balance between the psychological and the physiological: "What has Mind to do with brain substance?" He then lists the conceivable answers and arrives at the reasonable conclusion that the two work in parallel, although we cannot say exactly how. The final paragraph of the chapter, however, has the study of the Brain as its sole topic. The best method for this study, Bain writes confidently, is to "begin at the outworks, at the organs of sense and motion, with which the nervous system communicates; we can study their operations during life, as well as examine their intimate structure; we can experimentally vary all of the circumstances of their operation; we can find how they act upon the brain, and how the brain re-acts upon them. Using all this knowledge as a key, we may possibly unlock the secrets of the anatomical structure; we may compel the cells and fibres to disclose their meaning and purpose" (4-5).

The promise of that statement, that Bain will proceed by such a scrutiny, is violated in the next chapter, where Bain offers little more than folk wisdom as evidence for the interdependence of mind and brain. Is it really true that "the memory rises and falls with the bodily condition; being vigorous in our fresh moments, and feeble when we are fatigued or exhausted" (9)? Or that "Protracted and severe mental labour brings on disease of the bodily organs" (11)? These propositions cannot survive reflection. Is it true that "in all cases of pronounced mental aberration, disease of the brain is present in a marked form" (14)? Certainly not, as research even before 1875 was showing. The point is that Bain is really not interested in examining the evidence. Instead, he is elaborating a metaphor that has physical processes and substances as its vehicle and the mind-body relationship as tenor.

In his fifth chapter, "The Intellect," Bain draws at length on neural physiology, some factual and much admittedly hypothetical, to prove that the brain can accommodate complex intellectual life; his endeavor makes sense only in light of an underlying conception of a mental entity that has location and extension and operates as a physical system. Bain asserts that our "complex and modified consciousness" results from "the separate consciousness of separate nerves [for example optic nerves cannot receive sound impressions], and the changing intensity of the currents," plus "the countless combinations of these simple elements" (85-86). Physical reality and memory both suggest that renewed feelings occupy the same brain parts "and in the same manner as the original feeling" (89), although the "re-induced currents" are seldom "equal in energy" to the original (91). Bain contends that the physical system makes localization possible: his calculation of the number of "Acquisitions" in a person's mind and the number of nerve cells and fibers in the brain proves there can exist "an independent nervous track for each separate acquisition" (107-8). He makes an estimate of the number of "cerebral growths" required for bodies of knowledge such as the multiplication table, the repertoire of a good musician, the written characters of the Chinese language, and finds that even for the "most retentive and most richly-endowed minds" with a likely total of 200,000 acquisitions, there are "for each nervous grouping 5,000 cells and 25,000 fibres" (107). The physical system also makes possible the fixation of trains of thought: there must exist "a *strengthened connexion or diminished obstruction*" where the related nerve-currents meet, "a preference track for that line over other lines where no continuity has been established" (117). Bain's next statement indicates how strongly he is impelled to ground mental phenomena on this hypothetical physiology: "This is merely a hypothetical rendering of the facts: yet it is a very probable rendering. In the nature and number of the nerve elements, and their mode of connexion, there is nothing hypothetical; and there is no departure from fact or strong probability, in assigning special and distinct tracks for the currents connected with each separate sensation, idea, emotion, or other conscious state" (117).

Although he does not equate mind with these neurological phenomena in so many words, his concern to link them with mental phenomena suggests that he sees mind as constructed like a physical system, as the mind-as-entity metaphor suggests. He definitely expects to find, in the mind, phenomena and structures like those in the body; he does not investigate the physiological system for analogues to mental phenomena. He assumes that if "complex consciousness" is composed of the consciousness of individual sensations combined in varying ways, then a place or substance or entity must exist wherein the combinations can occur. The same reasoning holds for the supposed likelihood of "renewed feelings" occupying the same place in the brain as the original, and for the correlation between "nervous tracks" and "acquisitions." And it holds for more mundane phenomena such as the "seemingly inseparable association" between facial gestures and states of feeling (6).

In describing the capacity of the physiological organ, as in discussing the Laws of Relativity and Diffusion, Bain demonstrates the acceptability of hypothetical reasoning based on the mind-as-entity metaphor. Unlike the psychologists of the eighteenth century, Bain does not assert the autonomy thesis, but like them he views the mind-body problem as at least partially a language problem: although "there is something unique, if not remarkable, in the close incorporation of the two extreme contrasted facts, termed Mind and Matter, we must grant that the total difference of nature has rendered the union very puzzling to express in language" (*Mind and Body* 134). He goes on to say, "When I speak of mind as allied with body—with a brain and its nerve currents—I can scarcely avoid *localizing* the mind, giving it a local habitation." But in fact he attends no more consistently to the problem than did Hobbes and Reid. In one section he points out that we can use analogies such as the telegraph wire or the electric circuit to discuss the locale of consciousness, but if we do so "we are not speaking of mind, properly so called, at all" (134-35). The reality is that "Our mental experience, our feelings and thoughts, have *no extension*, no place, no form or outline, no mechanical division of parts" (135). But in his earlier description of two fundamental principles, the Law of Relativity and the Law of Diffusion, he conveys the opposite impression, that if we had the right instruments we could observe our mental experience in the brain: "Change of impression is necessary to our being conscious" (45) and "When an impression is accompanied with Feeling, the aroused currents *diffuse* themselves freely over the brain, leading to a general agitation of the moving organs, as well as affecting the viscera" (52). These two principles combine to cause "the really fitful nature of the mind; the stream of consciousness is a series of ebullitions rather than a calm or steady flow" (50).

These descriptions imply that we should be able to measure the changes of impression either directly or by measuring their associated currents, hence that we should be able to measure the type or amount of consciousness associated with any given external or internal stimulus. But this logical extension would be unacceptable to Bain, who asserts that "mental and physical proceed together, as undivided twins" (131). The mind-as-entity metaphor, operating here hand in hand with rapidly expanding knowledge about the nervous system, leads the psychologist to create an extended metaphor using terms from the harder sciences. The internal consistency of this extended metaphor convinces the psychologist that he has described the system scientifically, when he has actually failed to heed his own caution about descriptive language.

What then is the language most appropriate to the "unique conjunction" of mind and body? How can the psychologist resolve the "paradox" or "contradiction" in our experience, that "we understand union in the sense of local connexion; here is a union [of mind and body] where local connexion is irrelevant, unsuitable, contradictory" (136)? How can we best describe what happens when we shift between what Bain calls the "object attitude" (in which our attention is directed outward, to objects) and the "subject attitude" (in which we are simply feeling)? Bain's answer:

> The only adequate expression is a CHANGE OF STATE a change from the state of the extended cognition to a state of unextended cognition. . . . When, therefore, we talk of incorporating mind with brain, we must be held as speaking under an important reserve or qualification. Asserting the union in the strongest manner, we must yet deprive it of the almost invincible association of *union in place*. An extended organism is the condition of our passing into a state where there is no extension. A human being is an extended and material mass, attached to which is the

power of becoming alive to feeling and thought, the extreme remove from all that is material; a condition of *trance* wherein, while it lasts, the material drops out of view—so much so, that we have not the power to represent the two extremes as lying side by side, as container and contained, or in any other mode of local conjunction. The condition of our existing thoroughly in the one, is the momentary eclipse or extinction of the other. [137]

This section has for its controlling metaphorical vehicle the theme of change-of-state. The tenor is twofold: what happens in the mind, and the mystery of what happens. This second aspect is embodied in such odd images as the human being consisting of a mass and a power, and the equally odd possibility that conditions are extinguished and recreated from one moment to the next. Supporting and elaborating this metaphor are terms drawn from the physical realm but used in a non-physical sense. Bain's contention is much like that of Reid a century earlier concerning the term "substance" applied to mind. Although the terms here are "union," "association," and "change of state," rather than "substance," the point is the same—the terms cannot be avoided but must be used in the special metaphorical sense: "union" cannot mean "*union in place*," just as for Reid "substance" applied to mind did not mean "having extension and mass." "Change of state", like "diffusion," derives from the scientific language in use at the time and enhances the pseudo-scientific quality of the description while conforming to the mind-as-entity conception of thoughts as corpuscles and minds as containers.

In contrast to Bain's description of the physiological conditions of consciousness, this presentation of his theory is metaphysical in the negative sense often attached to that word in the nineteenth century: vague, complex, speculative, unrelated to how mental phenomena are actually experienced and described. The contrast itself indicates that Bain is more comfortable with describing the mind first as a physical entity and only second as the complex of feeling, willing, and thinking experienced by human beings. His conclusion to the chapter makes this point even clearer: "without the extended consciousness the unextended would not arise. Without certain peculiar modes of the extended—what we call a cerebral organization, and so on—we could not have those times of trance, our pleasures, our pains, and our ideas, which at present we undergo fitfully and alternately with our extended consciousness" (138). It does not seem to occur to Bain to stress the dependence of the extended on the unextended. Mind-as-entity functioning as a theory-constitutive metaphor does not readily permit or invite such a perspective. The metaphorical language is most conducive to a habit of thought that consistently regards the mind as an extended substance, which means that while Bain in theory advocates the equality of the two modes, in practice, unless he attends closely to the words he uses, he departs from his preferred explanation of "the line of mental sequence" as "mind-body giving birth to mind-body" and lapses into what he calls the less "intelligible" explanation of "a constant interference, a mutual influence between the two" (130, 132). And from this unsteady position he tends to attribute more influence to the side of the extended. Bain fails to give equal voice to the mental aspect for the same reason that Carpenter failed to wonder about that large blank space between "the Will" and "motor impulses." Although two hundred years separate them from Descartes, Bain and Carpenter still accept the Cartesian focus on extension and substance and do not attempt to introduce new language that would conform to their new characterization of the mind as other than a limited entity.

The discrepancy in *Mind and Body* between clear, albeit hypothetical, statements about the physiological conditions of consciousness and the apparent paradox that the mind, being extensionless, can have no "local connexion" with matter, is one manifestation of the continuing influence of the mind-as-entity metaphor. A second manifestation can be seen in the structure of Bain's first text, *Senses and the Intellect* (1855). This work begins with neurology, a detailed discussion of the Bell-Magendie law, the speed of nerve impulses, and other purely physiological phenomena. As one of the first works thus to anchor "empirical associationism to the science of physiology" (Robinson, *Intellectual History* 325), *Senses* holds an important place in the history of psychology. But the neurological and physiological section, Bain labels "introductory." The first chapter of the body of the text begins thus: "We now commence the subject of Mind proper, or the enumeration and explanation of the States and Varieties of Feeling, the Modes of Action, and the Powers of Intelligence, comprised in the mental nature of mind" (1st ed. 65).

This small but significant rhetorical detail suggests the difficulty of representing a connection between physiological and mental phenomena. While working on the first version of *Senses*, Bain had written to John Stuart Mill that his greatest wish was "so to unite psychology and physiology that the physiologists may be made to appreciate the true ends and drift of their researches into the nervous system" (quoted by Robinson, *Intellectual History* 324). He was hoping to provide a system or theory by which the physiologists would see that their work was fundamental to an understanding of "the subject of MIND proper"—providing a physiological basis for characterizing the operations of the immaterial entity, mind. It was a vain hope and would remain so until the development of language that would permit a new characterization of what had traditionally been represented as the mental entity.

Some differences between the first two editions of *Senses* suggest that Bain may have recognized that he did not yet understand psychology and physiology well enough separately to effectively combine them. The concluding pages of the introductory section of the first edition are strident. Bain asserts that "there is no such chamber" as the sensorium, "where impressions are poured in and stored up to be reproduced in a future day." We must *discard* this notion, Bain declares; current knowledge is "sufficient to destroy the hypothesis that has until lately prevailed as to the material processes of perception." The present view of "current action" is not perfect but is "more exact" than the receptacle hypothesis (61). The second edition is moderate by comparison. There Bain urges that the notion of a sensorium be "modified and corrected," and instead of writing that we may now "say with great possibility, no currents, no mind" (1st ed. 61-62) he writes that "it seems as if" the statement is valid (2d ed. 66). A further retreat occurs in the final paragraph of this section. In his first edition, Bain insists that the natural course of the nervous currents is to influence action, hence that "the brain is only a part of the machinery of mind" with other parts extending "throughout the body" (62). The second edition makes the same point but much less forcefully: the brain alone could not generate movements and receive sensations, and "it is uncertain how far even thought, reminiscence . . . could be sustained without the more distant communications between the brain and the rest of the body" (66).

A third manifestation of the influence of the mind-as-entity metaphor in Bain is pointed out by Daniel Robinson: Bain's inability to describe experience credibly. Despite his praise for Bain as the designer of the first really thorough "*psychological* system," Robinson concedes that when Bain moves from discussing the physiology of sensation to mental phenomena, his analysis becomes "very dated, hesitating, sometimes foolish, and generally tortuous" (*The Mind Unfolded* 70, 79-80). Young makes the same criticism of Bain's *Study of Character*. In Young's words, the book's character descriptions "are pale shadows of individual human beings and bear little relation to the complex attributes of real men." Bain relies on anecdotes, introspection, and "the biographies of great men"; he includes "no original observations of the behavior of other men and no comparative data" (*Mind, Brain* 131). These limitations are present in all of Bain's work. His description of why we tend to repeat ourselves, for instance, could be directly borrowed from Hume or Sterne:

> Everything that we have ever done, we have a disposition or tendency to repeat. . . . The co-existence of thousands of such tendencies in the brain is sufficient to cause neutrality, until something occurs to determine a preference for one, or to remove the superincumbent pressure that all combined exert upon each. Now the existence of a present state formerly joined by contiguity to a past state, is one mode of opening up the crowd to allow this past state to re-assert itself. The other mode is when the past state is already *partially induced*, which is the case when something similar is present to the mind. To whatever extent the similarity holds, to that extent the past state is already re-enacted: the pres-

sure is removed from a part, and the remainder is then able to break out. [*Senses* 2d ed. 557]

Sensations able to break out, a crowd of sensations able to block the path, thousands coexisting in the brain and each exerting an equal pressure—it sounds as if the mind's activities are taking place in a specific locale and that the ideas or sensations are tangible entities, so many billiard balls of thought. As an explanation of the mental phenomenon, it is both tortuous and foolish. As part of Bain's extended metaphor of the mind, it illustrates the relative unsuitability of the mind-as-entity metaphor for the study of mental events that lie between simple reflex actions and mature reflection. The extended metaphor is vivid and compact but not sufficiently expressive when applied to large-scale phenomena such as memory. Bain relegates this explanation to a note at the end of a chapter in the second edition of *Senses* and drops it completely from the third, illustrating Robinson's point that he does not successfully join the physiological and psychological perspectives.

Mind-as-entity functioning as a theory-constitutive metaphor seems to limit Bain to a physicalistic conception of the fundamental laws of mental action and mental physiology alike. He repeatedly insists on the physiological basis of thought but at the cost of not developing a language of the mind more in keeping with the new discoveries and new emphases. A subsection of *Senses*, titled "Of the Nerve Force and the course of Power in the Brain," illustrates this limitation in a more physiological context:

This portable, or current, character of the nerve force is what enables movements distant from one another in the body to be associated together under a common stimulus. An impression of sound, a musical note, for example, is carried to the brain; this impression is seen to produce a responsive action and excitement extending to the voice, mouth, eyes, head, etc. This multiplex and various manifestation implies a system of connexion among the centres of action, whereby many strings can be touched from one point. . . . Supposing the corpora quadrigemina to be a centre for the sense of vision, an impression passing to this centre propagates a movement towards many other centres . . .

and through these various connexions an extensive wave of effects may be produced, ending in a complicated chain of movements all over the framework of the body. Such a system of intercommunication and transmission of power is therefore an essential part of the bodily and mental structure. [*Senses* 1st ed. 57-58]

This physical system is essential, but that strictly mentalistic item the sensorium is not. Sensation takes place through the impression and transmission of currents, and these currents "may have all degrees of intensity, from the fury of a death struggle to the langour of a half-sleeping reverie, or the fitful flashes of a dream, but their nature is still the same" (61). He has already demonstrated that enough is known about nerve-force to qualify the analogy between nervous and electric currents: nerve-force does not require a closed circuit, and neural conduction is a "wasting operation" (58). This second statement is especially significant for any theory of the relationship between mind and body: the nerve "influence conveyed is much more beholden to the conducting fibres than electricity is to the copper wire. The fibres are made to sustain or increase the force at the cost of their own substance" (59).

For Bain the essential feature of the system is physical action—it is as essential for the "mental" as for the "bodily" structure. He concludes this section thus:

Nervous influence, rising in great part in sensation, comes at last to action; short of this nothing is done, no end is served. However feeble the currents may be, their natural course is towards the organs accustomed to their sway. Hence the reason for adopting language, as we have done throughout the present chapter, to imply that the brain is only a part of the machinery of mind; for although a large part of all the circles of mental action lie within the head, other parts equally indispensable extend throughout the body. [62]

The mind's status as an entity guarantees it a place in the circles of mental action and ensures that it too participates in the action. As an entity, the mind quite logically has machinery and circles of action; Bain's chief concern is to see those circles extended throughout the body in a physicalistic system.

Both Carpenter and Bain share the problem that Young attributes to all of nineteenth-century physiological psychology: they separate "the organs of mind from motor functions" and view the cortex as a "unitary organ" which has as its "instruments" the sensory-motor centers ("Functions" 257). As Young has shown of this period, "when the study of mind came to be considered in physiological and biological terms, powerful philosophic constraints . . . narrowed the issue and impoverished the study of the mental functions of human and other organisms" (252). Young credits F.J. Gall with moving psychology from the realm of philosophy to that of biology and with moving psychological methodology beyond the study of brain by physiology or the study of the mind by introspection (254). Yet neither Gall nor his followers, although accepting that the brain is the organ of the mind, attempted to explore experimentally how the cortex might influence the sensory-motor centers, nor did they challenge the traditional faculty division of memory, reason, and will in determining the categories of mental operations (257). As Young observes, "philosophic constraints narrowed their study. For example, the assumption of the unity of the mind forestalled what now seems an obvious experiment—stimulating the separate areas of the cortex—until David Ferrier tried it in 1873. And according to Young, Ferrier even further separated brain functions from the behavior of real human beings: in order to apply to the cortex the same physiological experiments performed on the lower neural levels, it was necessary to forget about human nature (265-66).

The impoverishment extends down to the phrase level, as when Bain shifts from "enables us to say with great probability" to "it seems as if we might say." This small detail of language suggests that Young's analysis misses one essential point: those assumptions about the mind's unity and localization that limited investigations were effects as well as causes—effects of mind-as-entity functioning as a theory-constitutive metaphor. As long as psychology had as its constraining focus the *substance* mind, it was not likely to explore mental phenomena by using the language of the mind. In particular, it was not likely, as did the novelists of the same period, to consider how web-like relations form among human beings. This topic called for a new vocabulary and conceptual structure. However, the way was implicit in the figurative language of the philosophical psychologists.

Philosophical Psychology and Mind-as-Entity: Mill, Morell, Spencer, Lewes

The philosophical psychologists may have been more aware than the physiologists of the problems raised by the separation between physiological research and the study of living human beings interacting with their surroundings. They differed from the psychologists of the previous century in their relative unwillingness to assert that the mind is a thinking substance. They agreed that the rapidly growing empirical knowledge about the nervous system was still at best only knowledge about attributes of the mind and not about the mind itself. They confronted on a daily basis the discrepancy between, first, discoveries about nervous impulses, reflex arcs, and so forth, and, second, the phenomena of mind as actually experienced by living human beings, a discrepancy that was hardly apparent before 1830 but was dramatically evident by 1850. One set of facts will demonstrate this problem. Lewes pointed out that "it seems quite satisfactory" to know that colors are the products of wave lengths, "until we learn that although such vibrations [the waves] originate such sensations [of colors], it is through some intermediate agency which does not vibrate in these ways, but which is capable of effecting the sensations by vibrations that are demonstrably different" (*Study of Psychology* 185). Violet, for example, has one wave length, but the sensation of violet can also be produced by blending red and blue, whose wave lengths do not add up to that of violet. Likewise, several different combinations will produce similar sensations of white but will cause dissimilar physical reactions on photographic plates.

Yet perhaps because of their rather broad perspective, the philosophical writers began to correlate their figurative language with their theoretical statements and thus began to resolve the discrepancy between physiology and experience. Lewes was the most successful in this respect; John Stuart Mill, John D. Morell, and Herbert Spencer are instructive examples of relative failures.

Mill deals with the topic of psychology in the context of logic, following the common belief that to understand the rules of logic it was necessary to understand the human mind's structure, its patterns of thought. He devotes one of the six books of his *System of Logic* (1846) to "the logic of the moral sciences," concentrating on psychological matters in the first five chapters and then considering "social science." As Mill sees it, "the science of human nature" is not yet an exact science (528): "It falls far short of the standard of exactness now realized in Astronomy," for one; the "perturbations" which make each individual unique also prevent the prediction of "how an individual would think, feel, or act, throughout life" (528-29). Nevertheless, the general "laws of mind" are known. Introducing these, Mill adopts the autonomy thesis. He will not attempt to determine how the mind might be distinguished from its "sensible manifestations," and he will consider only states of mind produced by other states of mind (530): "When a state of mind is produced directly by a state of body, the law is a law of Body, and belongs to physical science." In opposition to Comte, Mill insists that it is far from proven that every mental state has an immediately antecedent physical state; even if it were proven, he believes, "we are wholly ignorant of the characteristics of these nervous states." Thus knowledge of mental phenomena must for a long time "if not forever" be sought through direct study "of the mental successions themselves" (531-32).

The subject matter of psychology is therefore "the uniformities of succession, the laws, whether ultimate or derivative, according to which one mental state succeeds another; is caused by, or at the least, is caused to follow, another" (532). The first of these laws is that "Whenever any state of consciousness has once been excited in us, no matter by what cause; an inferior degree of the same state of consciousness . . . is capable of being reproduced in us, without the presence of any such cause as excited it at first. . . . This law is expressed by saying, in the language of Hume, that every mental *impression* has its *idea*" (532).

In stating the second general law, Mill again follows Hume in his phrasing: "These Ideas, or secondary mental states, are excited by our impressions, or by other ideas, according to certain laws which are called Laws of Association," including the laws of contiguity and similarity (532). This sounds very similar to Thomas Brown's insistence on the possibility of a *mental physiology* that would focus on the mind's states and changes of state. Brown however would have opposed Mill's admission that the laws of mind "may be derivative laws resulting from laws of animal life, and that their truth, therefore, may ultimately depend upon physical conditions; and the influence of physiological states or physiological changes in altering or counteracting the mental successions, is one of the most important departments of psychological study" (532). Brown accepted the analogy between the laws of mind and those of the body, between mental physiology and human physiology, but he would not have agreed that the former might "ultimately" depend on the latter. Both Brown's *Lectures* and Mill's *System* were popular, respected, and often cited by their contemporaries, which suggests that during the twenty-three invervening years it became more acceptable to suggest the mind's dependence on the body, as long as the suggestion was suitably qualified—if the dependence is ultimate, it remains beyond human ken.

While Mill's theoretical pronouncements thus adhere closely to the autonomy thesis, he uses physicalistic figures to illustrate certain problems; these figures conform perfectly to the mind-as-entity metaphor. For example, a question that has always vexed association psychology is how humans perceive complex ideas as if they are seamless wholes, if it is true that all complex ideas are derived from discrete sense impressions. Mill answers in a figure drawn from chemistry: "When impressions have been so often experienced in conjunction that each of them calls up readily and instantaneously the ideas of the whole group, those ideas sometimes melt and coalesce into one another, and appear not several ideas but one; in the same manner as when the seven prismatic colors are presented to the eye in rapid succession, the sensation produced is that of white" (533).

This is a case of mental *chemistry* because the final complex idea seems to be generated by the simple ideas and because it seems to exist in the mind as a simple idea. It would be a case of mental *mechanics* if the complex idea were perceived as consisting of or composed by the simple ideas. Mill continues: "Our idea of an orange really *consists* of the simple ideas of a certain color, a certain form, a certain taste and smell, &c., because we can by interrogating our consciousness, perceive all these elements in the idea. . . . [But we cannot] discover those elementary ideas of resistance, derived from our muscular frame, in which Dr. Brown has rendered it highly probable that the idea [of extension] originates" (533). I have labeled Mill's references to mental chemistry "figurative," but in the next several pages Mill clearly demonstrates his belief that "there *is* such a thing as mental chemistry" (533). This assertion is really not necessary to Mill's treatment of laws of mind; deleting the discussion of mental chemistry would not detract from the quality of the explanation. Nor is the term itself helpful. The physicalistic connotations of "mental chemistry" and "mental mechanics" run counter to what Mill identifies early in the *System* as the basic assumption of his method, subjectivism: "every objective fact is grounded on a corresponding subjective one" and the only meaning possessed by the label is "as a name for the unknown and inscrutable process by which that subjective or psychological fact is brought to pass" (52). This discrepancy between connotations and theory is one of the identifying features of the continuing influence of mind-as-entity in the nineteenth century.

It is also worth noting that these chapters remain almost unchanged through the eighth edition of *System* (1872). Mill adds to chapter 4, "Of the Laws of Mind," a footnote recommending Bain's *Senses* and *Emotions* and Spencer's *Principles of Psychology*, and he concludes the chapter with the relatively optimistic statement, "If there be really a connexion between mental peculiarities and any varieties cognizable by our senses in the structure of the cerebral and nervous apparatus, the nature of that connection is now in a fair way of being found out" (447). These minor additions strengthen the work's physicalistic tendency. The figurative language went unrevised, implying that it is just as valid in 1872 as in 1846 to consider the mind as displaying both chemical and mechanical behaviors.

Mill's retaining this language is significant because it is open to some obvious criticisms. Lewes, without referring to Mill directly, remarks that the psychologist can never perform "real analysis" such as the chemist performs: feelings never exist in stages but only as completed states, and the very elements of the feeling are changed by the process, as are the "tissues which are its physical basis" (*The Study of Psychology* 180). The hypothesis of a mental chemistry is as erroneous as the one advanced by the Sensational School, which attempted to treat "the organism as a *mosaic*, or assemblage of organs . . . an error the consequence of which is seen in the conception of the Mind as an assemblage of impressions, a mosaic of experiences" (181). For Lewes, the organism always acts as a unity; this is the most important teaching of biology. "The notion of a *tabula rasa*, on which the Senses inscribe their impressions, is unbiological" for this reason: "A percipient organism must exist before impressions can become perceptions" (182). And once this transformation takes place, the impressions cannot be recovered, so any hypothesis about the elements of the mental-chemical reaction must remain chiefly speculation.

As I said, these criticisms are not subtle or intricate, but they are criticisms of concept and method rather than of language. If challenged, Mill would probably respond that "mental chemistry" is of course not intended to stand as a hypothesis but rather as an analogy; he would likely agree with Lewes on the problems of such an hypothesis. However, the habit of thinking fostered by the mind-as-entity metaphor leads him to offer the suggestion as he does, without qualifying it as analogy.

John D. Morell is almost forgotten today, but he was well known to his contemporaries, and his *Elements of Psychology* (1853) was the first work published in England with the word "psychology" in the title. (Friedrich Rauch's *Psychology, or a View of the Human Soul Including Anthropology* came out in America in 1840.) *Elements of Psychology* is Morell's attempt to combine Hegelian idealism with the psycho-physical realities necessary to any relatively complete psychology. The two are not intrinsically incompatible, but problems arise when Morell relies on the language of mind-as-entity.

Morell's commitment to the mind-as-entity concept is clear from his designating as the most important fact about the nervous system that "every individual nerve pursues its own way through the whole system, up to its final destination in the encephalon" (96). The nervous system is governed by a single basic law, "the law of nervous action," which Morell expresses in a pair of lengthy sentences that are almost entirely metaphorical:

> When any appropriate stimulus makes an impression upon the corresponding nerve at any point in the circumference [of the organism], the first tendency is for that impression to follow the pathway of the nerve or nerves affected, through every intermediate region up to the *cerebrum itself*; and, then, having excited the mind's attention, and roused the activity of the will, to be reflected back along the motor nerves, and give rise to any external movements which the case may demand or suggest. Just as in the electric telegraph, when the magnetic current is once excited, the impulse impressed passes all the various stations on the road, speeds on to its destination, gives an intelligent hint to the mind there located, and then elicits a response, which originates *anew* in that mind, back to the other extremity. [*Elements of Psychology* 97]

Continuity of effect is the essential assumption underlying this description; as with Hartley, the causal chain from impression to idea cannot be broken. The mind comes into play with the stimulation of the cerebrum itself, from which it can reflect a nervous impulse to the appropriate muscle groups. Morell then goes on to explain what happens when "the original impression cannot actually reach the brain" either because of "some physical impediment to it" or because "the nerves are expending their energy in some other direction. . . . In this case, the impression *stops short* at one of the other centres, and is reflected back from that centre, through the motor nerves, without exciting the mind's attention or awakening the energy of the *will*" (97-98).

Morell's description seems so straightforward and factual that we may not notice the many terms drawn from the mind-as-entity complex (impression, pathway, intermediate region, reflected back) or the shift to an explicit simile at the beginning of the following paragraph, "forming, as it were, a complete magnetic system." This shift makes it seem as if the preceding metaphorical discussion was not metaphorical but literal. The same sleight-of-pen was used by Locke, Reid, Mill, and the other psychologists I have considered; like them, Morell may use the explicit simile because he actually believes that he has already described the operation of the nervous system in a literal way and now needs to provide an illustrative figure.

Morell does not, however, localize the mental entity in the cerebrum. The title of this section of *Elements* is "Intelligence as Sensation," but there are very few references to the mind as such. Mind and will exist "above" the cerebrum, but this place they occupy may be a qualitatively different sort of space from that occupied by the nervous system. The verbal description permits the possibility of an extensionless place like the unextended mental substance hypothesized by Reid; the difference is that Morell leaves his description vague enough and refers so infrequently to the mind that he does not risk Reid's overt contradiction between everyday and metaphysical senses of key terms. He really is talking about the mind, as becomes clear when he summarizes this section at the beginnning of the next, "Second Stage of Intelligence.—Intelligence as Intuition." Suddenly the mind is the topic of every sentence and the grammatical subject of most: "Hitherto the mind has acted only in response to some physical impulse .... What, then, we have to inquire, will be the form of the human intelligence, when the mind has once broken loose from the physical impressions of the senses, and when it can view itself, and the universe, as *separate* and *opposed* realities?" (122-23).

The mental entity Morell most wants to discuss is precisely that which has "broken loose from the physical impressions of the senses." Having broken away, the entity begins to become self-determining, becomes an entity in its own right—an active, living entity rather than a mere participant in the physical process of taking impressions from the external world. Only when the mind "can view itself, and the universe, as *separate* and *opposed* realities" does it become discrete. Without crediting Morell with a conceptual revolution, we should appreciate how, by limiting his figurative language to the physiological realm in one section and then asserting the presence of the mind after the fact, he manages to sidestep the mind-body problem. His figurative rendering of the movement of impressions through the nervous system allows him to conceptualize the mind more easily as another kind of entity, albeit still an entity.

Morell's conceptual flexibility is also apparent in his adaptation of Carpenter's model of the movement of sensations and willed impulses. Figure 2 shows the model as altered by Morell (102).

Although his additions are speculative, Morell is responding to the incompleteness of the model devised by Carpenter. His distinction between the partially and the fully excited cerebrum attempts to correlate physiological states to mental states more exactly than Carpenter does, and while the division between "Regulating ideas" and "Regulating physical efforts" relates to nothing factual, it does signal Morell's awareness of the problems raised by the blankness of that side of Carpenter's diagram. With Morell it is at least possible that the model has begun to serve a generative function by pointing to questions about what it does not represent. Attending to those blank areas could be a first step toward shifting attention away from the mechanism of the flow and allowing the phenomena of the mind to be discussed in the language of the mind. A subsequent step would be to discard the model but preserve the concept it embodies—the interactive relations among the system's parts.

Except for these hints of a new language of mind, Morell gains little ground in representing the mental and the physiological aspects of human life. He localizes the mental entity in an interesting figurative way relative to the flow of nerve energy, but the

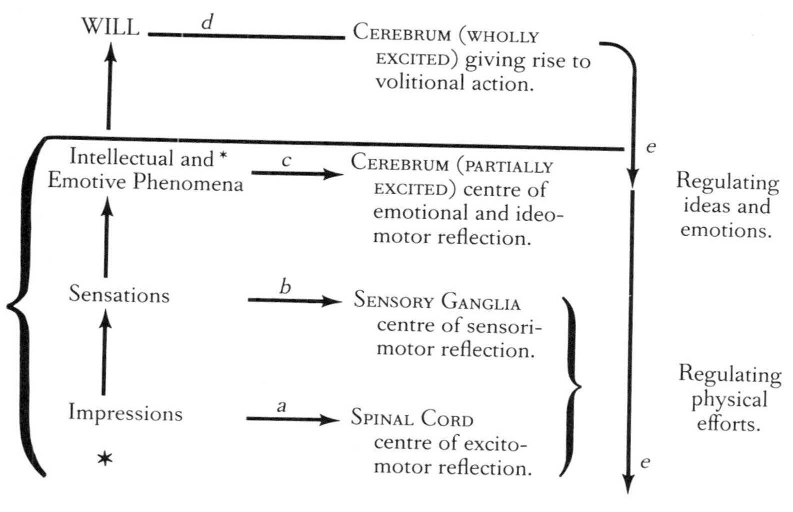

Figure 2. Morell's Diagram of the Flow of Impulse

entity itself still exists, still has a location, and perhaps has substance and extension. Herbert Spencer, in the important second edition of his *Principles of Psychology* (1870), denies the appropriateness of using such attributes, even as metaphors. Introducing his chapter on "the substance of mind," Spencer insists that if we understand by this phrase "Mind as qualitatively differentiated in each portion that is separable by introspection but seems homogeneous and undecomposable; then we do know something about the substance of Mind" (1:145). If we assume "an underlying something, it is possible in some cases to see, and in the rest to conceive, how these multitudinous modifications of it arise." But, Spencer continues, if we take the phrase to mean "the underlying something of which these distinguishable portions are formed, or of which they are modifications; then we know nothing about it, and never can know anything about it." In other words, although we can identify "the substance of Mind" as "resolvable into nervous shocks" and can say that these shocks "answer to the waves of molecular motion that transverse nerves and nerve-centres," nevertheless we still can't say "what Mind is" any more than we could claim to know what matter is if we could decompose it into its "ultimate homogeneous units" (1:156-57).

In contending that psychology can explain mental phenomena but cannot say anything about "the underlying something," Spencer exemplifies the larger problem, psychology's failure to articulate a coherent, non-hypothetical theory of the relationship between human experience on the one hand and physiology on the other. His movement toward such a theory represents one of the first sustained attempts to break free of the concepts and language associated with the mind-as-entity metaphor. The conceptual and metaphorical distance he had to travel can be measured by noting how the metaphor's key components of extension and impressibility dominate one of his early works, his 1860 essay "The Physiology of Laughter."

In this piece Spencer approaches laughter strictly as a psychophysical question: "Why, when greatly delighted, or impressed with certain unexpected contrasts of ideas, should there be a contraction of particular facial muscles and particular muscles of the chest and abdomen?" (452-53). His answer is based on the general principle that "nervous excitation always *tends* to beget muscular motion; and when it rises to a certain intensity always does beget it"; that is, "the nervous system in general discharges itself on the muscular system in general: either with or without the guidance of the will" (453-54). Not only muscles but also viscera and other components of the nerve-muscle system can receive a discharge from an excited portion of the system; nervous discharges from one part of the nervous system to another constitute consciousness (455). It is also important that a state of nervous tension seldom if ever "expends itself in one direction only" (456). For example, Spencer notes, "an agreeable state of feeling produced, say by praise, is not wholly used up in arousing the succeeding phase of the feeling and the new ideas appropriate to it; but a certain portion overflows into the visceral nervous system, increasing the action of the heart and facilitating digestion."

Furthermore, if some channels are closed, the discharge must be stronger along the others, and if one direction is determined as preferred by the existing conditions, the discharge along the others will be weaker.

Using the explanatory apparatus of nerve-force, channels, and preferred directions, Spencer can answer his opening question: Why are certain muscles involved in laughter? He explains that "an overflow of nerve-force undirected by any motive, will manifestly take first the most habitual routes; and if these do not suffice, will next overflow into the less habitual ones" (458-59). The muscles around the mouth are most frequently stimulated by moderate flows of mental energy, and as they are small they are also relatively easily stimulated; hence these are the "first to contract under pleasurable emotion" (459). If the nervous energy is so great that these muscles cannot drain it off, the respiratory muscles will next be stimulated, being "more constantly implicated than any others in those various acts which our feelings impel us to"; if the flow of energy is greater still, the upper limbs will be called into play, and finally the head will be thrown back and the spine bent inwards (459-60). The article's concluding sentence puts the whole investigative method in a nutshell: "We should probably learn much if in every case we asked—where is all the nervous energy gone?" (466).

The system of neural hydrostatics offered by Spencer as the cause of laughter is purely hypothetical. It is an expressive, compact, and vivid extended metaphor with a very plausible connection to the secondary domain of fluid mechanics. Spencer constructs this explanation in the essay exactly as Black says a scientific model is to be constructed, with one significant difference—the model is not used to predict results which are then tested against new data, but instead is buttressed with well-known facts of everyday life. For instance, "the suppression of external signs of feeling, makes feeling more intense," and intense mental action destroys appetite and arrests digestion (456-57). Constructing the extended metaphor constitutes normal science for Spencer, and the metaphor itself constitutes an expression of mind-as-entity.

"The Study of Laughter" does not display the evolutionary perspective that is now regarded as Spencer's main contribution to psychology. This perspective he first fully articulates a decade later in the second edition of his *Principles of Psychology* (1870), a substantial expansion of the first edition, which preserves "sundry of the cardinal ideas" of the first, as he mentions in the preface, but also incorporates more Darwinian material. In developing this evolutionary perspective, Spencer moves beyond the mind-as-entity concept but remains entangled in the metaphor's language.

The most revolutionary statement in *Principles* is Spencer's definition of life: "the definite combination of heterogeneous changes, both simultaneous and successive, in correspondence with external co-existences and sequences," or, more briefly, "the continuous adjustment of internal relations to external relations" (1:293). In his second most revolutionary statement, he insists that "every proposition" in psychology must recognize the "all-essential" influence of "environing actions" (1:390-91). But the revolution extends no farther. When Spencer works out the implications of these statements he reverts to expressions that sound like those of Hume, Hartley, or Thomas Brown. These expressions neither represent mental phenomena in the language of the mind (Spencer in fact does not advocate the autonomy thesis) nor, more significantly, suggest that the definition of life as an adjustment of relations corresponds to a metaphor serving a generative function.

One of the ways in which internal relations adjust to external is through "extension of space." Spencer declares: "It is a fact that the appearance of the higher senses, even in their most rudimentary forms, is accompanied by some extension of the space throughout which correspondences can be effected. It is a fact that the successive stages in the development of each sense imply successive enlargements of the sphere of space. And it is a fact that the advent of rationality is, among other ways, shown in the carrying of these enlargements still further" (1:318). In short, the "progress of life and intelligence" is a function of spatial extension. Life, Spencer goes on to say, increases in "amount" according to the "extension of the correspondence in space," since such extension adds to the number of external relations and hence to the number of internal changes (1:319). Spencer also asserts that the foundation of the extension is the sense of touch and that there is a direct relationship between the sensitivity of this sense and the degree of intelligence: "the most far-reaching cognitions, and inferences the most remote from perception, have their roots in the definitely-combined impressions which the human hands can receive" (1:362). Only the first of Spencer's "facts" is more than an opinion; the others are interpretations and assertions. All three, as well as the correlations between the amount of life and spatial extension, and between the sense of touch and intelligence, preserve an important quality of the mind-as-entity metaphor: the dependence of mental phenomena on physical processes and qualities of the external world.

As revolutionary as is Spencer's unswerving advocacy of *relation*, the relationships that he describes are all one-way, from space to life, "internal relations" adjusting themselves to "external relations." Consciousness, the irreducible center of mental life, is just as much a one-way relationship: "we can become conscious only through the changes caused in us by surrounding things," and our consciousness consists of these changes "*combined and arranged* in special ways" (2:291-92). Consciousness of complex things comes about the same way: "in proportion as a chain of such changes is consolidated into a single change, in the same proportion do the several sensations which form the antecedents and consequents of the changes, become present together" into a consciousness of the "complex thing" (2:295). In contrast to Upham's statement that there comes a time in the development of the individual mind when "the soul finds knowledge in itself," Spencer actually seems to deny an important human experience, that sensation of turning inward.

Spencer's preference for physicalistic terms is also apparent in his discussion of "the nature of intelligence," which is basically identical in the 1855 and 1870 editions. For Spencer the key distinction between physical and psychical life is that the former is characterized by successive and simultaneous changes, but the latter consists primarily of "successive changes only" (1:405). He remarks that images of many things are always being impressed on the retina, "yet these are not appreciated internally" and "do not undergo that co-ordination with others which constitutes them psychical changes." The "seriality" of consciousness, especially "as it rises to a higher form" (intelligence), is not essential to his theory, but it is consonant with a commitment to mind-as-entity: one simple substance in one location, capable of existing in one state at a time. Spencer concludes the paragraph with a metaphor of consciousness as something woven: "In brief, we may say that while the outer strands of changes which constitute the thread of consciousness, are indefinite and loosely adherent, there is always an internal closely-twisted series of changes, forming what we may consider as consciousness proper" (1:406). Spencer uses this metaphor casually to illustrate the seriality of consciousness. As he presents it the metaphor is neither very vivid, nor very expressive, nor very apt.

Spencer's presentation of the concept of *relation* is best regarded as derived from the mind-as-entity metaphor rather than as a new metaphor able to generate new theories. His language consistently connotes a mind that is impressible and localized, an entity in which changes in the nervous system correspond to changes in the external world and impressions from that world. Life consists in the adjustment of inner *to* outer; Spencer does not seem to ask if mental life might have its own laws and processes radically different from those of the external physical world, or if the outer might adjust itself to the inner.

Spencer is by no means isolated in his approach. All of the philosophical psychologists roughly contemporary with him exhibit the same discrepancy between, on the one hand, a relatively clear understanding of the physiology of perception and motor stimulation and, on the other, a vague idealistic description of the phenomena of experience as subjectively perceived. The discrepancy is equally present in the works of psychologists with a fairly strong sensationalist orientation such as Mill and in the works of those with a more idealistic orientation such as Morell. Spencer is unusual because his concept of *relation* occupies an important position in his theoretical statements; in addition, it is a much more intelligible expression than for example Bain's "mind-body giving birth to mind-body." Lewes moves one step closer to a revolutionary perspective by not only insisting on the inseparability of life and mind but embodying that inseparability in some of his figurative language.

Like Spencer, Lewes classifies psychology among the life sciences; Lewes does so, as he explains in *The Study of Psychology* (1879), because he conceives of the mind as an entity like other biological entities. According to Lewes, psychology should be defined as "the science of the facts of Sentience," which is a "more precise and comprehensive" definition than the usual "science of the facts of Consciousness" (7). This latter definition is restricted because it ignores what to Lewes is self-evident, that despite the existence of "what are called spiritual facts" and although "no deductions from what is known objectively of the material mechanism will explain the phenomena of sensibility, as states of consciousness," nevertheless there can be no rational grounds for separating Mind from Life" (8). Thus psychology is correctly defined as a branch of biology and its method that of the physical sciences. Lewes feels that it is totally artificial to "classify certain phenomena as psychical, and others as vital. . . . all psychical phenomena are vital, and in all of them sensibility is a factor" (9). Taking a cue from the agreed subdivision of all biological sciences into two components, "Morphology, the science of form, and Physiology, the science of function," Lewes comes at the identification of psychology with biology from another direction: psychology is concerned not with the organism's structure or evolution but with its "sentient functions and faculties" (9).

These general principles contain two elements with potential to revolutionize the concept of the mind. First is Lewes' contention that mind and life cannot be separated and that the proper focus of psychology is *sentience* rather than the more restrictive *consciousness*. Second is his identification of psychology as a biological science, thus a science concerned with function more than with form. Yet as with Spencer, the revolutionary promise is hindered by habits of language based on the mind-as-entity metaphor. Lewes begins *The Study of Psychology* by defining psychology as a discipline that "investigates the Human Mind, not an individual's thoughts and feelings; and has to consider it as the product of the Human Organism not only in relation to the Cosmos, but also in relation to Society. For man is distinctly a social being" (5). While a product can be something intangible, like a *function*, the connotations of "product" and "function" are not entirely congruent; Lewes' characterizing the mind with a term that first connotes something tangible is an early hint that the promise will not be fulfilled in this book.

As Lewes explains "the study of psychology" in more detail, he remains within the limits of the mind-as-entity metaphor despite the contradictions that result. His revolutionary tendency pulls him in one direction, hence he dismisses Hamilton's "metempirical postulate of a 'something behind or under the phenomena'" of thought; the only way it is "permissible in a scientific treatise to speak of Soul or Mind, as substance or subject," is from the perspective of "the organism in relation to the external world and to the social world" (12-13). His tendency to remain within what was then considered normal science in psychology leads him to insist on the "identity of molecular and sentient changes" (14), so that psychology should be considered as "the science of the products" generated by the operation of physiological mechanisms. It would be methodologically unsound to separate the two sciences psychology and physiology, he writes, because that would mean "excluding all the processes known to be physiological and known to be unconscious" (19).

Lewes also holds with the physicalistic hypothesis of a sensorium, and he uses physicalistic language to describe its operation: "Subjected to varying stimulations, and combinations of stimulation, it acquires new aptitudes, new modes of response; and is incessantly modified, if not in its elementary structure, at any rate in the fluctuating disposition of its elements. It thus forms, as it were, a spiritual mechanism superadded to the material mechanism" (32-33). He arrives at this description by following the principle of the "identity of molecular and sentient changes," even though the molecular changes are "entirely hidden from our present means of detection" (33). Lacking any idea of precisely how these changes occur, Lewes nevertheless adopts the figurative language of mind-as-entity: the sensorium's "plasticity" allows it to be modified by experience (34). The best organization of the study of human life is quite clear to Lewes: physiology must first generate a "theory of the mechanism," and psychology can then "trace the operation of this mechanism in the functions and faculties which spring into existence through its adaption to the Cosmos and Society" (38). The "material mechanism" generates the "spiritual mechanism."

In a later chapter Lewes defines "the General Mind" as the "abstract conception" consisting of the shared features of all minds. This mind is shaped by and can be studied through language. An individual can only feel the emotions of the group "when his soul is moved like theirs; he cannot think their thoughts so long as his experiences refuse to be condensed in their symbols" (160-61). It would seem then that every mental phenomenon can in principle be explained as the interaction of a number of elementary particles, substances, or atoms of thought under a few general laws. This is the same atomistic approach characteristically induced by the mind-as-entity metaphor. However, Lewes has earlier spoken against this kind of analysis. It would indeed be possible, he writes, to construct "out of the facts of Consciousness alone" an "abstract science of Feeling, to stand beside the abstract science of Force—an *Aesthetics* parallel with *Dynamics*. The general facts of Feeling formulated in abstract laws would then be disengaged from all concrete manifestations; the organism and the medium would be left out of account, as Matter and its Qualities are disregarded in Dynamics" (64-5). Sensations and thoughts could be reduced to "cerebral vibrations," and some "psychological Lagrange might arise who would reduce all these vibrations to a single equation." This would be a powerful instrument but would not be a psychology; "it would no more expound the facts of Human Nature than Dynamics expounds the facts of Nature." His explicit point is that psychology must incorporate much more than just the facts of consciousness, which do not include the facts of physiology as they influence unconscious mental operations. The less obvious point is that the concept of a general mind as Lewes presents it is reductive after the fashion of the psychology of the eighteenth century, whereas his insistence on "the organism and its medium" derives from his more revolutionary tendency.

In *The Study of Psychology*, Lewes seems most consistent in his inconsistency: if he articulates a revolutionary premise in one section, he will likely advocate the normal-scientific opposite in another. The mind-as-entity metaphor and the concept of relation are incompatible. *Study* is the first of Lewes' "Problems of Life and Mind." He considers three others: "Mind as a Function of the Organism," "The Sphere of Sense and Logic of Feeling," and "The Sphere of Intellect and Logic of Signs." In the prefatory note to the volume in which these appear, the editor (George Eliot) says that Lewes had intended to rewrite much of the material. He would certainly have re-ordered the chapters in the third problem, "the actual arrangement being partly the result of conjecture. The Fourth Problem, of which the later pages were written hardly more than three weeks before the Author's death, is but a fragment." Because of its title and its relatively finished state, "Mind as a Function of the Organism" would presumably contain the same level and type of inconsistency as *The Study of Psychology*. Surprisingly, Lewes' figurative language indicates much less constraint by mind-as-entity. In attempting to represent certain phenomena of mind that were becoming of more interest to psychologists (especially those phenomena that occur outside immediate conscious awareness) and in attempting to correlate these phenomena with the "theory of the mechanism" constituting physiology, he is groping toward the elements of a generative metaphor that serves as an important structuring principle in the novels of George Eliot.

The potential generative metaphor in these pages is that of the web of relations used to represent sentience. Lewes specifies it in criticizing the notion of "double consciousness": "We have seen that the discriminated experiences comprised under Attention must be regarded as a *series*; but the true comparison for sensorial reaction is that of a *web*" ("Mind as a Function of the Organism" 217). This explicit naming draws together concepts and figures from the previous two hundred pages in a compact, vivid, and expressive metaphor. As early as the opening chapter Lewes uses the word "network" four times in three sentences, making clear in the last that the network is web-like: we cannot know an organism's precise "disposition . . . in any one case, nor in what degree the various *threads* of the network are in action" (16, my emphasis). Among the most important of these threads that will concern Lewes in the following pages are what he calls "neural tremors," which influence feelings and dispositions; when he refers to the "escort of nascent sensations and thoughts" he means this network of threads (17). It follows from this concept that a change in any part of the organism is transmitted throughout the whole (40), and it follows from the metaphor that "we cannot have one sentient state that is not *enmeshed* with other sentient states, so that each wave of stimulation sets going a multitude of connected stimulations" (41, my emphasis). One of the reasons this metaphor is so expressive is that the subsidiary vehicle of "wave motion" describes the dynamics of the web; Lewes frequently refers to "waves" of sensation washing through the system, receding, and recurring.

Likewise follows the "Law of Grouping," which Lewes labels "the fundamental law of mental action": neural tremors group themselves into a sensation, sensations into perception, thence into conception, thence into judgments (159). True, "we are never conscious of the *formation* of any product, only of the *group formed*." This disclaimer would be enough to undercut the law of grouping itself except for the law's metaphorical validity. Lewes does not explain his derivation of the Law, but it could certainly be generated by a model of sentience-as-web. The physical model alone would not generate the law, but Lewes' examples stress the subjective, psychological experience in conjunction with what can be objectively, albeit hypothetically, inferred from a model. He precedes this statement of the law by reminding his readers that when listening to a symphony we easily and quickly alternate between awareness of the whole ensemble of sound and awareness of the "component masses" (158-59). We know that the component masses group themselves into the ensemble, and this knowledge viewed in light of the sentience-as-web model implies the law of grouping.

As I said, this metaphor is only potentially generative for Lewes. When explaining other phenomena that could be effectively described in these terms, he may use other metaphors. Thus personality is the psychological analogy of the influence of the center of gravity on the physical system: "The position of the centre of gravity is a continually shifting point. The attitude of the Personality is likewise a continually shifting point" (197). Thus "motives are determined by motors lying deep down in the mental structure," whereas unconscious cerebration can in part be explained by "the silent growth of *tendencies*" (138-39). Both metaphors derive from the mind-as-entity concept, and Lewes' easy mixing of them suggests that he has not yet really been struck by the relational metaphor.

Lewes' uncertainty about the theoretical role of the relational concept is even visible in the sentence following his naming of the web metaphor:

> The attitude of the Sensorium is a fluctuating attitude which successively traverses and retraverses all the positions of the sensorial field, and which thus successively brings now one and now the other point into the daylight, leaving the others momentarily obscured though still impressing the sentient organism; we can understand, then, how among the numerous impressions many are so rapidly brought under focus that they seem simultaneous; and how two or more strands of quite different impressions shall be alternately fixed by the "yellow spot" of Consciousness, and yet, owing to their disparity, seem like two personalities. [217]

The "yellow spot" refers to the one spot on the retina capable of distinct vision, the spot to which by reflex we move the image of any object that makes a sufficiently strong impression on the outer zones of the retina, thus enabling us to see that object distinctly (194). Lewes refers to research showing that the reflex action can be overcome and concludes that there exists "an inner or sensorial visual point (*Blickpunkt*) which dominates that of the retinal point" (195). The yellow spot is a physical reality whose function in perception is well understood. Lewes develops this extended metaphor to explain our occasional sensation of experiencing a double consciousness. But the sensation could as well be explained by remaining within the relational metaphor; the physicalistic metaphor embodies assumptions about the sensorium that are as hypothetical as the concept of mental chemistry or of the mind as a blank slate. Even more telling, the metaphor itself is confused. Is the "sensorial field" the one encompassed by the retina or a hypothetical one within the sensorium? Where are the "strands of impressions" located?

That Lewes was sensitive to the problem of the language used to talk about the mind there can be no doubt. This is why his consistent inconsistencies, his repeated contradictions, may be viewed as symptoms of a conceptual tension that might have resulted in a radically new way of talking about the mind. It is also possible that his awareness of the key role played by language in human inquiry kept him from going beyond the limitations of the mind-as-entity metaphor. He understood that figurative language and hypotheses could be used as exploratory tools; this understanding may have prevented his seeing that a different type of metaphor can project us into a new realm or transform a perspective. He grasped the principle, as in this lucid discussion of the role of hypothesis and figurative language:

> What takes place in the nervous system under stimulation and reaction is neither demonstrable to Sense nor discernible by Intuition; it is, and will long remain, mere guesswork. This may seem a hard sentence to those who have been relying on the hypothesis of vibrations, wave-movements, chemical or electrical processes, cell-functions, seats of sensation, seats of emotion, seats of volition, and seats of thought. . . . All that has gained currency on this subject the student will do well to accept as provisional imagery which may assist exposition, not as data from which conclusions may be drawn. The hypotheses are not terms of knowledge, but terms to fill our gaps in knowledge. [*Study* 184]

This is an excellent explanation of what would be called, a century later, "theory-constitutive metaphor." Such a metaphor helps us, as Boyd says, accommodate our language "to as yet undiscovered causal features of the world." The psychologist who makes conscious use of such a metaphor, however, may risk forcing all data to fit the metaphor, just as normal science tries to fit data to existing theories. Indeed, it may be left to the fictional imagination, operating in a novelist or even in a psychologist, to reconceive the paintbrush as a pump, so to speak—to not just describe but represent in new metaphors a web-like sentience or a fully textured mind-scape.

Achievements and Limitations of the Psychologists

Most of the psychologists discussed in this chapter contributed significantly to the development of the discipline as we know it today. Bain showed that a psychological system could be erected on a physiological basis—that is, on the basis of an actual rather than a hypothetical physiology. Spencer and Lewes, along with Bain, helped develop the evolutionary perspective that finally placed psychology within the biological sciences and stimulated systems such as the functionalism of William James. Young points out that Spencer, in his psychological theories, combined phrenology and associationism in an evolutionary context, thus moving to integrate two important strands of thought in "the debate on man's place in nature" ("Psychology in Evolutionary Debate" 96). Lewes' works also "formed an important contribution to the later stages of the psycho-physiological trend," and Morell was "the first of a number of nonmedical writers who shared the basic problematic of the medical psycho-physiologists while analyzing its implications in a more philosophical manner" (Danziger 123). Mill revised and improved his father's radical associationism.

Nevertheless, the psychologists remained limited by the mind-as-entity metaphor to the extent that they failed to develop a language for talking about the mind separate from the language used to discuss other human endeavors: they did not come much closer to achieving Reid's goal of a distinct language of the mind than did their forebears Berkeley, Locke, Hume, and Reid. Rather, the main emphasis in the established psychology was shifted "from the extreme of allowing the terms of everyday experience to dictate how the nervous system must be organized and must function, to that of allowing the categories of physiological analysis to dictate the elements from which the phenomena of everyday life would have to be synthesized" (Young, *Mind, Brain* xiii-ix). These two extremes are well represented, according to Young, by Gall's *The Functions of the Brain* (1826), which placed the study of mind in the context of metaphysics, and the second edition of David Ferrier's work of the same title, published in 1886, which placed it in the context of biology (7). (Young notes that even today the methods of psychology and physiology have not been unified, 246-47.) Scientific research in the nineteenth century was dominated by the languages of physics, biology, and geology, which supported the theory-constitutive function of the mind-as-entity metaphor, both because these studies were well developed and accessible (useful for model-making) and because they were after all components of the century's normal science and were not until late in the century challenged to explain anomalous data.

The nineteenth-century psychologists of the English tradition, like their earlier counterparts, remained disinterested in that component essential to the psychological novel, "a separable or at least radically distinguishable *inner world*" (Williams 209). Far from being separable or radically distinguishable, mental phenomena were primarily analogous to if not actually driven by phenomena of the external world. This was the import of association psychology, of physiological investigations, and of neurological chapters in works as professedly idealistic as Morell's *Elements*. The one mental faculty that was preserved from such external influence was the will, and this was preserved in order to maintain the special status of the human being within Creation. (See Daston.) Thus Carpenter, for example, "was clearly at pains to preserve an area of action for the will so as to provide a psychological guarantee of the possibility of individual moral action" (Danziger 130). Both Carpenter and Thomas Laycock, as well as other physiological psychologists of their era, were dedicated to solving this problem: "How to conceive the principles of automatic action whose existence scientific psychology had demonstrated in such a way as to leave room for the operation of a divinely ordained natural order" (Danziger 141). In preserving the will as a faculty outside the psycho-physiological network or at most having only one hand in that network, so to speak, the psychologists were not introducing an "inner world" of the kind Williams refers to. While Spencer and Lewes (most notably) argued for the unity of life and mind, their physicalistic orientation prevented them from conceiving of the unity as implying more than the dependence of mind on life.

Because of these particular features—the lack of a separate language for talking about the mind, the lack of interest in an inner world, the stress on consciousness and will, the unfulfilled promise of some of the metaphors used by Morell and Lewes—psychology was surpassed by fiction in one endeavor that was increasingly important in the nineteenth century: the development of a way to understand and represent the life of the mind. This development in fictional works is described in the next two chapters. There I will show how the concepts of mind-scape, as discussed in Chapter 3, and sentience-as-web, as embodied in metaphors used by the philosophical and physiological psychologists, combined into the generative metaphor mind-as-a-living-being.

V

REVEALING SURFACES, PREDICTABLE DEPTHS: MIND AS ENTITY IN BRONTË AND DICKENS

The most obvious characteristic shared by the psychologists and novelists of the eighteenth century and the psychologists of the nineteenth century is a concern with "the substance mind." This concern derived from the problems raised by the mind-as-entity metaphor. It manifested itself in the novels' focus on how particular ideas were formed and in the psychological works' development of laws of mind analogous to the laws of the physical world. It was seen as well in an ongoing debate over the degree to which mind could be termed a substance, an entity, or a power and still retain the immateriality necessary for its connection with God. The principle of continuity, fundamental to all the sciences, imposed two demands when applied to the study of the mind: to receive sense impressions from the physical world, the mind had to have a physical component, and to respond to sublime and divine experiences, it had to have an immaterial, divine component. Since the mind was experienced as unified and indivisible, these demands were in conflict.

In addition to this metaphysical aspect (as it was termed), the question of mind had a practical aspect represented by the name of one of psychology's ancillary disciplines, moral science. Both the novelists and the psychologists were responding to their society's desire for an explanation of behavior that would be internally consistent and at the same time would contribute to the improvement of society. Thus both took as their starting point for analysis the mature mind (always male, of course) reflecting on the genius of God's design; that design, in turn, was manifested not only in perceivable phenomena but also in the means by which the phenomena impressed themselves on the mind and stimulated its growth. Because psychologists attempted to understand this interaction between the mind and the world, they claimed for their discipline the first place in the hierarchy of the sciences. Undergirding this whole structure of theories and goals was the mind conceived of as a thinking substance and figuratively represented as a malleable, localizable, and discrete entity.

After about the first third of the nineteenth century, people began to realize that this structure could not accommodate some mental phenomena that were becoming more and more interesting. Two particular areas of experience remained relatively inaccessible: powerful, apparently innate feelings (usually characterized as "the heart"), and the sense of the mind as a complex being governed by laws perhaps very different from those of the physical world (a sense that now pervades everyday usage with the terms "the unconscious" and "the subconscious"). In this chapter I show that Charlotte Brontë and Charles Dickens attempted to represent the first area of experience by modifiying the mind-as-entity metaphor; their attempts attest to the lingering attractiveness of that metaphor. In the following chapter I focus on the techniques developed by George Eliot and Henry James to represent the second area, methods which for the first time show an explicit concept of the life of the mind as a living, sentient whole.

If these four novelists were imagined as psychologists, Brontë and Dickens were within the limits of what I've called normal science, relying on the theory-constitutive metaphor mind-as-entity, whereas Eliot and James were moving toward a conceptual revolution with their metaphors of mindscapes and sentient webs. All four, however, were engaged in the "epistemological quest" that Michael Timko identifies as one of the main traits of the Victorian era, in contradistinction to the "metaphysical quest" of the Romantics (610). Timko writes that the Wordsworthian "certainty of knowing, this apprehension of a metaphysical certainty, is gone in the next generation"; the Victorians were more concerned to understand the human being in a pragmatic way—how the human body, mind, and society work together (613).

The reception accorded Dickens and Brontë demonstrates the importance of "the heart"; their works were judged in part by how convincingly the life of the heart was presented. Dickens fared poorly in this respect, Brontë much better. Dickens was regarded as someone who could tell a story so well and people it with such interesting caricatures that the uncritical reader seldom noticed how *un*true-to-life these caricatures really were. According to one anonymous critic writing for the *Rambler* in 1854, the "great intellectual characteristic" of Dickens was his "most unusual power of observing the external peculiarities of men and women, as distinguished from all insight into that hidden nature whence flow the springs of their conduct" (in Ford 82). This critic also declared that "morally there is probably not another living writer, of equal decency of thought, to whom the supernatural and eternal world simply is *not*." George Eliot spoke explicitly of Dickens' "false psychology" in her essay "The Natural History of German Life." She felt that he could render the externals but was unable to render the "psychological character" of his figures (271). Trollope, in a masterful piece of faint praise, commented, "It has been the peculiarity and the marvel of this man's power, that he has invested his puppets with a charm that has enabled him to dispense with human nature" (in Ford 106).

These negative voices were calling for the presentation of a single human nature, like Lewes' "General Mind," with a clear connection between its "hidden" component and the "eternal world." In his important essay "Dickens in Relation to Criticism" (1872) Lewes attempted to explain the source of Dickens' power and popularity, which he felt had not been adequately acknowledged by critics. Despite this positive approach, however, Lewes labeled the Dickens world "a fantastic absurdity" and its characters "caricatures and distortions of human nature. . . . Unreal and impossible as these types were, speaking a language never heard in life, moving like pieces of simple mechanism always in one way (instead of moving with the infinite fluctuations of organisms . . .) these unreal figures affected the uncritical reader with the force of reality" (in Ford 61-62). Lewes' distinction between "moving like pieces of simple mechanism" and "moving with the infinite fluctuations of organisms" implies two important criteria for credible characters: they must be organisms, and they must demonstrate finely modulated responses to slight variations in stimuli. In assessing the achievements of Brontë and Dickens I will show that their metaphors of mind did not enable them to meet these criteria.

It is useful to consider a dissent from the general evaluation of Dickens' fictional world as unreal, in order to better understand what Dickens' contemporaries took to represent reality. David Masson, writing in 1859, placed Dickens in what he called the "ideal, or Romantic school" (34). What this meant, Masson continued, was that Dickens was able to take a "hint from actual fact," generalize it, and develop it "into a character to match; which character he then transports, along with others similarly suggested, into a world of semi- fantastic conditions, where the laws need not be those of ordinary probability. . . . The Ideal or Romantic artist must be true to nature, as well as the Real artist; but he may be true in a different fashion. He may take hints from Nature in her extremest moods, and make these hints the terms of creations fitted for a world projected imaginatively beyond the real one, or inserted into the midst of the real one, and yet imaginatively moated round from it" (35-36). As one example, Masson offered Micawberism, remarking that although "there never was a Mr. Micawber in nature" yet nature was pervaded with the "essence," which Dickens "extracted." But in disagreeing with the negative evaluations Masson still accepted their reading of Dickens' fictional world: it is moated round from the real world, it contains characters that no one will ever meet in nature, and it is governed by other laws than those of ordinary probability.

Masson's description of Dickens' creative technique reminds

us that the term "reality" did not mean quite the same thing in 1850 as it does today. For all of the critics, reality meant nature, and nature was agreed to have a component above, beyond, or behind the tangible everyday reality, an "eternal" component that correlated with the characters' "inherent necessity" and "hidden nature." This is John Romano's basis for contending that Dickens is best regarded as a realistic novelist, attempting to signify "with only partial coherence but with great longing, the world that lies beyond the farthest border of his power to portray" (7). Romano believes that Dickens' works imply an epistemology: "reality is forever escaping our grasp, forever going deeper than, forever superseding and outdistancing, the forms provided by the chasing mind" (47). The mind, with its forms derived by rational processes or else impressed in a physical way by the external world, can never "grasp" that larger reality. One element must be added to make Romano's depiction complete: although the intellect cannot rationally understand this deeper level or higher realm, the heart can sense it. Dickens knew that the realm of depth could not be perceived as the surface details could be, nor could it be *rendered*, but it could be sensed or intuited and could be *signified.* Metaphor was an indispensable tool for this signification; only by means of metaphor could Dickens express the otherwise inexpressible experience of depth.

This is not to say that he did a particularly good job even then. His conception of such experience was limited by the mind-as-entity metaphor, which did not invite him to portray those infinite fluctuations of organisms that Lewes said were so important. Reality forever escapes the grasp of characters in the Dickens world as well as the grasp of the novelist because the greater part of the interaction is "always in one way," from the external world to the mind: mind is *impressed by* the world and has little if any life of its own. Dickens' contemporaries were dissatisfied with his world, insofar as it allowed little place for the sensed connections between human depths and "the supernatural and eternal world"; Dickens simply asserted such connections. Dickens' psychology was primarily based on associationism and the hypothesis of an impressible mind, with the heart as a rather passive kernel of goodness underneath the layers of character impressed by the world. Bringing the heart into the metaphorical structure in this relatively programmatic way allowed Dickens to represent powerful, irrational, benevolent feelings better than the psychology of the eighteenth century had done, but it did not correct the deficiencies of the mind-as-entity metaphor.

In contrast to the resistance met by Dickens' psychology, Charlotte Brontë's psychology was regarded favorably because she preserved the connection between the springs of human nature and the eternal fountains while also giving her main characters a fuller life. The reviews included in Miriam Allott's *The Brontës* frequently mention the author's skill in developing character and her ability to focus on the workings of a single mind. The phrases "anatomy of mind" and "anatomy of the female heart" occur several times in descriptions of the author's method and achievement (74, 118, 141, for example). These physicalistic statements are usually accompanied by explanations of the moral value of or the moral intent behind the author's attention to particulars. Thus, one reviewer praised *Villette* for that "actuality" in portrayal of human beings which is "the very genius and spirit of modern English fiction"; actuality allows readers to feel "the thrill of sympathy" and learn, from the characters' thoughts and actions, how to "think and act" (213). According to another reviewer, the "soul" of the author of *Villette* saw "men and things with the correct glance of science, only warmed and made more piercing by a genial sympathy" (182-83). A third, discussing *Shirley*, emphasized Brontë's ability to represent both the everyday real and the transcendent real: "A sharp relish for the beauties of external nature, no mean power of reproducing them, and occasional glimpses of ideal imagination of a high order, are visible throughout" (129).

Again, Lewes' comments are instructive as an index of the criteria upheld by the progressive psychology of Brontë's time. He identified the "significant characteristic" of *Jane Eyre* as its "deep, significant reality." He went on to explain that the author's "faculty for objective representation is also united to a strange power of subjective representation. We do not simply mean the power over the passions—the psychological intuition of the artist, but the power also of connecting external appearances with internal effects—of representing the psychological interpretation of material phenomena" (Allott 84, 86). He praised Brontë's ability to describe how surface appearances affect a mind and how the mind in turn misrepresents or misconceives the appearances by correlating rather precisely each fact of external appearance with an internal effect. In other words, Brontë was able to render those infinite fluctuations that Lewes regarded as equivalent to life.

The second power Lewes attributed to Brontë was her response to the developing interest in what he would later call sentience—the interest in the infinite number of fluctuations experienced by an organism, in the psychological impact of physiological fluctuations, and in the physiological impact of psychological fluctuations. This power exceeds in degree but does not differ in kind from that of Defoe, Richardson, and Austen. Brontë gave passions a more coherent voice than did these earlier writers, but the voice itself was still one element of a rather simply conceived, relatively passive mental entity.

Brontë's Psychology of Surfaces and Depths

The four novels of Brontë's mature period show a development away from a psychology that assumes a straightforward connection between surfaces and the mind beneath, to a psychology that stresses the difficulty of reading surfaces accurately. In *The Professor* (the earliest of her novels but not published until 1857) she relied on physiognomy, the revealing glance, and clearly defined character types to portray her characters and their interactions. In her later works she emphasized how characters develop toward self-understanding while calling into question the psychological truisms of that first work. Her criticism of Jane Austen provides the metaphorical key to her concept of the mind: "What sees keenly, speaks aptly, moves flexibly, it suits her to study, ut what throbs fast and full, though hidden, what the blood rushes through, what is the unseen seat of Life and the sentient target of death—*this* Miss Austen ignores; she no more, with the mind's eye, beholds the heart of her race than each man, with bodily vision sees the heart in his heaving breast" (in Knies 48).

The vehicle of the metaphor here is the heart as a physical organ, throbbing, pumping blood, constituting the body's most important vital sign. The tenor is emotional life or the passions. With the word *sentient*, Brontë located emotional life outside of the relatively limited realm of consciousness and within the broader realm of sentience, which incorporates unconscious facts, those which "lie outside the range of Introspection" but can be studied through observation and inference without the necessity of hypothesizing a "mystic Unconsciousness" as Lewes explained (*Study of Psychology* 91). The attempt to bring the realm of sentience within the novel form was potentially revolutionary; Lewes no doubt had this attempt in mind when he praised Brontë for "representing the psychological interpretation of material phenomena." But her continuing reliance on figurative language derived from the mind-as-entity metaphor prevented her fulfilling this potential. She referred to the minds of her characters as impressible and discrete entities; she insisted on a point-for-point connection between external appearances and the internal reality, although her characters have to learn to read the appearances; she conveyed no sense of a distinct inner life, although her characters discover inner springs and fountains.

The Professor is a study in unendearing self-control. Its narrator, William Crimsworth, never allows himself any extremity of feeling. The passions of rapture and despair only impinge on his life through the agency of the young lace-mender, Frances, whom he comes to love. Because his feelings for her are phlegmatic and controlled, he is puzzled by her excesses. Only once is he mastered by impulse, when he asks if she will marry him: "There are impulses we can control; but there are others which control us, because they attain us with a tiger-leap, and are our masters ere we have seen them. Perhaps, though, such impulses are seldom altogether bad; perhaps Reason, by a process as brief as quiet, a process that is finished ere felt, has ascertained the sanity of the deed Instinct meditates, and feels justified in remaining passive while it is performed" (228).

His mind, to Crimsworth, consists of separate entities which can initiate and regulate deeds. Assuming that all minds are similarly constructed, Crimsworth can explain Frances' outbursts of passion only by imagining her as two separate beings. Thus after their marriage he feels possessed of not one but two wives, one firm, active, and enterprising, the other full of "poetic feeling and fervour," one a "submissive and supplicating little mortal woman" and the other a "mere vexing fairy" whom he must "dose" with the "deep, serene, and sober mind" of Wordsworth (255, 258). Crimsworth's inability to understand that such a wide range of behavior can come from only one being is a characteristic limitation of the mind-as-entity metaphor. The mental entity is necessarily unified at least to the extent that Crimsworth feels his own mind to be—under the control of reason. A person who seems possessed of two dramatically different personalities must be two separate selves; a single mental entity could not contain both.

Readers usually resist accepting Brontë's favorable view of the narrator, a man who understands little of other people and who seems to know nothing of the unseen seat of Life. Frances is not two persons but one, and objectively her moments of passion need be no more puzzling than Crimsworth's. Further, she understands that her passions are real and important. As she tells him after one outburst, when he asks where "all that wild vigour" has disappeared to, "I cannot tell where it is gone . . . but I know that, whenever it is wanted, it will come back again" (261). Brontë clearly intends readers to approve both of Frances and of Crimsworth, whose character is the opposite of hers.

One explanation for Brontë's demands on her readers is her desire to strike out in a direction completely different from that taken in her Angrian romances. She writes in her preface to *The Professor* that as a writer she has come to prefer the "plain and homely," hence her hero "should work his way through life" as real men do: "As Adam's son he should share Adam's doom, and drain throughout life a mixed and moderate cup of enjoyment" (3). A second explanation is that Brontë has not yet found language to represent the location of that "wild vigour" and the way it operates. When describing the impact of passions on plain and homely minds, she does use figures of speech that differ from those common in the novels of the previous century. Crimsworth remarks that when Frances disappeared for a time, he did not allow the disappointment and grief "engendered" in his mind to "grow there to any monstrous size" (164). The organic connotations are rather new here, but the image is still an extension of the mind-as-entity metaphor rather than a new metaphor with generative potential. Most psychologists before Brontë adopted something similar to Reid's comparison of the growth of the mind to the growth of a plant from seed to fruit-producer: "In our progress from infancy to maturity, our faculties open in a regular order appointed by nature" (*Intellectual Powers* 807). Brontë appropriates the metaphorical concept, only changing it by applying it to an individual idea rather than to the faculties.

Jane Eyre (1847) puts the passion of the main character at the novel's center and dramatizes the impact of her passion on her sentience and her conscious awareness. But the lesson the novel teaches is similar to that illustrated by Crimsworth: passion has to be brought under control. Jane the mature retrospective narrator sees that her younger self has grown in her ability to recognize the constants in her personality and control the variables, which she was able to do because she always understood that her mind was impressible. The young Jane is always seeking ways to control her mental shape and thus nurture her developing sense of "what throbs fast and full." If she correctly represents to herself the surfaces of events, she will have a much better chance of imprinting herself in the most constructive way. The need for this tactic is dramatized in her encounter with Mrs. Reed after that woman has slandered her to her new teacher. Jane's child-mind cannot defend itself against the lies, thus she feels as if her mind has been physically abused: "The whole tenor of their conversation," Jane remembers, "was recent, raw, and stinging in my mind; I had felt every word as acutely as I had heard it plainly, and a passion of resentment fomented now within me" (68). Jane releases this passion by shouting out the truth about Mrs. Reed's injustice, but the release brings its own alienation. "My soul began to expand, to exult," Jane remembers, yet even while speaking she was conscious of her "savage" voice and felt quite strange in her new "sense of freedom" (69). Jane must learn both how to protect herself against such attacks and how to control her outbursts if she hopes to preserve her sense of identity.

Particularly useful to Jane in achieving these goals and useful to Brontë in presenting that achievement is the image of the mind as separable from the self. Describing her feelings when she first realizes that her friend Helen Burns is near death, Jane writes: "And then my mind made its first earnest effort to comprehend what had been infused into it concerning heaven and hell: and for the first time it recoiled baffled; and for the first time glancing behind, on each side, and before it, it saw all round an unfathomed gulf: it felt the one point where it stood—the present; all the rest was formless cloud and vacant depth; and it shuddered at the thought of tottering, and plunging amid that chaos" (110-11). The psychological event here is clear: a feeling of mental vertigo caused by an irresolvable conflict between a well-learned lesson and the reality of death. Writing "my mind" instead of "I" allows Jane to preserve some distance—she does not have to acknowledge that the confusion overwhelmed *her*. Likewise, the tactic allows Brontë to localize the confusion—it is specifically in Jane's *mind*, not generally in her self. When perched on a ridge or pinnacle overlooking formless cloud and vacant depth, Jane's mind is an entity separate from Jane herself.

The same tactic serves when Jane explains her later attempt to find a way of getting out into the world and seeking "real knowledge of life amidst its perils" (116). The question is, how to do this: "I could not tell: nothing answered me. I then ordered my brain to find a response, and quickly. It worked and worked faster. I felt the pulses throb in my head and temples; but for nearly an hour it worked in chaos, and no result came of its efforts" (118). After a quick walk around her room the answer comes "quietly and naturally": she should advertise for a position as a governess. The experience Brontë describes is a common one, but her language is unusually specific about the process: giving an order to the brain and then watching it try to carry out this order, with the physiological sensations that folk psychology typically attributes to strenuous mental effort.

This personification of the mind is a significant step toward representing the life of the mind as a living being in its own right, but its source is still identifiable as the mind-as-entity metaphor. Locke had represented the mind as having a "presence-room," and Upham represented the mind or soul as able to turn its attention inward; the faculty of sight has always been attributed to the mind ("the mind's eye"). As I will show in Chapter 6, there is a qualitative difference between placing the self as a mind within a mindscape and representing the mind as even an active, willful entity within a landscape. Brontë retains the mind-as-entity hypothesis of separate mental faculties by representing mind as separate from the self and also separate from the passions. Moreover, even this rather coarse division into self, mind, and passions meets the moral imperative of the psychology contemporary with Brontë, that the mind be able to retain a divine component or be in some way connected to the divine. The language of these passages specifies *mind* as that which does the work of thinking, leaving the "I" to occupy the divine corner.

Jane Eyre's later development consists of learning to analyze her impulses and learning when and how to repress them, when to give them free reign. In short, she is learning to manage her brain, her passions, and her other mental components. And note that while I use the term "repression," it is not Brontë's term and does not carry the negative connotations it does in our century. What Jane must learn is to increase her mental health by *management* of her impulses. Jane most needs to manage herself whenever she is in danger of becoming emotionally involved with an apparently unattainable object, because otherwise she risks making herself too open to external impressions that will ally with her passions and overcome her precarious self-control.

An example of her management occurs when she becomes convinced of Mr. Rochester's infatuation with Blanche Ingram.

Realizing how dangerous this situation is for her fragile self, she examines the "thoughts and feelings" of her heart and attempts "to bring back with a strict hand such as had been straying through imagination's boundless and trackless waste, into the safe fold of common sense" (190). This examination takes the form of a trial in which the "I" is prosecutor, judge, and jailor (191). She *arraigns* her faculties of memory and reason and comes to the "judgment" that "a greater fool than Jane Eyre had never breathed the breath of life." She also pronounces her sentence: to look into a mirror, draw in chalk her own portrait, omitting "no harsh line" or wrinkle, and title it "Portrait of a Governess, disconnected, poor, and plain," then to imagine the most beautiful face she can paint, and call that Blanche Ingram. This is a sanative activity for Jane; it keeps her "head and hands employed," and more important it gives "force and fixedness to the new impressions" she wants to "stamp indelibly" on her "heart." She turns to account what can be a weakness, her susceptibility to impressssions; having determined what new shape her heart should bear, she uses a pair of external, tangible, surface images as the press.

In learning to manage her mind Jane achieves a greater loyalty to her "nature," as becomes clear when St. John Rivers proposes that she marry him and accompany him on his missionary work. She could easily dedicate her life to the mission, she realizes, but not as his wife. "As his curate . . . there would be recesses" in her mind which he could not touch, "sentiments growing there, fresh and sheltered, which his austerity could never blight." If they were married, however, she would be "forced to keep the fire" of her nature "continually low, to compel it to burn inwardly and never utter a cry, though the imprisoned flame consumed vital after vital—*this* would be unendurable" (432-33).

By referring to the fire of her nature and to her mental recesses, Jane shows that she has assimilated her passions into her self-image. Having done so, she is able to resist St. John in his most forceful moment, when he insists so strongly on his plan for the two of them that she feels physically impressed, as with Mrs. Reed. But this time her resistance is passive, not passionate, and her reward is a kind of freedom of sensation and action: the very next instant she is able to "hear" the cry of the distant Rochester: "Jane! Jane! Jane!" Her intuition tells her immediately that the voice is not witchcraft but the "work of nature," her own nature. The cry she hears is not merely a plot device, an emanation from her unconscious which signals "Rochester's new humility" as Sandra Gilbert asserts (801); the man after all did cry out in the words Jane hears. Nor is it the less actual because it represents a "truth" of Jane's "psyche" (Yeazell 128). What is being dramatized here is the moment when a character accepts the reality and strength of her passion and discovers her own power, stressed in the next passage by the first-person emphases: "I broke from St. John, who had followed, and would have detained me. It was *my* time to assume ascendancy. *My* powers were in play and in force" (445).

But Brontë's use of first-person here is still within the limits of the mind-as-entity metaphor; she assigns different reactions to different faculties. Jane's heart was the specific organ that first perceived Rochester's cry: "My heart beat fast and thick: I heard its throb. Suddenly it stood still to an inexpressible feeling that thrilled it through, and passed at once to my head and extremities" (444). In retrospect she attributes her "moment of ascendancy" to her "soul," which "neither feared nor shook, but exulted as if in joy over the success of one effort it had been privileged to make, independent of the cumbrous body" (447). Brontë's decision to refer to Jane's "heart" and "soul" preserves the distance between her *self* and these passionate responses; Brontë does not allow Jane, as "I," to identify her *self* with that which thrillingly responds and exults. The self is something greater than the faculty responsible for these inner, observable, discrete responses. More than this Brontë's figurative language does not permit her to say about Jane's progress toward self-understanding and self-management. The "seat of Life" remains unseen; the details of its sentience remain unexplored beyond the moments of crisis and of decision, when Brontë does very effectively render the "psychological interpretation of material phenomena."

In *Shirley* (1849) Brontë turns her attention more toward surfaces but still attempts to connect them with depths. She takes on a new task in this novel—creating a rural society with a variety of characters and social interactions—that requires her to attend more to the subtle variations of human behavior.

Reading surfaces is an important activity in the novel. All of the major characters either reveal their own depths or learn to read someone else's, or both, during the course of the story. And all of the readings are presented in language that assumes an impressible mental entity. The proto-industrialist, Robert Moore, reflects that he saw only the surfaces of people and events until he went away to the cities, where, he says, "I looked a little into reality . . . I saw what taught my brain a new lesson, and filled my breast with fresh feelings" (555). This "new lesson" replaces the set of characters "impressed" on his mind by childhood experiences, characters that had clouded his eyes and his sympathetic faculty. Once they are replaced, his vision is clearer: he is able to see his proper role in society as well as his ideal mate, Caroline Helstone. Brontë's description of Caroline stresses the eye, the sense organ by which external appearances and internal effects are most often connected. Caroline's perception is of such a high order that she seems able to look into people's minds. She sees that "certain ideas" have become fixed in Robert's mind regarding how best to attain happiness and how best to handle the local people (72). She sees that the apparent "bad spirit" of an elderly woman's eye is only a "figment of fancy" and that the eye actually reveals the presence of a "canker somewhere, and a canker not the less deeply corroding because concealed" (186). Her eyes are not only penetrating; they are also expressive, "gifted at times with a winning beam that stole into the heart, with a language that spoke softly to the affections" (75).

Yet Caroline's perception is not so penetrating as Shirley Keeldar's. Shirley possesses a deep spring of human and religious feeling, a "still, deep, inborn delight . . . the pure gift of God to His creature, the free dower of Nature to her child" (398). This spring complements her "piercing" eye and enables her to read easily and accurately the depths represented by most surfaces. Like Caroline's, Shirley's eyes are also expressive of what lies beneath her own surface: "so long as she is calm, indolence, indulgence, humour, and tenderness possess that large grey sphere: incense her,—a red ray pierces the dew,—it quickens instantly to flame" (398). Louis Moore, as perspicuous as Shirley, is able to read this surface. In his journal he writes that he wants to "read a line in the page of her heart"—to read whether she is attracted to him (630). To accomplish this he sets up an actual experiment. While watching her face, he tells her of his plan to go to America and find a wife. Brontë attributes to Shirley's face the following statements: "I see the line which is my limit—nothing shall make me pass it. I feel—I know how far I may reveal my feelings, and when I must clasp the volume. I have advanced to a certain distance, as far as the true and sovereign and undegraded nature of my kind permits—now here I stand rooted" (632). Louis reads these statements as easily as if they were written in words.

Brains being taught lessons, minds afflicted with cankers, and reading someone's heart by reading the face—these images all evoke the mind-as-entity metaphor through the concepts of expression and impression, with their physicalistic connotations of a force acting on a body to bring about change of motion, state, or shape. This is the case even with the "red ray" image—a visible phenomenon within the eye resulting from a change of mental state. But Brontë also draws on a second set of images that suggests an important new element in the understanding of the mind. This set can be seen in two passages. One describes what happens to Louis when he proposes to Shirley and she accepts: "All creation was exaggerated: colour grew more vivid; motion more rapid; life itself more vital: (641). The other describes Shirley in a contemplative mood: her "eye seeks, and her soul possesses, the vision of life as she wishes it. No—not as she wishes it; she has not the time to wish: the swift glory spreads out, sweeping and kindling, and multiplies its splendours faster than Thought can effect his combinations, faster than Aspiration can utter her longings" (397-98).

The language of both passages suggests that Louis and Shirley are experiencing a truth about depths. Shirley seeks and possesses, but the vision she possesses, Brontë insists, does not depend on her desires—the vision shows life "not as she wishes it" but *as it is*. The perception is intuitive; it takes place even before her pre-formed "Aspirations" would have time to color the scene. Louis's heightened emotional state does cause him to see exaggerated color and motion, but Brontë's choice of "life itself" to complete the description indicates that surfaces have become transparent so that he sees "life itself" as Shirley sees "the vision of life as she wishes it." In both cases the mind is more than just a collection of faculties and more than a passive recipient of impressions. Although separate parts are mentioned (eyes, soul, inner spring), the whole mental being has the vision, and both Shirley's mind and Louis's can project themselves into the world and apprehend the living depths.

What probably keeps Brontë from more fully realizing the potential in these images is her continuing conscious reliance on the language of physiognomy. This language, the single most notable embodiment of the mind-as-entity metaphor in Brontë's novels, has been fully discussed elsewhere (Jack, Senseman); I need only add that the language restricts action to that of the external world on the mind. Passages like those describing Shirley and Louis demonstrate Brontë's interest in richer possibilities of ex-pressing the relationship among mind, surface, and depths, but the relative infrequency and inarticulateness of the passages shows her language to be too limited. "As she wishes it. No—not as she wishes it" shows a writer whose conceptual reach may be exceeding her linguistic grasp.

In *Villette* (1853), Brontë shifts the direction of her exploration. Whereas in *Jane Eyre* and *Shirley* she is concerned to represent the reality and significance of the depths, of "life itself," in *Villette* she concerns herself almost exclusively with the persistent and troublesome tendency to see depths where there are only surfaces. The mature Lucy Snowe comments thus on the struggle of her younger self to come to terms with her character: "These struggles with the natural character, the strong native bent of the heart, may seem futile and fruitless, but in the end they do good. They tend, however slightly, to give the actions, the conduct, that turn which Reason approves, and which Feeling, perhaps, too often opposes: they certainly make a difference in the general tenor of a life, and enable it to be better regulated, more equable, quieter on the surface; and it is on the surface only the common gaze will fall. As to what lies below, leave that with God" (255). This is a pragmatic accommodation to the demands of everyday existence ("the common gaze") and to the impossibility of making much change in "what lies below." The narrator understands this impossibility because she has repeatedly experienced how unreliable are those sensations that in *Jane Eyre* and *Shirley* are associated with the apprehension of truth: shortness of breath, quickening of the pulse, throbbing at the temples.

Each of Lucy's four encounters with what she supposes to be an actual ghost of a nun named Justine Marie dramatizes her tendency to assign too much truth to phenomena that elicit from her a rush of feeling. The first encounter takes place when she is excitedly and nervously preparing to read a letter from a man she has become infatuated with; it overwhelms her physically: "I cried out; I sickened" (351). The second occurs in the ghost's reputed wandering place when she is burying his letters. This time she faces the ghost for five minutes and then tries to touch it (426). She is able to remain calm because she believes that she has buried her dreams and passions along with the letters. But she still does not consider questioning what her senses tell her. The apparition looks like a ghost; it came upon her the first time as a ghost, and it causes an overwhelming rush of physiological sensations—therefore it must be what it seems.

Brontë criticism frequently notes that Lucy must find her identity in a balance between passion, including sexual passion, and reason (e.g., Martin 154) and that many of her actions can be read as symbolic sexual acts, such as her impassioned reading and later burying of the letters (Goldfarb 150, 153). She may be, as Goldfarb claims, frigid in the clinical sense (157); self-repression is certainly part of her nature. But just as effective in helping her deny her passion is her projection of her inner turmoil into the external world. This is what she is doing during the third encounter. She has just whispered a farewell to the long-buried letters and has been surprised by Paul, for whom she has come to feel a strange attraction. He further upsets her by sharing his own experience of the strange "something" that haunts the garden and by asserting a "rapport" between himself and Lucy, an "affinity" that extends even to a similarity of foreheads, eyes, and tones of voice. Since the ghost appears at this moment, it is no wonder that Lucy perceives all of nature to be charged with special significance: "the wind rose sobbing; the rain poured wild and cold; the whole night seemed to feel" the ghost (534). Even this late in her story Lucy still does not see that it is part of her "natural character" to link the terrible, the thrilling, and the passionate, so it does not occur to her to question the meaning she immediately assigns to the phenomena. In this encounter her passions are given free reign and completely transform the external world into a terrible and thrilling scene, where in the second encounter they are completely repressed and allow her to calmly confront the apparition. In neither case is Lucy finding a way to regulate the "quick" of her nature.

Lucy's equation of emotionally colored perceptions with truth is the aspect of her character she has the most difficulty coming to terms with. In leading up to the fourth encounter, the narrator is much more critical than before of this weakness of her younger self. Lucy has been drugged by her most dangerous enemy, Madame Beck, but instead of being knocked out she is stimulated by the opiate and goes wandering through Villette late at night. Drawn to a strange festival at the center of the city, she finds herself near all of her enemies. When someone cries out that Justine Marie is about to arrive, Lucy undergoes a "presentiment of discovery," certain that all mysteries are about to be solved. The mature narrator asks, dryly, "When imagination once runs riot, where do we stop?" It is not Lucy's nun who appears but a young woman of the same name, accompanied by Paul. Lucy's presentiments were "all falsities—all figments" (671-72). What is revealed is not a gothic mystery but an unpleasant fact of real life, so she assumes—that Paul and the young girl are to be married. Painful as the sight is, Lucy gives thanks for the drug which has sparked this excursion, because now she is sure she knows everything. The narrator, however, presents her younger self's thoughts in such exaggerated diction that the effect is ironical: "I always, through my whole life, liked to penetrate to the real truth; I like seeking the goddess in her temple, and handling the veil, and daring the dread glance. O Titaness amongst deities! The covered outline of thine aspect sickens often through its uncertainty, but define to us one trait, show us one lineament, clear in awful sincerity; we may gasp in untold terror, but with that gasp we drink in a breath of thy divinity; our heart shakes, and its currents sway like rivers lifted by earthquake, but we have swallowed strength" (674).

This passage shows that Lucy is being ridiculous to view truth as that which shakes her heart and terrifies her. The narrator remarks that she might have deliberated before drawing her conclusions about the scene before her, "but far from me such shifts and palliatives, far from me such temporary evasion of the actual, such coward fleeing from the dread, the swift-footed, the all-overtaking Fact" (676). Her judgment is clear: the younger Lucy actually would have had a less distressing life if she had been able to overcome her submission to the constructs of her heated imagination. The judgment also constitutes a criticism of the common assumption that certain physiological sensations accompany a perception of the goddess Truth.

Sensations, any sensations, Brontë would say at this point in her life and career, can only reflect the truth about states of mind, and even those states may not be easy to read from the surface. As Robert Heilman points out, the novel's style conveys this problem effectively: Brontë uses "sensory specifics" to present events in a way that can even make the reader temporarily unsure of their "objective reality" ("Tulip-Hood" 245). The language used to present the fourth encounter reinforces this point. Returning from the festival, Lucy finds the nun on her bed, or at least what she finds is momentarily a real entity. But then comes the reversal that stresses Lucy's tendency to misread surfaces: "In a moment, without exclamation, I had rushed on the haunted couch; nothing leaped out, or sprung or stirred; all the movement was mine, so was all the life, the reality, the substance, the force; as my instinct felt" (681). It was nothing but a dummy. Set against the ironical exaggerations of the "shifts and palliatives" passage, Lucy's discovery here is the only appropriate one—not only are the movement, life, and force hers at the present moment, but there has never been anything else. This is the only truth to be discovered.

Robert Colby calls this event Brontë's "last word on the Gothic novel"; as Lucy "clears her mind of the phantoms from the past that have haunted it, so Brontë exorcises the gothic novel that once fired her imagination, even as Miss Austen had exorcised it earlier in the century" in her novel *Northanger Abbey* (419). She has definitely exorcised the sensationalism and supernaturalism associated with the gothic. From another angle, however, *Villette* is a logical extension of the psychological perspective taken by gothic novelists. Robert D. Hume notes that gothic works show a concern with "*interior* mental processes" and particularly with the experience of "moral ambiguity" (283, 285). He contrasts the romantics with the gothic writers in their use of the imagination. This faculty served the romantics as "their vehicle of escape from the limitations of the human condition." Gothic writers, on the other hand, "though possessed by the same discontent with the everyday world, have no faith in the ability of man to transcend or transform it imaginatively. Their explorations lie strictly within the realm of this world and they are confined to the limits of reason" (289).

These criteria for the gothic tale aptly summarize the psychological components of *Villette*. It concentrates on "the limitations of the human condition," especially the tendency to misread surface appearances and to misinterpret sensations. Lucy Snowe finally gains enough self-understanding and self-control to influence events in her everyday world: she is able to defend her fragile relationship with Paul. Before her discovery about the real nature of the ghost she is not able to do this. Her most dramatic failure occurs when Paul, looking for her, is hurried out of the room by Madame Beck, while Lucy remains immobile and speechless (643). Later, after her concurrent discovery of the ghost's real nature and her own "force," the same situation recurs, but this time Lucy's feelings deny "suppression" and force her to cry out that her heart will break (695). The cry brings Paul to her side, and they are united from that moment on. Lucy responds to this assault on her feelings as she did to the ghost's first appearance, with a cry, but at that time she was disturbed in her private and hopeless dream-world whereas now her possibility of happiness is threatened by the all-too-tangible and imposing form of Madame Beck, with her eye "like a steel stylet." The rightness of her reaction is demonstrated by what follows—the two lovers do spend a brief happy time together.

Lucy's emotional maturation is paralleled through the novel by a progression in her description of her emotions: "The method of exposition becomes less theatrical" in the second half (Martin 170). The emotional and physiological state of Lucy crying out to Paul is similar to states described in the earlier novels: she experiences a rush of tears punctuated "with many a deep sob, with thrilling, with icy shiver, with strong trembling," although this time there is also "relief" (695). The difference is that in *Villette* such rushes of feeling do not signal a sublime reality but a simple personal truth about a human relationship. Brontë no longer needs to modulate this truth through the mechanisms of a preternatural event such as Jane hearing Rochester's cry.

For this reason I regard *Villette* as Brontë's best achievement as a psychological novelist, her most carefully thought-out presentation of sublime emotions associated with "rapport" and "affinity" among human beings. She demonstrates that sensations pointing to the existence of "what throbs fast and full" are valid, that sensations of "affinity" are generated within this hidden fountain, and that there is no other meaning to the term "the real truth." The mind-as-entity metaphor helps her in this endeavor by providing a language in which to render the sensations and discuss some of the mind's activities. The metaphor is most manifest in *Jane Eyre* and *Shirley*, with their emphases on learning to read surfaces correctly; it is less manifest in *The Professor*, in which Brontë is still searching for the best perspective from which to present her themes; it is again less manifest in *Villette*, when she becomes more critical of the metaphor's basic premise that sensations can be connected point-for-point with the external world.

Lucy Snowe's hard-learned lesson is that this premise is not always valid, especially not with sensations of the thrilling sort. She has unfortunately failed to learn the next lesson in her self-prescribed course of regulation: that when she links sensations with the abstract notion of the "goddess Truth," she does not comprehend "what lies below" her own surface. She remains fundamentally confused about her own nature. On the one hand she claims to prefer a chill and dim life. On the other hand, she seems to be participating in an anthropomorphic melodrama. When Paul sails away, Lucy knows that she has had, as she says, her one allotted taste of Eden; even the anticipated "Juggernaut" of woe at his three-year absence proves only a "chilling dimness" instead of an awesome, crushing force (711). This is the calm side of her nature. When Paul is to return, however, another storm shakes her quiet life, a storm more terrifying than the others because it endangers him. Thus it roars, "frenzied," for a week, until the deeps have "gorged their full of sustenance" and the "destroying angel of tempest" has "achieved his perfect work"—that is, has taken Paul's life (715).

The goddess Truth still lurks behind these sentences as the source and rationale of Lucy's references to a "destroying angel" and the sentient, vengeful sea; it is a distorting goddess because it prevents Lucy from directly observing her own reaction. The conclusion frames Lucy's story perfectly. She has pictured eight years of her early life metaphorically as a storm: it was "a long time, of cold, of danger, of contention" which still recurs to her in nightmares as a tangible sea storm ("the rush and saltness of briny waves in my throat") and which she claims actually did include a storm in which "the ship was lost, the crew perished" (46-47). When she found a position as companion to an elderly woman and thought her life would be stable and calm for the next twenty years, "Fate" intervened, and on a stormy night that accompanied the death of her first benefactress, Fate showed that it "would not so be pacified" (51). The language Lucy uses to describe these events at the two ends of her narrated life, more than the events themselves, shows that her "natural character" has not changed significantly.

After the emotional climax, the novel swings back to the other extreme, concluding with two calm paragraphs. "Here pause: pause at once" Lucy tells herself at the beginning of the penultimate paragraph. Instead of expressing her emotion she mocks the need of some "sunny imaginations" for a happy ending: "Let them picture union and a happy succeeding life." The final paragraph similarly mocks the conventional summing up by giving details only of the novel's despicable characters: "Madame Beck prospered all the days of her life; so did Pere Silas; Madame Walravens fulfilled her ninetieth year before she died. Farewell" (715). To the end Lucy is caught in a rhythm of "inner passivity and acceptance on the one hand, emotional excitement and turmoil on the other" (Hook and Hook 147). That Brontë chooses this kind of conclusion may indicate her own continuing uncertainty about the psychological reality she wants to portray. Despite her belief in the existence of "what throbs fast and full," Brontë does not present a single coherent perspective on the dynamics of that inner depth in relation to the rest of the individual's mental life.

The Shaping of the Heart in Dickens' Novels

Dickens' novels, like those of Brontë, tend to portray the mind as a being with a life, and his psychology, like hers, was limited by the mind-as-entity metaphor. He conceived of the mind as shaped (literally "impressed") by the external world through the mechanism of the senses and according to the laws of association. His novels dramatize how an individual's mind is shaped in opposition to the urgings of the heart and how this shape, usually imaged as layers, can subsequently be stripped away to allow the formation of a new shape that better suits the heart's best urges.

Although Dickens never declared his allegiance to association psychology, both the language and the concepts of this psychology are so prominent in his character portrayals that he can fairly be termed an association novelist. He made extensive use of the central metaphor of associationism, that the mind is a blank slate or piece of clay shaped by external forces. But he went far beyond his contemporaries' use of associationism in the extent to which he showed minds to be impressed by environment and *re-formed* through the agency of the heart. In most cases this reformation is prepared for by an associational complex that the character has experienced but never acknowledged. The heart remains a mystic entity; it is linked by association to elements of the phenomenal world and exercises its power through this link. This was Dickens' new accommodation between association psychology's view of human development as continuous and the common experience of sudden changes and reversals, his adjustment between that psychology's insistence on the power of the external world over the life of the mind and the belief that inner forces, collectively characterized as "the heart," can counteract the external world's power.

David Copperfield (1849-50) reflects this general pattern. Associationism is referred to early in the novel and is present in some of the striking events of David's adolescence, even in the statements that convey what J. Hillis Miller calls a "providential" ordering of experience, an ordering that seems to bring together past and future "in a time out of time sustained by God" ("Three Problems" 36). In the opening chapter David mentions his "first childish associations" with his father's gravestone and takes care to point out that he cannot claim any direct knowledge of the arrival of Aunt Betsey, that is, knowledge "founded on the evidence" of his "own senses" (3). The chapter's concluding sentence is heavy with a providential ordering: "I lay in my basket, and my mother lay in her bed; but Betsey Trotwood Copperfield [his aunt's name for the girl David was supposed to have been] was for ever in the land of dreams and shadows, the tremendous region whence I had so lately travelled; and the light upon the window of our room shone out upon the earthly bourne of all such travellers, and the mound above the ashes and the dust that once was he, without whom I had never been" (11). This passage's prophetic tone, knotty syntax, and references to light and "earthly bourne" suggest a realm of experience quite apart from the phenomenal.

This noumenal realm fills a place occupied in Brontë's fictional world by the goddess Truth. The realm may even be more "real," since in the Dickens world it is more accessible and is an occasion for self-deception. From the perspective of David's later life, however, this sentence makes significant associations: it links aunt, mother, newborn, dead father, gravestone, and light together in a syntactic structure that is the embodiment of the associational complex formed by these elements in David's mind. From this point on, each element suggests to him the whole, and like any idea in the mind this idea of the whole can stimulate a sensation—in this case the feeling that he is perceiving a "tremendous region," a noumenal realm of a "time out of time." While David consciously prefers the providential ordering, Dickens gives him language that relates the ordering to a complex of impressions whose formation was purely a matter of chance.

The second chapter of the novel draws on the Lockean concept of impressions inscribed on a blank slate and then combined into ideas and beliefs. David states that his goal is to search his mind for its earliest memories: he will look "into the blank" of his infant mind (11). This search yields his "earliest impressions," which, as any Lockean knows, qualify only marginally as ideas: they were "the first opinions—if they may be so called" that he remembers having "derived" from what he saw (13-14).

These "first opinions" include specific details about the appearance of their house, the churchyard, and the church, as well as an awareness of his mother's pride in her beauty. His sense of himself in relation to these elements of his world begins to be eroded when Mr. Murdstone appears, courting Mrs. Copperfield. David becomes aware that his mother is changing under the influence of the suitor; she begins to withdraw her kindness except in surreptitious moments.

After the marriage, David is assailed by powerful impressions that threaten his early shape—his sense of himself in relation to his family. The change comes when he bites Murdstone's hand; afterward he feels a guilt that lies heavily on his "breast." This metaphorical weight begins to impose its shape of criminality on his character, and its force is augmented by a five-day imprisonment in his room, where David is isolated and never even hears himself speak. "All this," David reflects, "appears to have gone round and round for years instead of days, it is so vividly and strongly stamped on my remembrance" (52). And no wonder it is so stamped; solitude was considered a grave danger in the psychology of Dickens' time. David's case is especially serious because his child mind is extremely malleable, susceptible to the stamping. He is also confused by contradictory impressions from his mother and from Peggotty (the family servant who is like a second mother to him). His mother believes that his "heart" contains "bad passions," whereas Peggotty continues to believe in his innate goodness (52-53). As strange as it feels to the young David to think of himself as a criminal, the balance of impressions seems to him to lie on that side. Dickens' figurative language effectively conveys David's sense of having a shape forced on him from the outside, a shape that begins to determine his character.

According to associationist principles, David can hardly avoid conceiving of himself as a criminal. The association between feelings of guilt and the self-concept of criminality is intrinsically powerful, and its effect on David is reinforced by a beating, by five days of isolation from all potentially corrective associations, and by hearing his mother accept the Murdstones' judgment of his character. The more powerful the initial association, the more likely it is to shape the character. When subsequent events seem to confirm the shape, it becomes even more binding. The language Dickens uses, like Brontë's language, demonstrates the continuing usefulness of the mind-as-entity metaphor. The image of a tangible, impressible mind helps him not just to represent but explain such problematic mental phenomena as the development into belief of a young person's sense of himself as a criminal. David goes through the early stages of this development when he is sent away from home, ostensibly for education but in fact as punishment. Separated from all the familiar associations of his early life, he is totally open to external impressions.

And Murdstone has taken care that they will be harsh, having informed the school of David's bestial behavior. Thus when the boy arrives at Salem House, he is immediately forced to wear a sign: "Take care of him. He bites" (67). The result of this external influence is that he begins to dread himself "as a kind of wild boy who did bite."

Although the evidence of David's senses pushes him to believe that he really is a criminal, his heart remains strong enough to oppose that external evidence, as demonstrated by his later decision to flee the firm where Murdstone has employed him and seek a home with his fairy-godmother aunt in Dover. This is the time in his life when David's heart becomes a more dominant part of his character and begins to play an active role. As Dickens' language makes clear, however, the heart must exert its influence through the mechanism of association—it works through rather than transcends the mental entity. David's heart generates the initial idea from early associations, imbues it with conviction derived from the power of those associations, and places it in the brain. All of these operations are in keeping with the metaphor mind-as-entity, although attributing them to the heart constitutes an important addition to the ways that the manifestations of mind were described before Dickens. David points out that the idea of running away entered his "brain" where it "hardened into a purpose . . . my mind was thoroughly made up that it must be carried into execution" (151). He does not write "I had made up my mind" but separates his self and his mind, just as Brontë has Jane Eyre do. The next paragraph reveals more exactly how the idea arose: "Again, and again, and a hundred times again, since the night when the thought had first occurred to me and banished sleep, I had gone over that old story of my poor mother's about my birth . . . there was one little trait in [Aunt Betsey's] behavior which I liked to dwell on, and which gave me some faint shadow of encouragement. I could not forget how my mother had thought that she felt her touch her pretty hair with no ungentle hand. . . . I made a little picture, out of it. . . . It is very possible that it had been in my mind a long time, and had gradually engendered my determination" (151). The idea thus arises from a complex of associations. The components of the story (especially the ideas of mother and aunt), associated with sensations of motherly gentleness, have been linked in a mental picture that has taken on a tangible reality for the boy. After a hundred late-night repetitions this reality is as strong as that of the external world which is trying to shape him into a criminal.

Dickens' language insists that David's decision does not rise mystically out of an unconscious realm but is engendered, although not consciously and intentionally. David's professed inability to understand his idea ("I don't know how it came into my head," 148; "I don't know how this desperate idea came into my brain," 151) reflects his desire to believe that his life has been organized by an external providence, while the language he selects indicates that his major decisions have resulted from complexes of associations.

The "tremendous region" complex surfaces again when David is safely in bed at Aunt Betsey's. It is called up because he finds himself in an environment emotions that replicates the one he knew the Murdstones appeared and because some of the same elements of the first "tremendous region" scene are present: a path of light (here the moon on the sea, earlier a lighted window), a window through which another realm of existence seems visible, and a similarity of idea (traveling and being houseless is like "the earthly bourne of all such travellers"):

I remember how I still sat looking at the moonlight on the water, as if I could hope to read my fortune in it, as in a bright book; or to see my mother with her child, coming from Heaven, along that shining path, to look upon me as she had looked when I last saw her sweet face. I remember how the solemn feeling with which at length I turned my eyes away, yielded to the sensation of gratitude and rest which the sight of the white-curtained bed—and how much more the lying softly down upon it, nestling in the snow-white sheets!—inspired. I remember how I thought of all the solitary places under the night sky where I had slept, and how I prayed that I never might be houseless any more, and never might forget the houseless. I remember how I seemed to float, then, down the melancholy glory of that track upon the sea, away into the world of dreams. [170]

The paragraph is like an incantation with its repeated "I remember how." The verb "remember" is the main verb in four of the paragraph's five sentences; this, along with the length and cumulative nature of the sentences, sets off the moment from the flow of David's day-to-day existence. Instead of action or movement, the sentences convey "time out of time," the same quality conveyed by the first "tremendous region" passage. The sentence structure in both passages suggests a momentary abrogation of ordinary physical reality and its laws, including laws of association. The scene evokes in David a complex of associations that calls up in him the earlier sense of a "tremendous region" and momentarily lifts him out of the realm governed by the laws of association. When the complex is evoked, David feels at one with his heart (his drive toward a morally respectable life) and briefly seems to transcend the external physical world.

A second prominent complex of associations centers on Agnes Wickfield and shares some key elements with the "tremendous region" complex. When they first meet, David is struck by Agnes' "tranquillity." As she leads him to his room, pausing at the top of the stairs, he suddenly thinks of a stained-glass window he has once seen, and he remembers that he "associated something of its tranquil brightness with Agnes Wickfield ever afterwards" (191). The phrase "ever afterwards" suggests that Agnes exists for David in a timeless realm, an impression conveyed even more strongly in the following description of a moment in the narrative present: "I see her, with her modest, orderly, placid manner, and I hear her beautiful calm voice, as I write these words. The influence for all good, which she came to exercise over me at a later time, begins already to descend upon my breast. . . . I feel that there are goodness, peace, and truth, wherever Agnes is; and that the soft light of the colored window in the church, seen long ago, falls on her always, and on me when I am near her, and on everything around" (198).

Unlike most of the associations David has formed in his life, this one has the power of softening him and thus causing the past to blur in his memory. Like the "tremendous region" complex, the Agnes complex lifts him out of the phenomenal realm, with its linear time and its tendency to harden character in ways detrimental to the individual's growth. Agnes' very face seems to bridge the phenomenal realm and the "tremendous region": it is "bright and happy" on the one hand, and on the other tranquil, displaying "a quiet, good, calm spirit" (191).

The life of David's mind is structured by an interaction between the principle of association (which shapes particular ideas, self-conceptions, and complexes of images) and the power of Agnes (which can begin to erase the whole of his mind's slate and endow certain complexes with a "tremendous" hue). Dickens focuses primarily on the surface of David's mind, but his psychology also incorporates associations that can be recognized retrospectively as working beneath the character's conscious awareness to influence moral growth.

These associations operate "unconsciously" in the sense Lewes gives that term: incorporating physical and physiological processes of which the individual is not aware. Dickens' figurative language shows that the associational process is physical and has a physical influence on the shape of David's mind (impressing, smoothing out, re-forming) as well as on the ideas within the mind. The mind-as-entity metaphor applied to the unconscious in this way helps Dickens explain not only David's decision to flee to Dover but also his sudden insight that he loves Agnes. He says of this second discovery, "I cannot so penetrate the mystery of my own heart, as to know when I began to think I might have set its earliest and brightest hopes on Agnes" (817). This sentence indicates both that the seed was planted long ago and that some details of its growth will forever remain beyond his ken. Immediately after Dora's death, reflecting on his suffering, he suspects that he may attribute to Agnes the plan for his trip abroad, but "her influence was so quiet" that he knows no more than this. He also suspects that in his "old association of her with the stained glass window in the church, a prophetic foreshadowing of what she would be to me, in the calamity that was to happen in the fullness of time, had found a way into my mind" (659). His understanding of Agnes' role extends no farther.

However, he does understand the process that brings about his revelation during his wanderings in Europe, a process involving first a destruction of the old shape of his mind (a return to the blank-slate or smooth-clay condition) and then the impression of a new shape congruent with his heart's urges. David first describes the accretion of bits of a new idea (his bereavement) that gives him a new and bleak picture of his present state: the new idea comes "little by little, and grain by grain. . . . At first it was a heavy sense of loss and sorrow. . . . By imperceptible degrees, it became a hopeless consciousness of all that I had lost—love, friendship, interest; of all that had been shattered—my first trust, my first affection, the whole airy castle of my life; of all that remained—a ruined blank and waste, lying wide around me, unbroken, to the dark horizon" (696). The new idea is like a physical burden he carries from place to place, and he has a sense of traveling with an "ever-darkening cloud on [his] mind" (697). He is unable to respond to "the old abiding places of history and Fancy" as he passes through them, and he lacks any "sustaining soul."

This description stresses the tangible quality of David's thoughts and emotions, especially his sense of himself as a blank and his corresponding inability to respond to anything around him. His physicalistic imagery clearly portrays the weight and magnitude of his despair and the emptiness at the core of his being—the lack of a sustaining soul. Yet because he is blank again he can be re-formed. This process begins one peaceful evening when a chord in his "breast" seems to stir in unison with the surrounding "beauty and tranquillity" and sets in motion a train of impressions that will evoke the "tremendous region" complex (697-98). At this moment David chooses to open the letter from Agnes. It is a trusting, exhorting, sisterly letter. David's response: "I put the letter in my breast." This does not simply mean that he puts it in his breast pocket; it means that David feels he has inserted the idea of his love for Agnes into his consciousness—the physicalistic language serves Dickens well to illustrate how one can add to one's stock of ideas. After David has placed within himself this "sustaining soul," the shadows clear from his mind. From this time on he has a will and a goal: simply, to "try"—try to follow her suggestions, to turn suffering into good, to reach out to others, to draw on nature. His success in this endeavor is marked by an ability to further control what ideas and interests he takes into himself. His decision to "try" represents his heart's accession to the ruling position in his mental life, from which it selects the experiences that shape his new character.

Throughout his career Dickens was committed to a psychology based on the mind-as-entity metaphor, as can be seen in the figurative language of his second novel, *Oliver Twist* (1838) and his last completed novel, *Our Mutual Friend* (1865). In contrast to *David Copperfield*, *Oliver Twist* does not rely explicitly on associationism, but the psychological dangers faced by the young hero are dangers precisely because of the impressibility of his mind. Fagin, the leader of the gang that has captured and is trying to corrupt Oliver, says to his cohorts "once fill his mind with the idea that he has been a thief; and he's ours" (126). The "dear old man" counts on the thieves' environment and the usual lack of resistance in young minds to make his project successful: "In short, the wily old Jew had the boy in his toils; and, having prepared his mind, by solitude and gloom, to prefer any society to the companionship of his own sad thoughts in such a dreary place, was now slowly instilling into his soul the poison which he hoped would blacken it, and change its hue for ever" (120).

Oliver Twist does not carry out the experiment, suggested by these passages, of leaving Oliver with Fagin long enough to test whether Fagin's attempt to fill the boy's mind could work. The sentences imply that it might; there is no question that Oliver's mind has been prepared or that the poison is being introduced. The only question is whether the hue of the boy's soul could be forever darkened. On the other hand, Fagin's influence is opposed by a "good sturdy spirit" in the boy's "breast," "implanted" there by "nature or inheritance" (5). Inheritance is the more likely choice; late in the novel his father's will is revealed, with its provision that the yet-unborn child could receive his estate only by keeping his name pure as a way of validating the father's "confidence in the mother, and his conviction . . . that the child would share her gentle heart, and noble nature" (351).

Dickens' choice of words suggests that these qualities Oliver's mother passes down to him are every bit as tangible as the gold locket and ring which were to have proved his identity: it was not just her gentleness but her gentle *heart*, not her nobility but her noble *nature*. This heart is able to respond directly to benevolent stimuli from the external world. A loving, sisterly woman sheds a tear on Oliver's forehead as he sleeps, and he smiles as if there is awakened in him "some pleasant dream of a love and affection he had never known," a phenomenon similar to the "sudden dim remembrances of scenes that never were, in this life; which . . . no voluntary exertion of the mind can ever recall" but which are brought suddenly to mind by a melody, sound, or odor (191). Similarly, when the wounded, weak boy is moved to a place of rustic beauty whose "scenes of peace and quietude sink into the minds of pain-worn dwellers in close and noisy places, and carry their own freshness, deep into their jaded hearts," he seems to "enter on a new existence." The narrator avers that "the memories which peaceful country scenes call up, are not of this world" but are from "some remote and distant time" (210). Echoes of Wordsworthian pre-existence aside, these passages suggesting a noumenal realm also imply through their figurative language that the realm acts on the mind or heart through the apparatus of perception—the passive-impression theory of the eighteenth century still operates for Dickens.

From a psychological point of view, an important difference between Oliver and David is that the former's intellect is not sufficiently developed for him to be aware of and reflect on the kind of associational complex that David evokes during his first night in Dover. This does not mean that Oliver cannot be aware of a "terrific region." Quite the contrary—he never really departs from such a realm and is able to sense it directly, without needing an associational complex. His heart seems never to have lost touch with that "remote and distant time." The purity of Oliver's mind is also evident in that he is never divided like Copperfield, feeling that something is wrong but choosing to do it anyway.

This point has often been made, for example by Miller, who observes that at the end of the novel Oliver is "willing to exist as the image of his father, willing to take as the definition of his essential selfhood those traits which are the repetition of his father's nature. . . . He lives happily ever after, but only by living in a perpetual childhood of submission to protection and direction from without" (*Charles Dickens* 83).

But Miller grants Oliver too much self-direction in describing him as willing his essential selfhood. Oliver does lose consciousness at crucial times rather than allow his mind to be filled by the brutalizing impressions of the orphanage and Fagin's den of thieves, as if some central executive power recognizes the dangers and switches off his awareness of the external world. These fainting fits are not consciously willed, however; Oliver cannot be said to take on his father's traits precisely because the combined natures of father and mother have always possessed him. The only sense in which he takes on their traits is the associationist one, having had a shape impressed on his blank slate even before birth. Unable to open his mind to new impressions, he cannot form new associations and therefore cannot grow. Nor does his heart ever become so covered over with soiling impressions that he needs to undergo Copperfield's transformation. His character has been so rigidly determined that his intellect and will cannot develop beyond the rudimentary level necessary for his physical survival. Oliver, it seems, could have been changed only by Fagin's experiment or a similar exterior power. He may be the only one of Dickens' main characters of whom Lewes' criticism is undeniably true—he moves like a "simple mechanism always in one way."

Eugene Wrayburn of *Our Mutual Friend* is far removed from Oliver not only in the chronology of Dickens' career but in his susceptibility to blackening and poisoning by the external world, and whereas Oliver never fluctuates, Eugene's only steady characteristic is his inability to hold to one direction. Eugene seems to have received very little from his parents in the way of a heart or nature. He and his brothers did receive educations, but of an arbitrary sort having nothing to do with what might have suited their talents or inclinations: their "respected father" has determined in advance for each of the sons "what the devoted little victim's calling and course of life should be" (193). The results of such arranging come as no surprise: Eugene is selfish and easily bored, the second brother is only a shaky "pillar of the church," and the third "was pitch-forked into the Navy, but has not circumnavigated" as planned (193). Having to follow a rigid plan, Eugene has lost touch with his heart; nor has he been able to gain the self-understanding that might be expected of someone his age. His friend Mortimer asks if he is concealing something, and Eugene answers, "I know less about myself than about most people in the world, and I don't know" (338). He refers to himself as a "troublesome conundrum" (349). Again, much later, Mortimer tries to determine whether Eugene cares for Lizzie Hexam; Eugene responds, "I thirst for information. What do I mean? If my taking so much trouble does not mean that I care for her, what does it mean?" He says these things "with a perplexed and inquisitive face, as if he actually" has no idea what to make of himself (599-600). He views his own actions as he might view the actions of any other human being; those actions indicate that he must care for Lizzie; yet he feels no such loving attachment. He can stand outside himself and form an "impression" of the substance of his activities, but he claims to be unable and certainly is unwilling to penetrate into his own heart and explore his motives. His knowledge about himself is literally superficial: he attends only to surfaces, to his words and actions, resolutely refusing to attempt to penetrate within. He had once joked about expecting to derive a "moral influence" from his well-equipped kitchen (337), a joke that highlights the tragedy of a person who sees himself as subject to any chance impressions from his surroundings. Eugene can explain his behavior only by denying responsibility for it: his "nature" drives him toward Lizzie. He also insists that her nature causes her to love him: "She must go through with her nature, as I must go through with mine" (764-65).

Like the re-formation of Copperfield, the re-making of Eugene depends on the metaphor underlying associationism, mind as a tangible and impressible entity. Eugene, however, loses his old character in an instant, with none of the gradual softening undergone by Copperfield. His character seems to be so hardened that nothing short of a physical smashing of his skull can reform it. This event takes place by a river, which functions as a psychic mirror to reflect Eugene's state of mind and the sudden shattering. The scene is set with Eugene strolling along while his mind reaches the familiar dilemma that has always blocked its progress: what to do about Lizzie. He is incapable of forcing his thoughts in a different, more moral direction; they have traveled in the same pathways for too long. At the instant when he formulates the dilemma, he is attacked by Bradley Headstone and his ossified character is shattered:

> The rippling of the river seemed to cause a corresponding stir in his uneasy reflections. He would have laid them asleep if he could, but they were in movement, like the stream, and all tending one way with a strong current. As the ripple under the moon broke unexpectedly now and then, and palely flashed in a new shape and with a new sound, so parts of his thoughts started, unbidden, from the rest, and revealed their wickedness. "Out of the question to marry her," said Eugene, "and out of the question to leave her. The crisis!"
>
> He had sauntered far enough. Before turning to retrace his steps, he stopped upon the margin, to look down at the reflected night. In an instant, with a dreadful crash, the reflected night turned crooked, flames shot jaggedly across the air, and the moon and stars came bursting from the sky. [766-67]

In simply following what he deems his nature, Eugene has remained on the surface of his mind and has been unable to act on his occasional awareness that his intentions are wicked. His heart tells him he should either marry Lizzie or leave her, while his ill-formed character makes both impossible. It is indeed a crisis, because he feels he must act yet cannot. When the reflected night shatters with the blow, it is as if, simultaneously, his repressed heart has burst forth and he has been sucked into its depths. The water represents his mind; the moon and stars bursting toward him signal the shattering of his consciousness. From remaining strictly on the surface of his mind, he is plunged into the core of his being.

The violence of the destruction of Eugene's conscious character is paralleled by an especially long sojourn in a "tremendous region," during which he wanders in what he calls "endless place" (807). Except for brief periods of consciousness, his "crushed outer form" shows none of his "spirit" (806). Yet the re-formation has already taken place, because in his moments of consciousness he acknowledges his guilt and responsibility to Lizzie, telling Mortimer to place Lizzie and his "reparation" before everything else, even to the extent of letting his assailant go unaccused (808). Bradley's murderous act has allowed Eugene's heart to break out of its crypt.

Dickens also relies on the mind-as-entity metaphor in presenting characters who do not undergo the trials of David, Eugene, or Oliver. The best example is Esther Summerson (*Bleak House*, 1853), who from early in her life has the ability to control her emotions by literally impressing herself with reminders of her decision to devote her life to "duty." Esther's godmother prescribed "submission, self-denial, diligent work"; for Esther this means to be "industrious, contented, and kind-hearted, and to do some good to some one, and win some love to myself if I could" (19-20). She can keep to this path because she intuitively understands the force of external impressions even when those impressions are created by the individual. When Esther must lock in her emotions, her intellect and will order her housekeeping keys to be jingled, but the Esther who wills the action and the Esther who is reminded of her duty are not identical, as the structure of Dickens' sentence shows: "I gave the housekeeping keys the least shake in the world, as a reminder to myself" (90).

Her understanding of this law of the mind is most evident in the way she protects herself from too much of a shock after a fever ravages her former beauty. The reader at least infers that she was beautiful; Esther always denies herself any positive characteristics except a certain "noticing way" (17). The reader must also infer that the fever has left her truly scarred; certainly she is changed. But her elaborate preparations for her first confrontation with a mirror are designed as self-protection and based on her awareness of her mind's facility for taking impressions. First she must remove herself from familiar surroundings, which is to say from familiar associations; this means a trip to a friend's house. The night of her arrival, after giving her maid a tour of the house and being repeatedly overwhelmed by the thoughtfulness of her absent host, she sends the maid to bed. Alone, she then reminds herself that her happiness depends on keeping her promise to herself (to give up her infatuation with a certain young man), reflects on her blessings, and lets down her hair. This passage follows:

> I drew [the curtain of the mirror] back and stood for a moment looking through such a veil of my own hair, that I could see nothing else. Then I put my hair aside, and looked at the reflection in the mirror; encouraged by seeing how placidly it looked at me. I was very much changed—O very, very much. At first, my face was so strange to me, that I think I should have put my hands before it and started back, but for the encouragement I have mentioned. Very soon it became more familiar, and then I knew the extent of the alteration in it better than I had done at first. It was not like what I had expected; but I had expected nothing definite, and I dare say anything definite would have surprised me. [444-45]

Esther has guaranteed for her senses the most favorable possible reception of the new face, knowing how easily sense impressions can quicken uncontrollable passions and destroy all capacity for the submission, self-denial, and diligent work that are important to her. The details of this action emphasize just how impressible her mind is. She first looks out through a curtain of what remains of her former beauty, and when she parts this curtain, she sees a new face already composed by the calming influence of her spoken reminder and her hair. Had she not so encouraged herself, she might have rejected the face and thus destroyed her carefully-built structure of duties and limitations. For the same reason she has kept herself from expecting to see anything definite, knowing that the associational law of contrast (here, contrast of expectations with actual impressions) would force her to perceive her change as a loss.

One reason Esther understands the power of the external world is that she has seen what happened to her cousin Richard when he became too involved with the Chancery case of Jarndyce and Jarndyce. As explained by Mr. Jarndyce, the suit "warped him out of himself . . . it is in the subtle poison of such abuses to breed such diseases. His blood is infected, and objects lose their natural aspects in his sight. It is not *his* fault" (434-35). Not only did Richard come to distrust Mr. Jarndyce, but he even allowed that distrust to extend to Esther. He was truly poisoned by setting his interest too narrowly on one subject, the court of Chancery, and thus flooding himself with associations relating to that social and moral disease.

Only when actually afflicted with her own disease is Esther unable to control her mind: "Dare I hint at that worse time when, strung together somewhere in great black space, there was a flaming necklace, or ring, or starry circle of some kind, of which *I* was one of the beads! And when my only prayer was to be taken off from the rest, and when it was such inexplicable agony and misery to be a part of the dreadful thing?" (432). The perception of existing in a void, the desire to cease to exist, the sense of unity as something dreadful, however, are all "sick experiences," Esther insists. She recalls them not to "make others unhappy" or because the memory causes her present discomfort but because "if we knew more of such strange afflictions we might be the better able to alleviate their intensity." Whether the affliction is an actual fever or Chancery, the natural interdependence among human beings becomes abhorrent. This is clearly a "sick experience." Such interdependence is one positive aspect of the impressible nature of human minds; the sanative influence of nature on such minds is another. Both depend on the mind-as-entity metaphor.

Achievements and Limitations of the Novelists

Both Brontë and Dickens were working toward accommodating mind-as-entity with the mental phenomena deemed important by their contemporaries. Both drew on explicit tenets of the psychology of their age, tenets based on the mind-as-entity metaphor: Brontë on the physiognomical hypothesis (surfaces shaping interiors) and Dickens on the underlying premise of associationism (external trains being replicated within and affecting the shape of the mind, thus influencing the individual's habits of thought). Both described mental phenomena in figurative language that demonstrates the continuing attractiveness of the metaphor as an explanation of mental phenomena. Brontë wished to represent the power of the depths, the hidden springs, the "quick," but she could do this only by granting that area of the mind the status of an entity separate from the lives of her characters, separate from the "I." Dickens linked moral transformations to the power of the human heart, which he conceived of as separate from the associationally formed character of an individual; such figures as Copperfield and Wrayburn sometimes seem to have no selves of their own but rather to exist as stages on which the forces of associationism and the heart struggle for dominance.

It is worth asking what a language of the mind might have looked like, developed by either of these novelists—a language that would have met Reid's criterion of being solely based on the mind rather than on physical analogies and would also have accommodated the new interest in other-than-rational experience. Two metaphors that might have helped generate a new conception of the mind are mind-as-light and mind-as-water. These were present in the psychological traditions out of which Brontë and Dickens were writing and were also present in germinal form in their novels. The metaphor of the light of reason as a specific kind of mental illumination dates at least from the time of Locke. For Locke, this light was both something that the mind could direct and something that might flash forth on its own; in the latter case it would be felt as an intuition. Light remained a standard metaphor as late as the middle of the nineteenth century. It was an important device for Emerson, for example, who described the human soul as a light rather than an organ, a function, or a faculty: "From within or from behind, a light shines through us upon things, and makes us aware that we are nothing, but the light is all" (161). The metaphorical connection between thoughts and water was of long standing. Thomas Brown noted a "very obvious, but a very beautiful similitude" between the relationship of brain to nerves and "the parent Ocean, receiving from innumerable distances the waters of its filial streams" (*Lectures* 185). Robert Langbaum remarks on the link made by Wordsworth between the flux of thought in his "veins" and "the external river that was his first sensation" (42). The more general metaphor likening the flow of thoughts to the circulation of some kind of current began to look more literal, less metaphorical, with the increasing research into the nervous system and charts of stimulus-and-action loops such as Carpenter's. As Bain noted, speaking of neural currents, "no currents, no mind."

Dickens made explicit comparisons among water, light, and mind in his description of the shattering of Eugene's mind. Throughout *Our Mutual Friend* water is strangely compelling both to the characters in the novel and to Dickens' imagination; water's symbolic connections with death, rebirth, and baptism are never far from Dickens' image-hoard. Evening light and moonlight are crucial components of David's associational complexes. Brontë's main references to light are those implicit in her descriptions of eyes flashing and sending rays, although she too worked with the image of moonlight as a signal of other-than-rational understanding. (See Heilman, "Charlotte Brontë.") Brontë relied heavily on the metaphor of the internal spring and the current of life flowing from it in depicting her main characters' growth.

Either metaphor could have adequately represented some of the unconscious phenomena that were becoming important in the nineteenth century, but neither was complete. Brontë drew on the fluid metaphor as the best way to represent what she regarded as the "unseen seat of Life," just as Upham had recourse to inner "fountains" in describing the progress of a soul's knowledge of itself and its relationship to God. Dickens' characters experience a particular kind of light as part of their transformations, and Copperfield's association of Agnes Wickfield with a stained-glass window is an interesting variation. But neither of the metaphorical vehicles was in itself sufficiently complex or textured to represent the whole body of phenomena effectively. Both departed from the concept of mind-as-entity, but neither could represent more than a single faculty or single kind of mental experience.

What was needed was a metaphorical vehicle that could render the mind as a complex and living being, in particular, a being with a full range of sentient experience. Neither water nor light displays any variation of structure or organizing pattern, so neither could render one of the most important received facts about the mind, that it has a structure designed by God for a specific purpose, and neither could render one of the most important subjective experiences, the felt texture within the stream of ideas and sensations. The metaphors remained limited to representing specific experiences—water associated with the sense of a continuing mental life, and light with the sense of intuitive understanding or discovery—for which they were well suited. The development of metaphors that go beyond this limitation is the story of the next chapter.

VI
TOWARD THE LIFE OF THE MIND: JAMES AND ELIOT DISCOVER SENTIENCE

Brontë and Dickens differed from earlier novelists in paying more attention to the springs of mysterious mental phenomena which are now usually associated with "unconscious" mental processes. To represent the development of these phenomena, they used the earlier psychology—mental faculties, associations, physiognomical "readings"—and that psychology's underlying metaphor of mind-as-entity. But these materials were used in new ways to demonstrate the inescapable subjectivity of some experiences, in Brontë's case, and the inevitable pressure of external events on character, in Dickens' case. Both novelists gave fictional voice to the new emphases of some psychologists who saw a complex of sentient relationships weaving every individual into the web of nature, society, and history.

Each writer displayed at least one characteristic limitation of the mind-as-entity metaphor, however: Dickens insisted on a qualitative separation between his characters' experiences of the phenomenal and noumenal realms, and Brontë similarly separated each character's "I" or executive power from the other operations and sensations. These limitations may not seem at first to be characteristic of the mind-as-entity metaphor, but as I have shown, they can be correlated with the difference between everyday and metaphysical senses of such terms as "substance" and "entity." The doctrine of an immaterial mental substance is not something most people can apply, although it is easy enough to speculate about. In everyday usage, in order for the mind to preserve its divine component, there must exist a discontinuity somewhere in the stream of experience, in either what or how one experiences. Thus Dickens represented the experience of the "tremendous region," David Copperfield's land of dreams and shadows, as different from other experiences, and Brontë consistently represented the executive faculty as endowed with awareness and will: "*I* ordered my brain to find a response." These two novelists lacked what the psychologists also lacked—language that could bridge the gap between the new wealth of experimental data on neural anatomy and physiology and the inescapable subjective data of experience. They lacked metaphors that could serve a theory-generative function, that could precipitate and then guide a revolution in the concept of mind.

George Eliot and Henry James were better placed. While not engaged, as were their psychologist associates and relations, in advancing the field's scientific understanding and respectability, both imbibed on a daily basis the most advanced psychological theories and discoveries of their time—Eliot through Lewes and James through first his father and then his brother. These links may explain the appearance in both writers' works of mental metaphors that represent, better than anything in the psychological literature, a life of the mind as a sentient being in every significant respect identical to the person with whose physical body it is associated. The speculation about sources is secondary; of primary importance is that Eliot and James used new metaphors and renewed the old metaphors to present the mental history of sentient beings. Eliot and James portrayed the operation of all identifiable forces—those external to the individual, those related to the association of ideas, and those which remain ultimately mysterious—within the field of sentient awareness. Their metaphors show that all forces have an immediate influence on that awareness and a longer-term, formative influence on the sense of self.

Like Brontë and Dickens, James and Eliot acknowledged the importance of sensations felt to be welling up from some subterranean source, the importance of sympathy with the external world, and the importance of feeling connected with other human beings and with the rest of the external world (a feeling that was usually called "sympathy"). They continued to make use of the language of mind-as-entity where appropriate. But to a far greater extent, they were concerned to represent mental experience across a full range of sentient experiences.

The revolutionary nature of this attempt should be clear. Well into the nineteenth century, psychologists and some novelists wrote as if most important mental experiences could be analyzed as the effects of sensory stimulation and nerve-force transmission. So conceived, the mind is a physical system, a collection of states and changes of states in the brain cells. When Spencer, Bain, and Lewes insisted that life and mind were inseparable, they were calling for an approach like that of David Ferrier, who interpreted principles of human behavior from physical and biological phenomena. As Lewes repeatedly stated, physiology must be the basis for all other human sciences. Eliot and James made the leap directly from physiology to mind, easily clearing the mind-body barrier with which the theorists were forced to contend. They took as a given the organic nature of mind and the mind's relationship to the external world, a relationship characterized by various levels of sentient experience, and they worked from this experience to the outside world. Their novels provide the applications which the theories were not quite able to realize. Both the literary and scientific endeavors were important, although from the point of view of metaphors of mind the novelists were more successful because they achieved a new figurative language to give vivid and compact expression to what was literally inexpressible.

Mindscapes, Webs, and Affairs of the Senses in Henry James

In his famous essay "The Art of Fiction" (1884), Henry James responds to Walter Besant, who advised writers to "write from experience." This is inadequate advice, James contends:

> What kind of experience is intended, and where does it begin and end? Experience is never limited, and it is never complete; it is an immense sensibility, a kind of huge spider-web of the finest silken threads suspended in the chamber of consciousness, and catching every airborne particle in its tissues. It is the very atmosphere of the mind; and when the mind is imaginative . . . it takes to itself the faintest hints of life, it converts the very pulses of the air into revelations. . . . The power to guess the unseen from the seen, to trace the implication of things, to judge the whole piece by the pattern, the condition of feeling life in general so completely that you are well on your way to knowing any particular corner of it—this cluster of gifts may almost be said to constitute experience. . . . If experience consists of impressions, it may be said that impressions *are* experience, just as . . . they are the very air we breathe. [12-13]

This description is puzzling when looked at closely. In what way can experience be equated with sensibility? In everyday language "experience" usually means "what one has experienced," what has happened. How can this be separated out, "suspended in the chamber of consciousness"? How can it be both an atmosphere and impressions? William Veeder has noted that in his criticism James relies on multiple metaphors as one way of expressing "his perceptions in a style adequate to their intricacy" (1). Veeder's point is well illustrated by this passage, in which experience is equated with an immense sensibility and the very atmosphere of the mind, is likened to a spider web and a cluster of interpretive abilities. In the paragraph I'm quoting from, James' last but probably not final word is that "If experience consists of impressions, it may be said that impressions *are* experience" (13).

The concept here expressed by James is certainly intricate. The metaphors suggest that experience is identical to sensibility yet different from consciousness. The mix of metaphors suggests that James is being pulled in two directions to represent mental phenomena. Characterizing experience as a web and associating it with the perceptive faculties ("an immense sensibility") sound like variations on the mind-as-entity metaphor, as does referring to consciousness as occupying a chamber. From this perspective *Experience* is that mental entity or component which records the particles of sensation and thought—it is the blank slate. But several features of the description evoke Spencer's definition of life as "the continuous adjustment of internal relations to external relations" (*Principles* 1:293) and Lewes' emphasis on *sentience* as the proper term for psychology because it is more inclusive than *consciousness* ("Mind" 5). The web must necessarily change with each particle it captures; as long as the consciousness lives, experience changes—"it is never complete." Because the web of sensibility is "suspended in the chamber of consciousness," some impressions, some particles of experience, may be trapped in the web without the individual being aware of them. Lewes' "sentience" and James' "sensibility" both refer to the full range of mental experiences, from the impressions or particles that may be captured but not consciously perceived, to the perceptions and conceptions that are present in conscious awareness. Taken together, James' details suggest two important claims about the relationship among sensibility, experience, consciousness, and impressions. First, the sensibility responds to each faint hint taken in, so that experience can never be complete, concluded, finished. Second, consciousness is separated from impressions both structurally and functionally.

Paul Armstrong, in a detailed discussion of this passage from "The Art of Fiction," remarks that what seem "transcendent powers of revelation" attributed to the person who can "judge the whole piece by the pattern" are no more than "an extreme instance of the general workings of consciousness as both James and phenomenology understand them" (39). Reading James as a phenomenologist is attractive, but Armstrong severely weakens his position by seeing James as committed to "penetrating to the essence of existence" (47). The phenomenologist's concern with such essences, especially when expressed in language that grants them them a transcendent reality, is at odds with James' stated concern with relations. For the same reason, the analyses of Fred See and Stuart Johnson are not entirely on the mark. Johnson sees James implying a "prelinguistic consciousness" that is "completely independent of the conditions of the world" (248), and See attributes to James' language a similar urge to represent the transcendent, to "restore the order of the signified while neutralizing its theological reference" (134).

Reading James in light of the psychology of Spencer and Lewes provides a useful corrective to this transcendental orientation and preserves the Jamesian emphasis on sense impressions and what one makes of them. Spencer and Lewes wanted to understand the individual in relation to the natural and social environments and also to the individual's total experience over time. James' metaphor of the experiential web implies that the novelist's attention has shifted as Spencer and Lewes said the psychologist's attention must shift. No longer does it suffice to represent the individual mind as shaped and impelled by relatively coarse external forces, consisting mostly of ideas and emotional pressures. The mind must now also be represented as part of a human web of sensitivity involving impressions ranging from those clearly perceived to those not at all perceived by the individual yet detectable in the direction of the individual's thoughts and actions. Seen from this angle, James' famous dictum, "Try to be one of the people on whom nothing is lost!" truly differs from Besant's "Write from experience" in what it suggests is possible—awareness of every quantum of (impressed) experience.

Experience is thus inescapably "an affair of the senses," to borrow a phrase from *The Ambassadors*, where "senses" has the most general possible meaning—not just what enters the mind through the five senses but what the mind senses in itself and creates for itself. This affair incorporates the totality of sentient life as Lewes defines it: the full range of activity of the sentient organism ("Mind" 5). But James adds a crucial element with his references to the "gifts" of the "imaginative" mind, the power to convert even the minutest sensory impressions into ideas about the whole phenomenon from which they originate. It is as if he grants sentience to the web itself, making possible for the first time a complete life of the mind as a single entity. This mental life manifests itself in two ways in James' novels: in his technique of representing the mind of a character as a whole individual within a mindscape, and in his close analysis of what his characters construct from the impressions they receive. Figurative language suggesting the mind-as-a-living-being metaphor is the connective tissue throughout.

Just how revolutionary is James' placement of the mind within the mindscape can be appreciated by looking again at several passages from *Jane Eyre* in which mental states or phenomena are described in terms of landscapes. First, this: "A ridge of lighted heath, alive, glancing, devouring, would have been a meet emblem of my mind when I accused and menaced Mrs. Reed: the same ridge, black and blasted after the flames are dead, would have represented as meetly my subsequent condition, when half an hour's silence and reflection had shown me the madness of my conduct, and the dreariness of my hated and hating position" (69-70). This ridge is explicitly not Jane but her mind, an emblem rather than her inner life itself. As an emblem, it has no claim to continuity in the novel; other mental states call up different images.

Brontë does not develop the image to parallel Jane's mental development, nor does she repeat it as a way of measuring Jane's subsequent changes. Thus, of a later event, Jane writes that her mind "made its first earnest effort to comprehend what had been infused into it concerning heaven and hell: and for the first time it recoiled, baffled; and for the first time glancing behind, on each side, and before it, it saw all around an unfathomable gulf: it felt the one point where it stood—the present; all the rest was formless cloud and vacant depth" (110-11). Or, later still, she describes herself as bringing back such of her thoughts "as had been straying through imagination's boundless and trackless waste, into the safe fold of common sense" (190).

The images of ridge and peak serve the author's immediate need—to represent Jane's mental states—but are not connected in a way that shows the ongoing life of the mind. Mind in both cases is an entity subordinate to and distinct from Jane herself. Likewise, her thoughts are relatively independent elements which are pulled one way or another depending on the relative strength of imagination and common sense.

Karen Chase attributes to Brontë a "new interest in psychological depth, an interior space that will serve as a highly charged dramatic arena" (52). In support of this astute observation she notes that Jane Eyre's changes of location are psychologically "resonant" acts and that "the self has emotions, faculties, and dispositions only because it also has a geography" (65, 91). But Chase does not show Brontë actually working with this interior space as much as she shows that she manipulates location and change of location in interesting ways. This limitation highlights a key difference between Brontë and James: Brontë reveals her characters' "inner lives" but does not "analyse their consciousness as James does" (Holder-Barell 81). The best example is *The Portrait of a Lady* (1888), whose heroine James places in a mindscape at a crucial moment in her life and returns to it several times to demonstrate the psychic distance she travels during her story; the images are what Alexander Holder-Barell calls *iterative*—they contribute to the novel's structure (117). They contribute to the motif of *seeing* that dominates the entire novel (Van Ghent 215).

The mindscape first appears when Isabel Archer is being courted by Gilbert Osmond but before she has decided exactly what that courtship will mean to her. He has just openly expressed his love for the first time; it has troubled her because she feels herself being forced to choose, and the pressure seems to her like "the slipping of a fine bolt—backward, forward, she couldn't have said which" (263). He leaves, and she sits alone, reflecting: "What had happened was something that for a week past her imagination had been going forward to meet; but here, when it came, she stopped—that sublime principle somehow broke down. The working of this young lady's spirit was strange, and I can only give it to you as I see it, not hoping to make it seem altogether natural. Her imagination, as I say, now hung back: there was a last vague space it couldn't cross—a dusky, uncertain tract which looked ambiguous and even slightly treacherous, like a moorland seen in the winter twilight. But she was to cross it yet" (265).

And cross it she does, realizing its full extent when she learns not only that Osmond pursued her mainly for her money but that a woman she thought one of her true friends had been his mistress and had put him up to the plot. Again she is reflecting, this time while journeying to London to sit at her cousin's deathbed and with her new knowledge about Osmond fresh in her mind: "She performed this journey with sightless eyes. . . . Her thoughts followed their course through other countries—strange-looking, dimly-lighted, pathless lands, in which there was no change of seasons, but only, as it seemed, a perpetual dreariness of winter" (464-65).

Together these passages represent a whole world within Isabel's mind, a desolate but nonetheless more vital place than the propositional sea Sterne attributed to Dr. Slop or the impressing and copying device described by Hume. This world differs enough from the external world that other laws may prevail: there seems no passage of time. The two descriptions also demonstrate a continuity in Isabel's inner life. They clearly stand outside of but run parallel to the ongoing events of her external world. The second passage shows her mind crossing that uncertain tract earlier constructed by her imagination. "Imagination" in the first passage denotes not a separate faculty but the mind in its most attentive state, as the comment in "The Art of Fiction" makes clear. In the second passage, likewise, James explicitly designates Isabel's eyes as sightless to indicate that her corporeal self is an insentient shell—she *is* her thoughts as they perform that other journey.

James dips into this internal world again at the novel's end, using the mindscape imagery to dramatize a new stage in Isabel's inner life. Her first suitor, the unfortunately named Caspar Goodwood, insists that she leave Osmond and return with him to America. Hearing this proposal, Isabel feels as if she is floating "in fathomless waters"; to rescue herself from this rapturous near-drowning, "she seemed to beat with her feet, in order to catch herself, to feel something to rest on" (489). But her trial is not yet over; Caspar seizes and kisses her, and it is "like white lightning, a flash that spread, and spread again, and stayed" (489). The narrator comments: "This however, of course, was but a subjective fact, as the metaphysicians say; the confusion, the noise of waters, all the rest of it, were in her own swimming head" (489). The point of this bit of Jamesian irony is that to devalue Isabel's experience because metaphysicians would call it *subjective* would be a mistake. Although explicitly presented as similes, the inner flood and lightning are as tangible and real as the external world. It is such passages that lead Richard Hocks to connect Henry James with William James' radical empiricism, an empiricism which "must neither admit into its constructions any element that is not directly experienced, nor exclude from them any element that is directly experienced. *For such a philosophy, the relations that connect experiences must themselves be experienced relations, and any kind of relation experienced must be accounted as 'real' as anything else in the system*" (65-6). By excluding subjective relations, however directly experienced, the metaphysicians to which James refers leave out these essential details of Isabel's inner life.

One of the many ironies of *Portrait* is that Isabel's struggle does culminate in choosing to allow her mind to be rather like that of a character in a novel from the eighteenth century, a character whose mind is a relatively passive, impressible entity. The novel suggests pretty clearly that in turning her back on the inner fountains Caspar has caused to flow, hence shunning new knowledge of herself, she makes an immoral choice because she denies life. Most of the main characters regard other individuals' minds as things. The narrator notes that Gilbert Osmond wants to treat Isabel Archer's mind as a "polished, elegant surface" for reflecting his thoughts, her "intelligence" as "a silver plate . . . that he might heap up with ripe fruits" (296). Isabel herself regards Osmond's daughter Pansy as "like a sheet of blank paper" and hopes "that so fair and smooth a page would be covered with an edifying text" (238). Later she comes to understand that "Pansy was really a blank page, a pure white surface, successfully kept so; she had neither art, nor guile, nor temper, nor talent. . . . She would have no will . . . her force would be all in knowing when and where to cling" (268). At this point in the story Isabel does not think the less of Osmond for what he has done to his daughter; it does not strike her as wrong to treat an individual as a blank sheet to be covered with a text, however edifying to the people who will be reading it. She only understands when she falls victim to the same treatment: "Her mind was to be [Osmond's]—attached to his own like a small garden-lot to a deer-park. . . . so far from desiring her mind to be a blank he had flattered himself that it would be richly receptive" (362).

The Lockean language in these passages shows that James acknowledges the possibility of treating minds as blank slates. Pansy definitely has been kept blank and nearly without will, and Isabel in spite of herself has become a silver plate in Osmond's collection. But to treat minds *only* in this way denies their inner fountains and the importance of human interaction. It denies some of the components of sentience that were being raised to new importance in the nineteenth century. A discussion between Madame Merle and Isabel makes this point. Madame Merle insists: "every human being has his shell and . . . you must take the shell into account. By the shell I mean the whole envelope of circumstances. There's no such thing as an isolated man or woman . . . . What shall we call our 'self'? . . . It overflows into everything that belongs to us—and then it flows back again" (175). Isabel takes exactly the opposite view: she believes that nothing she owns or wears expresses herself and that "everything's on the contrary a limit, a barrier, and a perfectly arbitrary one" (175-76). Neither view is correct. The older woman sees only the "shell" of the individual; she sees the individual identity as nothing more than the expression-impression relationship between character and possessions. Isabel's response stresses the inviolability of the individual identity. She is here as naive as Madame Merle is worldly. Neither understands the most accurate view of the life of the mind, given much earlier in a description of Isabel as someone who "carried within herself a great fund of life, and her deepest enjoyment was to feel the continuity between the movements of her own soul and the agitations of the world" (41).

Isabel's end is tragically fitting because she is not able to raise to a conscious principle her intuitive understanding of the continuity between an individual's inner self and the outer world. Osmond, she learns too late, is a person who "lived exclusively for the world" despite giving the impression of being entirely indifferent to it (331); "this base, ignoble world, it appeared, was after all what one was to live for . . . indifference was really the last of his qualities; she had never seen any one who thought so much of others" (360). She wanted to transcend that world, to preserve her individuality in the face of what she regarded as arbitrary limits, yet her mind does become a garden-plot attached to Osmond's deer-park, cultivated solely for his pleasure. Like Pansy, she becomes a victim not only of Osmond but of the immorality always possible in the mind-as-entity view.

Following the "sightless eyes" passage, James drops the mindscape construction but continues to dwell on how Isabel *feels* her new knowledge:

> She had plenty to think about; but it was neither reflexion nor conscious purpose that filled her mind. Disconnected visions passed through it, and sudden dull gleams of memory, of expectation. The past and the future came and went at their will, but she saw them only in fitful images, which rose and fell by a logic of their own. It was extraordinary the things she remembered. Now that she was in the secret, now that she knew something that so much concerned her and the eclipse of which had made life resemble an attempt to play whist with an imperfect pack of cards, the truth of things, their mutual relations, their meaning, and for the most part their horror, rose before her with a kind of architectural vastness. She remembered a thousand trifles; they started to life with the spontaneity of a shiver. She had thought them trifles at the time; now she saw that they had been weighted with lead. Yet even now they were trifles after all, for of what use was it to her to understand them? [465]

Her known past life and projected future life seem to follow their own logic in rising into her awareness, in a language emphasizing that Isabel's perception of these new relations is very much an affair of the senses—the ideas have shape, weight, even a logic of their own. And the ideas do not just contribute to but also define her state. As the narrator goes on to say, "Nothing seemed of use to her to-day. All purpose, all intention, was suspended." She is only able to sense the impressions she has earlier missed and perceive the connections they have established among themselves. The paralysis of Isabel's will is all the more significant in view of her earlier vitality. This mental event is one way James marks her decline into passivity and subjection. Isabel may now have a full deck of cards, but as the relations among her impressions arrange themselves without her guidance, it seems that the game is still beyond her ability.

This affair of Isabel's senses is subjective and varying but nonetheless significant. The once-trifling ideas become weighty and then again trifling as her mood fluctuates from moment to moment. These are not the eighteenth century's independent and indivisible billiard balls of thought. Nor are they the "sick experiences" of Dickens' characters or the scorned "figments" of Brontë's. As James insists, the fact that metaphysicians would label Isabel's thoughts subjective makes them no less real a part of her world. Indeed, for the period of this reflection, what passes outside the window of the train simply does not exist for Isabel or for the reader either. Her subjective world is the only one that she knows and we know, and it is as rich in opportunities for sensual experiences as the real Rome or Florence. The internal realm is as active and functional as the external. In the Jamesian world, perception is never disembodied but is always a sensual experience, the most important component of the individual's sentient life. To render this sensual quality, James uses figurative language based on the mind-as-entity metaphor because this language can vividly and compactly represent subjective experiences within the sentiences of his characters, experiences that have equal or greater claim to validity. This language is a constant throughout James' career, as present in the early *The American* (1877) as in *The Ambassadors* (1903).

Christopher Newman, the hero of the earlier novel, undertakes a journey like Isabel's to be at the side of a young friend on his deathbed. Awakening aboard a train, Newman "found his eyes resting upon one of the snow-powdered peaks of the Jura, behind which the sky was just reddening with the dawn. But he saw neither the cold mountain nor the warm sky; his consciousness began to throb again, on the very instant, with a sense of his wrong" (222). He has a *sense* of his wrong, and it causes him sensible mental pain, a throbbing consciousness; the sense is not a product of analysis or reflection. Throughout his wanderings after he loses Claire, his fiance, he preserves his "sense of being a good fellow wronged" (303); he is "filled with a sorer sense of wrong than he had ever known" (245). The simplicity of phrasing and the use of the word "sense" draw attention to Newman's heart pain as an affair of the senses.

In describing how his hero feels his way through moral problems, James preserves the consistency of this character who perceives his mind as a storage place, who desires to make an impression on the world and on the minds of other people, who searches for a wife to place on his pile of money "like a statue on a monument" and desires "to possess, in a word, the best article in the market" (44). This attitude may result from Newman's early life, of which he says, "I have never had time to feel things. I have had to *do* them, to make myself felt" (41). He makes this statement in the context of asserting himself to be a man of feeling, but this feeling is a matter of collecting impressions. He had gone to Europe for two reasons, first to get a wife and second to give "his mind a chance to 'improve,' if it would. He cheerfully believed that it had improved," especially during the six months he traveled while waiting for Claire to decide about his offer (74). But this improvement seems to consist mostly of having collected impressions. He writes to a friend that she could peruse his guide books and identify the places where he had "a sensation of some sort or other" by marks in the margins (75); the experiences seem to have made marks in his mind, or impressions, but they have contributed neither to a greater self-understanding nor to a greater awareness of that world which has produced Claire's family, the de Bellegardes.

Newman is satisfied to regard his period of traveling as nothing more than an attempt to "scrape together a few conclusions" of a very vague sort; he feels how far away is his earlier life, how prominent in his recent memory are Claire's eyes, and how lacking in beauty his life has been. These are "rather formless meditations" because Newman can only collect and record sensations; he cannot direct and shape them. He has made the external world yield him a substantial fortune, but he has no such ability within his sentient life.

Newman's lack of introspective power is especially noteworthy. Early in the novel he describes to a friend how he decided against revenging himself against the fellow who had played him a costly business trick—he had suddenly felt a "mortal disgust" for the revenge he had planned. He goes on to say that "this all took place quite independently of my will, and I sat watching it as if it were a play at the theatre. I could feel it going on inside me. You may depend upon it that there are things going on inside of us that we understand mighty little about" (34). On the one hand this curious description seems to indicate some kind of self-awareness; Newman's simile implies an inner eye that observes these "things going on inside of us." Yet the experience has not brought him any greater self-understanding; he remains as innocent of the causes behind this change of heart as he is unaware of any deeper principles guiding what he sees on stage. His senses in both cases take in what there is to be taken in, but the most he can do with it is to formulate a superficial truism like "there are things going on inside of us." It has certainly not helped him deal with Claire's decision to enter a convent: her conduct "struck him with a kind of awe, and the fact that he was powerless to understand it or feel the reality of its motives only deepened the force with which he had attached himself to her" (245-46).

Because he can only impress and be impressed, Newman is constitutionally unable to deal with the world of the de Bellegardes. One of his greatest frustrations about his relationship with the family is that he cannot make any impression on them, make them "feel" his "presence." Thus he enjoys a real triumph when he tells Claire's brother that he knows the family has a terrible secret. The latter "almost succeeded in looking untroubled; the breaking up of the ice in his handsome countenance was an operation that was necessarily gradual. But Newman's mildly-syllabled argumentation seemed to press, and press, and presently he averted his eyes" (252). This desire to impress himself also manifests itself once in his relationship with Claire; when she tells him their marriage is off, he first argues with her, to no end, and then forces a kiss on her (244). Of course neither act changes the outcome of the story; Claire enters the Carmelite convent and her family's name is never sullied by an alliance with a mere rich businessman.

The language used by James to describe his hero's thoughts and feelings stresses Newman's dominance by sensations and his inability to understand or empathize. James' imagery also suggests that Newman cannot reflect about himself. The depths of both his own mind and other minds remain for him unfathomable. He can no more understand such depths than he can the Carmelite nuns singing behind their wall: to his ears the music is only a "confused, impersonal wail" (277), the convent itself only a "high-shouldered blank wall" (305). Newman's resolution of the affair indicates that it has never been more than an affair of the senses. His first meeting with Claire had been for him like opening a book and being captured by the first lines (82). At the novel's end, after standing outside the convent, he visits Notre Dame, where he realizes that "the most unpleasant thing that had ever happened to him had reached its formal conclusion, as it were; he could close the book and put it away" (306). It is not likely that this formal conclusion would have been different if he had been more self-aware, but it is possible that he would have obtained a different kind of knowledge from the experience.

For Newman, Europeans as well as his own inner life remain blank walls. He approaches them sensuously but can see little structure and can make no impressions. His story is a fictional analog to the wholistic principle enunciated by Lewes: "We cannot have one [single] sentient state that is not enmeshed with other sentient states, so that each wave of stimulations sets going a multitude of connected stimulations. Were it not so there would be no Experience; only a succession of isolated sensible affections" ("Mind" 41). This principle manifests itself in the two basic laws of sensibility. The first is that "every wave-impulse is irradiated and propagated *throughout* the system." But this law is an "*ideal construction*," Lewes points out: "there can never be an irradiation throughout the central tissue, because each wave-impulse must be arrested and deflected as it is compounded with multitudinous impulses from other sources" (44). The second law brings the ideal construction into conformity with the real world: "Every impulse is restricted, and by its restrictions a group is formed" (45). Arguably, all of James' stories can be read as working out this principle in structure and character. Newman might have set his goals differently had he understood just how complex was the system he was interacting with and how impossible it was that a simple pressure could pass through without deflection and combination.

Lambert Strether, the central consciousness of *The Ambassadors*, has been called by Susan Griffin "the prototypic Jamesian perceiver." According to Griffin, Strether adjusts to his environment "by selecting those perceptions which fulfill his needs," and for him "the moment of perception is a moment of engagement with the problems of life" (398, 409). Griffin correctly insists that Strether is an active perceiver; it is equally important to note that some of the perceptions on which he acts originally entered his memory through the activity of his sentient web, without his being aware of them. What separates Lambert Strether from Christopher Newman is twenty years of chronological age, a weight of additional impressions that would be impossible to quantify, and a sensory apparatus well enough developed to catch the nuances and complexities missed by the younger man. Strether is a sensory web that allows very little to be lost; he has been given the imagination to "guess the seen from the unseen" and "judge the whole piece by the pattern." When Strether realizes that he has never felt possessed of freedom, it is a sensible realization, "an affair of the senses." He juxtaposes the tangible quality of an hour he has spent in the apartment of a young man who does seem to possess freedom against the felt emptiness of his own youth (318). The awareness itself has a tangible quality, becomes itself a matter of sensation, and thus it can contribute to Strether's consciousness in a way that Newman's collecting of impressions and viewing of his mind as a theater cannot.

Strether's sensible perception of his mental states is difficult to illustrate by excerpt because his reflections go on for pages and only gradually settle down into what William James characterizes as "resting-places," which are "the 'substantive parts' of the stream of thought"—the definite ideas or conclusions that will lead to some kind of action (*Principles* 236). This is one reason why the quivering, web-like sensibility described by Lewes is a more accurate representation than the "stream" of William James. Each new thought or impression of Strether's influences the whole web, and James takes as his writerly duty the tracing of these vibrations.

Nevertheless, certain elements can be extracted from lengthy reflections such as that in the Luxembourg Gardens after Strether has been two days in Paris (59-67). This scene supplies background information important for understanding the reflections as they progress. Strether had visited Paris as a young man and had carried away great plans of preserving the sense of culture kindled in him there. But the death of his wife and child and a long period of relatively dependent living in Woollett thwarted the plans. He is now in Paris to "save" the son of his benefactress from an apparently sinful relationship; if he succeeds, his reward will be marriage with Mrs. Newsome. James presents few of these details directly, of course; the reader must function as a Jamesian perceiver. But in the Luxembourg Gardens both Strether and the reader gain understanding as Strether *feels* his way toward a number of new conceptions about himself and his past.

While reading the letters from Woollett, including those from Mrs. Newsome, Strether notices a "sharp" sense of escape, and he feels a "duty" to try to explain that freedom and account for the corresponding sense of being young again. He wants to work out the explanation like a sum in arithmetic, but what he comes to is a sensual awareness of his present state in contrast to his past. Only now does he become aware of his mental state of two weeks ago, when he was "one of the weariest of men." This sensation, as now perceived, leads him to the idea of the cause: a "crowded past" that has made his life in Woollett "empty." He now hears what has been sounding in his mind's ear subliminally for years, "the hum of vain things." His sensual awareness of his past is all the sharper because it contrasts with the impressions of the previous day in Paris, which "had really been the process of feeling the stirred life of connections long since individually dropped." This stirred life is manifest in his sensations regarding the lemon-colored volumes he has seen in a book shop and remembers having considered buying on his previous visit. Their impact on him is a "conversion of the subconsciousness that, all the same, in the great desert of the years, he must have had of them." That is, his sentient web has been vibrating all these years from that stimulus, but vibrating too gently to be perceived until reinforced with the present experience of seeing a similar set of volumes. Once reinforced, the subconsciousness—the unperceived but captured impressions in the chamber of consciousness—become *converted* into the idea of his emptiness and weariness.

These and other details cohere for Strether in a tangible awareness of some of the essential features of his past life that have led to the empty present, and he now has the sensation of being free from that present. Here in Paris he senses the possibility of recovering dignity and identity, of being more than just the Lambert Strether whose name is on the cover of the review he edits for Mrs. Newsome. He is put into contact with the very stuff of his consciousness: the stirred life of connections from his past and especially the unsuspected presence in his subconsciousness of the books he never bought, books that also represent his unfulfilled plans and unmet goals.

Having been awakened, this stirred life develops page by page in Strether's conscious awareness. Its growth gives him among other things a measure of the significance of events. Such an event is the hour he spends waiting for Chad in the latter's apartment, on the evening of the day he has admitted to Mrs. Newsome's elder daughter, another of the "ambassadors," that he actually approves of Madame de Vionnet, Chad's "virtuous" attachment. He knows that this is "perhaps the most positive declaration he had ever made in his life," and when their interview terminated he knew that "it probably *was* all at an end"—his potential marriage to Mrs. Newsome (279-80). The dramatic event, juxtaposed with his sense of being in possession of Chad's rooms while he waits, will cause this hour to loom in later memory as one among the "particular handful that most had counted." During this hour, the time since his arrival in Paris takes on a tangible quality:

> He had heard, of old, only what he *could* then hear; what he could do now was to think of three months ago as a point in the far past. All voices had grown thicker and meant more things; they crowded on him as he moved about—it was the way they sounded together that wouldn't let him be still. He felt, strangely, as sad as if he had come for some wrong, and yet as excited as if he had come for some freedom. But the freedom was what was most in the place and the hour; it was the freedom that most brought him round again to the youth of his own that he had long ago missed. He could have explained little enough today either why he had missed it or why, after years and years, he should care that he had; the main truth of the actual appeal of everything was none the less that everything represented the substance of his loss, put it within reach, within touch, made it, to a degree it had never been, an affair of the senses. That was what it became for him at this singular time, the youth he had long ago missed—a queer concrete presence, full of mystery, yet full of reality, which he could handle, taste, smell, and the deep breathing of which he could positively hear. It was in the outside air as well as within; it was in the long watch, from the balcony, in the summer night, of the wide late life of Paris, the unceasing soft quick rumble, below, of the little lighted carriages that, in the press, always suggested the gamblers he had seen of old at Monte Carlo pushing up to the tables. [281-82]

Strether's awareness of his intangible loss (freedom and what he might have had from it) is a queer concrete presence of voices heard, things seen, events lived through. By contrast, David Copperfield's awareness of his tangible losses (two friends, his wife, and so forth) is simply an abstract weight. Strether's awareness of the past he might have had is sensual, ranking equally with his awareness of the actual apartment where he waits. His consciousness of both incorporates the whole of his sentient awareness, hence the strangeness, the queerness, the mystery, hence his inability to treat the awareness simply as an element of rational consciousness.

Strether's encounter with the reality of the relationship between Chad and Madame de Vionnet—that it is sexual and involves, at the very least, nights in country inns—is just as sensual and subjective (307-13). Here too the essential impressions are not at first processed by his consciousness. The several paragraphs leading up to his seeing them on the river trace the events as they develop: Strether observes the two figures approaching in their boat, senses their intimacy ("The air quite thickened, at their approach, with further intimations"), and suddenly recognizes them as his two friends. But he does not yet see what their being together means. James then subtly shifts to Strether's later reflections: that he had been the one trying to explain how *he* had arrived there, without explicitly stating that he had not "plotted this coincidence." He felt the need to explain but did not then know why he had that feeling, since "nothing of the sort, so far as surface and sound were involved, was even in question." His sense of something not quite right, his feeling that the two have something to hide, is an "impression" that is "destined only to deepen, to complete itself." As the narrator makes explicit, only when the passage of hours has allowed this completion to take place does Strether know "how he had been affected—he but half knew at the time." The chapter's final paragraph reveals the result of this experience; Strether feels with his entire organism the reverse of what Paris has been to him until now: he feels "lonely and cold." His response to "the quantity of make-believe" in the performance of his friends is a psycho-physical sensation—a revulsion in his "spiritual stomach"—and he *feels* "the pity of [their intimacy] being so much like lying." In this event, as in others that are crucial to Strether's developing understanding of himself and of the life people lead in Paris, James relies on the language of sentience and on the concept of unperceived impressions to represent the workings of the mind.

This analysis of the recognition scene should demonstrate the problem with some modern critical statements, for example that Strether "has long been in the uncomfortable position of sensing more than he can allow himself to know," that the knowledge comes from "the depths of the psyche itself," and that in such moments "James's men and women confront what in some part of themselves they have long since known" (Yeazell 25, 33). This is definitely a twentieth-century reading; as Yeazell says, in James' novels "the deepest reaches of the psyche—at least as the twentieth-century understands them—rarely come into view" (17). When we read Strether's and Isabel's discoveries in light of the late-nineteenth-century emphasis on sentience and understand that this psychology allowed the possibility of uncognized sensations, we no longer need to labor at constructing characters' psyches and finding that such construction leads to the paradox of *knowledge* being limited to "some part of themselves." Lewes, Spencer, and possibly even Henry James himself would say that sensations by themselves do not constitute knowledge; sensations become knowledge only when they are combined into patterns by imagination and judgment.

Because of his attention to the subjective components of experience and the value he gives those components, James ultimately transcends the limitations of the mind-as-entity metaphor. He makes this point explicit in Strether's famous conversation with Little Bilham in which he tells the younger man "Live all you can; it's a mistake not to" (132). This injunction comes as part of a "quiet stream of demonstration" that Strether has not planned, that in fact "overwhelmed him with its long slow rush" (131). That is, it seems to flow out of his total sentient awareness, not just out of a logical consciousness. It leads Strether to make a very Lockean observation: the "affair of life" is like a tin mould "into which, a helpless jelly, one's consciousness is poured—so that one 'takes' the form." But it then carries him to a more fundamental truth, that what the metaphysicians would call not just subjective but illusory can be a formative influence: "Still, one has the illusion of freedom; therefore don't be, like me, without the memory of that illusion" (132).

Strether's experiences in Paris exemplify the power of this influence, the constructing aspect of his perceptions, as he realizes during his private visit to Madame de Vionnet's rooms. Standing in the antechamber, he looks back through the vista of the rooms, "full, once more, of dim historic shades, of the faint far-away cannon-roar of the great Empire." This historical perspective is "doubtless half the projection of his mind, but his mind was a thing that, among old waxed parquets, pale shades of pink and green, pseudo-classic candelabra, he had always needfully to reckon with" (236). He has to reckon with it because it will create the connections—now between the room and its resonances of Empire, and at another time between himself and his own empty past. And the echoes of history are only *half* the projection of Strether's mind. Without forcing one word to carry too much interpretive weight, we may at least speculate that such echoes still rebound in the room, there to be caught by a sensitive enough web.

George Eliot's Webs of Sentience

Although James named the metaphor, there are two reasons why the figure of consciousness as a sentient web is best attributed to Eliot. Most obviously, she elaborated it earlier. Second, she attended more to presenting a character's total sentient awareness. The Jamesian emphasis is always on consciousness; every affair of the senses in James either is or becomes an affair of consciousness. Eliot also stressed consciousness—it is after all the field of moral action—but she represented more fully the slow accumulation of half-cognized and uncognized impressions on the organism. And since Lewes also explicitly named the web metaphor, it is worth recalling the close intellectual relationship between him and Eliot. The two of them studied Comte and other continental philosophers together; he certainly helped shape her ideas about the possible relationships between fiction and psychology; and she edited the third series of his *Problems of*

Life and Mind. (See Collins, Kaminsky, Mason, Shuttleworth.) But as W. J. Harvey warns, for a thinker with Eliot's intellectual breadth and depth and independence of mind, we cannot make easy causal links between any given philosopher or psychologist and her choice of images (155). The question of influence is important, but the images must be understood first.

As comparing James with Brontë illuminates the revolutionary quality of the Jamesian mindscape, so comparing Eliot and Dickens illuminates the generative function of her metaphor of the sentient web. Through his plots and his language Dickens emphasizes the effect of surroundings on the individual and the interconnections among seemingly disparate parts of the world. An often cited example of this emphasis in a Dickens plot is Esther Summerson's fever, which she contracted from her maid Charley, who got it from Jo the Crossing-Sweeper, who brought it with him from the pestilential corner of London named Tom-all-Alone's. This is one answer to a question posed by the omniscient narrator of *Bleak House*: "What connexion can there be, between the place in Lincolnshire, the house in town, the Mercury in powder, and the whereabouts of Jo the outlaw with the broom . . . what connexion can there have been between many people in the innumerable histories of this world, who, from opposite sides of great gulfs, have, nevertheless, been very curiously brought together!" (197). Strange as it must seem to such figures as "the fashionable intelligence" of this novel, there are many such connections—familial, legal, and most of all moral. Esther's fever visibly manifests her legal tie to Tom-all-Alone's (she is a ward in the case of Jarndyce and Jarndyce, and Tom's is a property in the same case), her familial tie (her father died nearby and was buried there), and less explicitly but just as importantly, her moral tie as a human being. The connections are all-pervasive and as tangible as those in any ecosystem.

Dickens made the same point explicitly in *Dombey and Son* (1846-48) in accounting for "moral pestilence": "Those who study the physical sciences, and bring them to bear upon the health of Man, tell us that if the noxious particles that rise from vitiated air [of slums] were palpable to the sight, we should see them lowering in a dense black cloud above such haunts, and rolling slowly on to corrupt the better portions of a town. But if the moral pestilence that rises with them, and, in the eternal laws of outraged Nature, is inseparable from them, could be made discernible too, how terrible the revelation!" (619-20). The cloud results from "a long train of nameless sins against the natural affections and repulsions of mankind"; it spreads out from the slums and jails to create such perversions of the natural order as "infancy that knows no innocence, youth without modesty or shame." Dickens did not see the root causes of vice and fever as innate in the world; although his images may occasionally obscure the point, he holds people fully responsible for the cultivation of all souls with whom they associate. If a soul has grown too warped to be gradually corrected by fertilizing, pruning, and staking, then a cutting must be taken and rerooted, so to speak, in order to force the necessary change of heart. This is what happens to Eugene.

In the context of metaphors of mind, the key point is that for Dickens the change of heart, like the initial formation of the character, operates through the whole individual and has as much to do with physical as with moral influences. Certainly this is a reasonable perspective, but Dickens gives no indication of how the world's connections act on the minds of characters. Lewes' criticism of Dickens' characters as "moving like pieces of simple mechanism, always in one way (instead of moving with the infinite fluctuations of organisms)" pointed to this limitation. The pressures of the Dickens world are generally coarse; they permit only certain types of movements. Such pressures as act on the organism seem to act physically. They shape characters' minds and do not involve the mental organism except as the passive subject of the forces.

In contrast, George Eliot shows environmental pressures acting through the senses on the consciousness and more generally on the sentience of the individual. One critic even identifies "the basis" of Eliot's creativity as her "painfully direct sense of other selves and of the organic nature of society," a sense she seeks to represent through her characters' sensations (Beer 101). The following passage from *Middlemarch* (1871-72) is often cited as the paradigmatic instance of Eliot's concern in her novels with the webs of relations that shape and limit the individual: "For the first time Lydgate was feeling the hampering threadlike pressure of small social conditions, and their frustrating complexity" (124). The passage also hints at Eliot's conception of psychology, that her characters' minds could move "with the infinite fluctuations of organisms" in response to the complex threadlike pressures. The minds participate in a web of sensations in two ways: sensations are transmitted along the web (often without the direct awareness of the individual, which only comes later, when the pressures have created enough force), and the web itself seems to be a sentient organism, as when a social group comes to share a conclusion without having discussed it.

Early in her career Eliot presents these threadlike pressures as more real than any other forces, by means of the key image of Hartleyan associationism (updated by Spencer and Bain): vibrations passing along either tangible or intangible threads. The various declensions of vibration are important in her description of Maggie Tulliver's mental events in *The Mill on the Floss* (1860). In this novel Eliot also presents herself as a scientist, describing psychological and social conditions and then searching the environment and the personal histories for contributing factors. In *Middlemarch* the vibrations image is generalized into that of the web, and the web is presented more explicitly as something which shapes characters' choices. In her last novel, *Daniel Deronda* (1876), Eliot's primary psychological interest is in dramatizing the events her characters experience and then showing how these events create dispositions and reactions at all levels of sentience.

In *The Mill on the Floss* the sensitive web informs the structuring of whole scenes in a context of psychological analysis and also manifests itself in an image complex that incorporates vibrations, flows, fibers, streams, and rivers. Many scenes in this novel either begin or end, or both, with relatively general explanations of the psychological principles and forces underlying the dramatized behavior. Such a scene is Maggie Tulliver's secret meeting in the Red Deeps with Philip Wakem, the son of the man her father believes caused his bankruptcy. Like a natural scientist, Eliot isolates their meeting in a single chapter and magnifies it to fill the entire field of view. The long introductory paragraph identifies Maggie's principal psychological tension, her conflict between, first, the "severe monotonous warning . . . that she was losing the simplicity and clearness of her life by admitting a ground of concealment" and, second, her desire not to lose Philip's friendship and companionship as well as the external world he represents (286). This is a prominent theme in Eliot's work, the struggle of an individual (usually a woman) to reconcile the claims of externally-imposed duty, which seem to limit self-development, with the desire to grow freely.

The chapter proceeds almost analytically. A section of dialog is followed by a description of what the characters feel as they speak, and these moment-to-moment events are placed against the fixed qualities of the situation: Maggie's discontent, which Philip's words set "vibrating," and the "monotonous" voice that warns her against the temptation to preserve their relationship by continuing to meet in secret. It is a complicated situation, and Eliot's method renders it effectively. When Philip accuses Maggie of trying to "stupefy" herself by refusing to see him any more, Eliot shows not one but two responses in the girl: "Maggie's lips trembled; she felt there was some truth in what Philip said, and yet there was a deeper consciousness that, for any immediate application it had to her conduct, it was no better than falsity. Her double impression corresponded to the double impulse of the speaker. Philip seriously believed what he said, but he said it with vehemence because it made an argument against the resolution that opposed his wishes" (288). Philip's corresponding double impulse does not directly give rise to Maggie's conflicting responses. Rather, Eliot's language shows, they share the same set of motivations. A single statement can spring out of contending impulses and can evoke in a sympathetic and sensitive consciousness similar responses.

Near its end, the chapter focuses on Philip's internal struggle to determine whether he had been acting out of selfish motives or had Maggie's best interests foremost. The chapter closes as it began, with generalizations. The narrator begs the reader's indulgence for Philip, who does not understand the situation and causes Maggie pain: his seemingly selfish behavior results from his imperfect character, which in turn has been shaped by his physical deformity, the lack of a mother's love in his life, and a father affectionate and indulgent but also flawed: "Kept aloof from all practical life as Philip had been, and by nature half feminine in sensitiveness, he had some of the woman's intolerant repulsion towards worldliness and the deliberate pursuit of sensual enjoyment; and this one strong natural tie in his life—his relation as a son—was like an aching limb to him. Perhaps there is inevitably something morbid in a human being who is in any way unfavourably excepted from ordinary conditions until the good force has had time to triumph; and it has rarely had time for that at two-and-twenty" (291). These are ordinary psychological observations; indeed, they sound quite dated to modern ears. What is significant about them is their patterning: they bracket the dramatic presentation and cause the entire chapter to read something like a case study.

While Eliot may have arrived at this technique in any number of ways, it does conform both to her sentient web metaphor and to the accepted scientific method of her psychologist contemporaries. The whole human being and the whole context of action must be studied together, and an individual's actions and motivations must be related to general principles. The reasons are clear. An impulse stimulated anywhere in the web will be transmitted through the whole, will continue to vibrate for some indefinite time, and will condition the reception of subsequent impulses. But because she is writing fiction and not psychology, Eliot is free to supply what the psychology lacks by creating these case studies. Thus she demonstrates the reality of the sentient web more effectively than her psychologist contemporaries, with their continuing dependance on mind-as-entity language and images.

Eliot's distance from a psychology based on the mind-as-entity metaphor can be measured by the language she tends to avoid as well as by her dominant metaphors and her structuring of scenes. She employs very few images connoting mind as a passive substance that takes impressions or as a passive vessel to be filled. The one place such images occur in some density in this novel is in the description of Mr. Tulliver's recovery from his stroke, where the images underscore the damage to his mind's active power. "The impression [was] on his mind that it was but yesterday when he received the letter from Mr. Gore" (222). "The thought of Wakem roused new vibrations" in him (225). "They were just the words to lay the most painful hold on" Mr. Tulliver's mind (225). "In a mind charged with an eager purpose and an unsatisfied vindictiveness, there is no room for new feelings" (257). In these examples, Mr. Tulliver's mind is not that much different from those of Caleb Williams, Tristram Shandy, Pamela, and other characters created during the previous century, nor is it a mind that would challenge the psychology of Hume, Stewart, Bain, or Mill to explain. The mind takes in and is filled up by impressions; it can be literally gripped by stimuli from the external world; thoughts create impressions.

One other type of image present in the eighteenth century, the mind or brain as a separable, tangible, and subordinate entity, occurs occasionally in Eliot, but she uses it in isolation and applies it to a relatively simple mind or mental event. Shrewd but simplistic Bob Jakin remarks, "I think my head's all alive inside like an old cheese, for I'm so full o' plans, one knocks another over" (276). When Maggie and her brother are children, their minds can be "quite filled for the moment with the words 'beggar' and 'workhouse'" (178). These brief echoes of the mind-as-entity metaphor scarcely count in view of how Eliot elsewhere describes the development of young minds. Of "keen moments" she observes that each has left a "trace" in the individual, "but such traces have blent themselves irrecoverably with the firmer texture of our youth and manhood" (57). Again, an item from the past is to be cherished as "the long companion of my existence, that wove itself into my joys when joys were vivid" (134).

What these early experiences contribute to our texture, however, is not the whole story. There is also the long-term pressure of a textured psychological environment. Eliot explains how this pressure operates in describing the limited religious and intellectual life of the people in St. Ogg's, especially the Dodsons and the Tullivers, and the impact of that life on Tom and Maggie:

> I share with you this sense of oppressive narrowness; but it is necessary that we should feel it, if we care to understand how it acted on the lives of Tom and Maggie—how it has acted on young natures in many generations, that in the onward tendency of human things have risen above the mental level of the generation before them, to which they have been nevertheless tied by the strongest fibres of their hearts. . . . In natural science, I have understood, there is nothing petty to the mind that has a large vision of relations, and to which every single object suggests a vast sum of conditions. It is surely the same with the observation of human life. [238]

This passage may be compared to Reid's description of the problem of knowing our minds from their first awakening:

> If the original perceptions and motions of the mind were to make their appearance single and unmixed, as we first received them from the hand of nature, one accustomed to reflection would have less difficulty in tracing them; but before we are capable of reflection, they are so mixed, compounded and decompounded by habits, associations, and abstractions, that it is hard to know what they were originally. [*Inquiry* 7]

The two passages differ strikingly in the approach and in the metaphors they imply. Reid insists on introspection while Eliot scrutinizes the external context; Reid's metaphor of mind-as-entity leads him to concentrate on the contents of the mind in spite of their mixed state, while Eliot's metaphor of the web of sentience leads her to speak of "the fibres of their hearts" and to view mental life as a living tapestry into which sensations weave themselves.

As a student of human life, Eliot sets as her goal the tracing of the relations, the calculating of the vast sum of conditions. In conveying her results, she is well served by the image complex of webs, fibers, and vibrations, just as the concept of the sentient web serves her well in exploring the mental territory of Tom and

Maggie, territory so well known and yet so unknown. Tom's is the less interesting study, because for him "mere perception predominates over thought and emotion" (145); he suffers from a "congenital deficiency," having been "born with a deficient power of apprehending signs and abstractions" (148). Tom and his father are of a piece: "it's puzzling work, talking is" observes the elder Tulliver (10). Tom's mind seems not to vibrate at all; his father's apparently vibrates only to one note, the thought of his mortal enemy, Wakem.

Maggie, on the other hand, is continually sensing vibrations from the external world, and this makes her seem more alive than her father and brother. Eliot closely examines the interaction in Maggie between a physical state or change of state and a mental state, as these two examples show: "But they had reached the end of the conservatory and were obliged to pause and turn. The change of movement brought a new consciousness to Maggie" (387-88). Maggie "moved her arm from the table, urged to change her position by that positive physical oppression at the heart that sometimes accompanies a sudden mental pang" (363). In such passages, Chase sees Eliot providing "the mechanical equivalent of consciousness" (161), but in fact they show a much more subtle interaction between strictly physical and mental events. Maggie is susceptible to Stephen Guest because he can set her vibrating with his voice, his look, or even his mere presence in the same room. It is when describing the meetings of Stephen and Maggie that Eliot portrays most vividly the moment-by-moment impact of specific events on sentient awareness and the continuing modification of that awareness by events. These meetings are rich in moral and emotional complexities. Stephen is engaged to Maggie's cousin, whom Maggie loves, and Maggie feels that if she is to marry anyone it must be Philip Wakem, who was so much a part of her earlier life. Maggie insists to Stephen that "the real tie lies in the feelings and expectations we have raised in other minds" (394). It does sometimes seem to her "right" to follow her strongest feelings, "but then, such feelings continually come across the ties that all our former life has made for us—the ties that have made others dependent on us—and would cut them in two" (395). Eliot's references to Maggie's sensation of "beating at head and heart" and her "slight start such as might have come from the slightest possible electric shock" (392) may seem strictly within the limits of the mind-as-entity concept. But these metaphorical vehicles are transformed by their context, the metaphor of "ties" (elsewhere "fibres") lying in one direction and feelings trying to cross against the grain of this felt mental structure. They contribute to the overall presentation of sentient life rather than representing a primarily passive, impressible mental entity.

Eliot uses the image of vibration to describe Maggie when she feels most alive, and she uses this figure in a significantly new way. For Maggie, to vibrate is to live; her "mind glanced back once or twice to the time when she had courted privation. . . . [but] The music was vibrating in her still . . . and she could not stay in the recollection of that bare, lonely past" (338). One of the sentences most revealing of the connection of life and vibrations is the following, when Maggie has been dancing and is still excited: "Life at this moment seemed a keen vibrating consciousness poised above pleasure or pain" (387). Equating life with a keen vibrating consciousness evokes some of the key principles of Eliot's psychologist contemporaries, especially Bain's Law of Relativity. In *Mind and Body* Bain writes that the state of unconsciousness may be accounted for by supposing either that "the nervous mass as a whole is quiescent" or that "currents are still kept up, but at an even, settled, unaltering pace" (48-49). He suggests that the second is more likely in view of such analogous observations as the slight degree of muscular tension that is present even during sleep and in view of our experience of "the really fitful nature of the mind; the stream of consciousness is a series of ebullitions rather than a calm or steady flow" (40). Thus "when all the currents of the brain are equally balanced, and continue at the same pitch—when no one is commencing, increasing or abating—consciousness or feeling is null, mind is quiescent" (50). But Eliot does not just borrow from Bain; she uses this image of a poised and vibrating consciousness to bring his formulation into greater coherence with subjective experience.

Bain and others insisted that the essential characteristic of consciousness was movement plus change of state. This subjective reality, as explained by the psychologists, corresponds with the physiological reality of constant neurological activity: in Bain's words, "no currents, no mind." The problem is that introspection sometimes reveals exactly what Maggie feels—a lively yet motionless state. Eliot's "vibrating consciousness" accommodates the psychologists' insistence on movement while allowing the mental state to remain unchanged. The metaphor provides a vivid, compact, and expressive representation that combines psychological and physiological perspectives. The psychologists tend to calculate the amount of mental life at a given moment by the quantity of nervous flux, thus implying large changes in short periods of time. A vibrating consciousness exists from the subjective perspective in a single state full of life, although at the level of the nerve fibers there may well be vibrations. (That is, neural physiology of Eliot's time could admit them.)

One more important point must be made about these vibrations in light of Eliot's moral endeavor. As Maggie has told Stephen, the various channels of a mind do not all run in the same direction; hence feelings running in one way may cut another feeling in two. The vibrations do constitute a flow of feeling, which is potentially destructive. Chase points out that Eliot makes no easy equation between a given mental metaphor and a moral value; currents can both flow and flood, and structures can both channel and constrain (176-80). Each current in a character's psychic life must be evaluated by its effect on the character's internal and social lives. To Maggie, life "*seemed* a keen vibrating consciousness," and perhaps it was at that moment, but Eliot's point is that life is always much more than what one moment represents. In fact *states* of mind must be transient, but the main currents will always be present. Eliot makes this clear in her description of Maggie at the charity bazaar. Before this event Maggie was pleased by her appearance and indulged her vain feelings, but then Stephen and Philip argue, with her as the covert cause, and her triumph is spoiled. Eliot remarks: "If that state of mind [vanity, sense of supremacy] could have lasted, her choice would have been to have Stephen Guest at her feet. . . . But there were things in her stronger than vanity—passion, and affection, and long deep memories of early discipline and effort . . . and the stream of vanity was soon swept along and mingled imperceptibly with that wider current which was at its highest force today" (383). In this description Eliot gives fictional voice to Bain's suggestion that currents are always flowing, even in the quiescent mind. Maggie remains a moral being because her particular currents are moral and are stronger than the ebullitions; their moral value is further enhanced when they figuratively conjoin with the flood at the novel's end. For Bain neither type of current, steady or excited, is intrinsically more worthwhile, but for Eliot the two metaphors of streams and vibrations carry an inescapable valuation.

In *Middlemarch* Eliot attends even more to the lives of various minds as these lives are linked by an extremely fine web of relations and shaped by gentle (but nearly irresistible) pressures over long periods of time. The vibrations of *Mill* have almost disappeared from the psychological picture. The web metaphor is most explicitly articulated in parallel with Lydgate's research. He is portrayed as desiring to build on the work of Bichat, who "first carried out the conception that living bodies . . . must be regarded as certain primary webs or tissues, out of which the various organs" are constructed; it is fallacious to attempt to study living bodies as confederations of independent organs (101). Lydgate's method is not entirely sound: in seeking the "primitive tissue" he is like Casaubon seeking "the key to all mythologies." The two are "emblematic of the materialist and idealist positions pushed to their extreme," and each position is flawed by seeking "to become unitary" (Carroll 74). Both go against the precept of Spencer and others that it is impossible to get at what mind or life "really is" by identifying the stuff out of which it is made. Lydgate desires to "demonstrate the more intimate relations of living structure, and help to define men's thoughts more accurately after the true order"—a worthy goal, but as Eliot points out, his way of putting the question, his quest for the primitive tissue, is not "the way required by the awaiting answer" (102). There is no question that Lydgate is capable of exercising the same "idealizing imagination of the invisible" valued so highly by Eliot and Lewes (Putzell-Korab 17). He desires to approach physiological questions

> with the imagination that reveals subtle actions inaccessible by any sort of lens, but tracked in that outer darkness through long pathways of necessary sequence by the inward light which is the last refinement of Energy, capable of bathing even the ethereal atoms in its ideally illuminated space. He for his part had tossed away all cheap inventions where ignorance finds itself able and at ease: he was enamoured of that arduous invention which is the very eye of research, provisionally framing its object and correcting it to more and more exactness of relation; he wanted to pierce the obscurity of those minute processes which prepare human misery and joy, those invisible thoroughfares which are the first lurking-places of anguish, mania, and crime, that delicate poise and transition which determine the growth of happy or unhappy consciousness. [113]

But a criticism is implicit in the last few lines of this passage: the lurking-places, the poise and transition, do not totally define the individual. No matter how precisely the subtle actions are understood in themselves, they still must be seen in the whole environmental context. Lydgate would have better served his science by studying the tissues in relation to the external environment rather than searching for the "common basis from which they all started." Eliot follows her own implicit advice. She does not search for the starting points, although she mentions them when she finds them; she pays more attention to the threadlike pressures of society and each individual's personal history. She demonstrates what Vicar Farebrother tells Dorothea: "Character is not something solid and unalterable. It is something living and changing, and may become diseased as our bodies do" (507).

As in *Mill on the Floss*, Eliot uses the mind-as-entity metaphor to describe the minds of her lesser figures. Mr. Brooke, for instance, is not intended to be complex. He functions in the story as a rather comic spokesperson for the safe opinions of landed gentry. When campaigning, he must have his mind managed like a warehouse: "The only way in which Mr. Brooke could be coerced into thinking of the right arguments at the right time was to be well plied with them till they took up all the room in his brain. But here there was the difficulty of finding room, so many things having been taken in beforehand. Mr. Brooke himself observed that his ideas stood rather in his way when he was speaking" (348). Casaubon is described in a similar way: his soul "was too languid to thrill out of self-consciousness into passionate delight . . . [his] was that proud narrow sensitiveness which has not mass enough to spare for transformation into sympathy, and quivers thread-like in small currents of self-preoccupation" (193). Brooke could easily have occurred in a Dickens novel; the description of his brain is similar to the description of Bradley Headstone of *Our Mutual Friend*, who "had made of his mind a place of mechanical stowage" (266). Casaubon's mind is more like the minds implicit in Mill's mental chemistry and mental physics, but it is still very much an entity that can be separated from the individual and described in metaphorical language closely akin to that of the eighteenth century. The organic metaphor is evoked by "quivers thread-like" and the physical one by "has not mass enough".

But the major characters' minds are shown in sensitive response to external pressures or rebellion against them, and all achieve a greater conscious awareness of some part of life as a result of this activity of the entire sentient organism.

In Dorothea's case, new understanding comes when her dominant mental current combines with the pressure of certain new experiences as they sink into and become part of her memory. The narrator notes, "In Dorothea's mind there was a current into which all thought and feeling were apt sooner or later to flow—the reaching forward of the whole consciousness towards the fullest truth, the least partial good" (141). This is Dorothea's tendency even as a young woman. It accounts for her initial attraction to Mr. Casaubon: "All Dorothea's passion was transfused through a mind struggling towards an ideal life; the radiance of her transfigured girlhood fell on the first object that came within its level," the dried-out scholar Casaubon (28). But this flow or transfusion is not all-powerful, because her mind can take in new experiences that come to exert a significant pressure. One such experience is her Roman honeymoon with her husband. "The weight of unintelligible Rome" makes a deep impression on Dorothea, not least because she sees in Rome an analogy to her own situation, a confused mixture of what is "living and warm-blooded" with what is superstitious and degenerate, the sum being a "vast wreck of ambitious ideals." These perceptions "first jarred [Dorothea] as with an electric shock, and then urged themselves on her with that ache belonging to a glut of confused ideas which check the flow of emotion. Forms both pale and glowing took possession of her young sense, and fixed themselves in her memory even when she was not thinking of them, preparing strange associations which remained through her after-years. . . . in certain states of dull forlornness Dorothea all her life continued to see the vastness of Saint Peter's . . . and the red drapery which was being hung for Christmas spreading everywhere like a disease of the retina" (135).

Mind-as-entity elements are present in the images of ideas blocking a flow of emotion and of forms fixing themselves in her memory. But each of these images is also related to immediate and long-term mental processes that cannot be accounted for by an associational interpretation like those common in earlier psychological works. While the associations remain in Dorothea's mind, they are evoked not by a specific impression but by "certain states." Moreover, the original associations have affected Dorothea at other than a conscious level; they cause in her a psycho-physical ache but otherwise almost surreptitiously make their way into the memory. Insofar as this can be considered an associational process, it is of the highly modified sort described by Lewes which involves states of the whole organism. To describe these processes Lewes relies on terms such as "the ground tone of feeling" and "silent processes of growth in the soul which make up what is called the Character" ("Mind as a Function of the Organism" 136). Eliot's figurative language, with its forms and lingering visions of the mind's eye, is just as compact but more vivid and expressive.

Eliot goes on to explore more carefully the reasons for Dorothea's present forlorn state and its ramifications. The truism is that "the light had changed, and you cannot find the pearly dawn at noonday": exchanging the state of courtship for the state of marriage necessarily changes the appearance of the partner (135). Dorothea only imperfectly perceives the reality beneath the truism: "that new real future which was replacing the imaginary drew its material from the endless minutiae by which her view of Mr. Casaubon and her wifely relation, now that she was married to him, was gradually changing with the secret motion of a watch-hand from what it had been in her maiden dream" (135). The endless minutiae can scarcely be perceived but can be inferred from the reaction they induce; Dorothea is finding herself "a mere victim of feeling, as if she could know nothing except through that medium: all her strength was scattered in fits of agitation, of struggle, of despondency" (138). Eliot's method here is inseparable from her metaphor of webs of sentience: she assumes a cause for every event, but the cause in most average, normal lives is not a single dramatic event but "thread-like" pressures in minute quantities operating over a long time.

When dramatic events come, they still do so in a context of memories and social pressures. One such event is Dorothea's realizing that "it was really herself whom Will loved and was renouncing" (438). The immediate realization is triggered by his final words before he leaves the room, and it is represented metaphorically and also syntactically as a disconnected instant: "It was all one flash to Dorothea—his last words—his distant bow to her as he reached the door—the sense that he was no longer there" (438). However, her subjective experience of a flash is led up to by Will's words and her concurrent thoughts. Will feels unable to tell this widow outright that he loves her, and as he talks to her of being forbidden what he cares for most in the world, she must determine whom he is referring to—her or Rosamond: "The thought that she herself might be what Will most cared for did throb through her an instant, but then came doubt" (437). The doubt quickly transforms itself into "images . . . referring to" Rosamond. This is the context in which she achieves her moment of insight. Nor does Eliot conclude the scene with this moment; she goes on to trace Dorothea's subsequent feelings. There is first the "sense of loving and being loved," which to Dorothea "was as if some hard icy pressure had melted, and her consciousness had room to expand: her past was come back to her with larger interpretation" (438). Yet gradually her awareness of "the world" returns and weighs on her "heavily," because the world—her family—would not approve of any connection with Will. Eliot's message and method are clear: there are no *isolated* flashes in the world of Middlemarch.

With the minds of Lydgate and Bulstrode, Eliot has excellent material for presenting the web-like nature of psychological events. In the case of Lydgate the most important events happen after he arrives in Middlemarch: he meets Rosamond Vincy and finds in Dorothea the woman who probably would have been his ideal companion. His marriage to Rosamond is a mistake that works in him "like a recognised chronic disease mingling its uneasy importunities with every prospect, and enfeebling every thought" (408). It affects the life of his mind exactly as a physical disease affects the body, interfering with ordinary perceptual and intellectual processes. As he watches Rosamond prepare his tea and thinks about trying to discuss with her their financial troubles, his mind wanders to thoughts of Dorothea: "These revived impressions succeeded each other quickly and dreamily in Lydgate's mind while the tea was being brewed. He had shut his eyes in the last instant of reverie. . . . [Dorothea's] voice of deep-souled womanhood had remained within him as the enkindling conceptions of dead and sceptered genius had remained within him . . . the tones were a music from which he was falling away—he had really fallen into a momentary doze, when Rosamond said in her silvery neutral way, 'Here is your tea, Tertius'" (409). This brief moment of awareness is one of Eliot's best psychological touches, showing her conception of the past weaving itself into present awareness.

Eliot continues in this vein as she describes how Lydgate feels presenting their unpleasant financial situation to his wife: "Some of the angry desire to rouse her into more sensibility on his account which had prompted him to speak prematurely, still mingled with his pain in the prospect of her pain" (409-10). Her beauty "touched Lydgate now, and mingled the early moments of his love for her with all the other memories which were stirred in this crisis of deep trouble" (410). Again, the *mingling* is the immediate manifestation of the web of sentience; the verb suggests not only the conscious thoughts but also the half-remembered emotions and unverbalized desires at work in Lydgate. One of Eliot's points about this young doctor is that he is not as wise or experienced as he would like to think and definitely does not understand Rosamond well enough to know how she will respond: "Perhaps it was not possible for Lydgate, under the double stress of outward material difficulty and of his own proud resistance to humiliating consequences, to imagine fully what this sudden trial was to a young creature who had known nothing but indulgence, and whose dreams had all been of new indulgence, more exactly to her taste" (411).

For Bulstrode, the threadlike pressures extend far into the past and consist of not-quite-repressed guilt. Bulstrode has lived long enough in Middlemarch to seem in the town's eyes a person whose life began with his arrival there. But the earlier years have had their continuing effect, just like Lydgate's chronic disease of the mind. This point is made when Bulstrode's history is revealed, as he reflects back over his life and his early struggle to reconcile his pious inclinations with the opportunity to get rich through increasingly unsavory means: "Mentally surrounded with that past again, Bulstrode had the same pleas—indeed, the years had been perpetually spinning them into intricate thickness, like masses of spider web, padding the moral sensibility" (426). He experiences once again the "bare fact," the great lie of his earlier life that enabled him to realize his money lust. He sees that "bare fact" as it would look to outsiders, as it looked to him at the time, and as it still looks, "broken into little sequences, each justified as it came by reasonings which seemed to prove it righteous." Bulstrode's overall self-justification, as Eliot's language demonstrates, has been a matter of innumerable steps, so many that "his soul had become saturated with the belief that he did everything for God's sake" (426). He has kept his conscience in check with "mental exercises" and has made his immoral acts lie "benumbed in the consciousness" for nearly thirty years (428). Yet these acts have never been wiped away. When Raffles, his former accomplice, appears, the past awakens and floods his mind "as if with the terrible irruption of a new sense overburthening the feeble being" (427).

Eliot goes beyond the writers of the eighteenth century and their dependance on mind-as-entity as a theory-constitutive metaphor in three ways. She gives explicit attention to the psychological states resulting from the pressures of the past; she purposefully takes account of the full subjective history of a character in understanding the character's present psychological state; she uses descriptions that stress texture and connectedness. *Middlemarch* is not a Dickens novel in which the mind is a piece of soft clay whose shape can be totally changed or a Brontë novel in which the mind exists separately from the self. When Bulstrode reflects, *he* is "mentally surrounded" by the past. Bulstrode is one more example of a theme that Eliot announced as early as her first novel, *Adam Bede*: "Our deeds determine us, as much as we determine our deeds" (359). Thus when Bulstrode's carefully constructed outer life falls apart, he remains the same individual and cannot change in such fundamental aspects as the pattern of his thoughts. The old justifications still come to him as if they have been drilled in by mental exercises, and his tendency to secrecy remains as strong as before. He longs to confess to his wife the full extent of his misdeeds, so that she will not again be as shocked as when she learned that he was implicated in the death of Raffles. The narrator notes that he may do this yet, "but concealment had been the habit of his life, and the impulse to confession had no power against the dread of a deeper humiliation," that his wife would "recoil" in disgust at the new confession (568).

Eliot has left behind the atomistic mental analyses generated by the mind-as-entity metaphor, in which long-range effects were represented, if at all, as the growth of seeds planted in the mind. For Eliot, any early event must have an impact on the whole mind, although the impact might not be available to consciousness until much later. She has also gone beyond the tendency of earlier writers to regard development of a mind as either an isolated growth or a shaping by external forces. At the very end of *Middlemarch* it is remarked of Dorothea that the "determining acts of her life were not ideally beautiful. They were the mixed result of young and noble impulse struggling amidst the conditions of an imperfect social state . . . For there is no creature whose inward being is so strong that it is not greatly determined by what lies outside it" (577).

Eliot's metaphor of the sentient web leads her to attend consistently to threadlike pressures. This attention is a crucial element of her optimism, for a character can generate as well as receive such pressures. Throughout her life Dorothea's "finely-touched spirit still had its fine issues . . . the effect of her being on those around her was incalculably diffusive." George Levine rightly insists that such statements mark Eliot as both deterministic and optimistic: a character "can, in some limited degree, move counter to the push of external circumstance, and, by allowing himself to become aware of his own motives, can even at times overcome them by changing them" (357).

In *Daniel Deronda* Eliot places the sentient-web metaphor in a somewhat new context: the growth of consciousness. More than in *Mill on the Floss* and *Middlemarch* she attends to what individuals *know* and *do* consciously and how these actions and choices in turn reflect back on and change the individuals. By no means does she ignore the other-than-conscious levels of sentient experience, but her interest is now much more directed to how characters make informed ethical choices rather than how they are driven by un-cognized experiences to ethical or unethical acts. She uses the metaphors to texture the life of the consciousness *in* society (ideas and awareness extend outward to other minds) and *through* time. For such an endeavor, generalizations are not very useful. To try to explain a psycho-physical phenomenon with terms such as "sensitiveness" and "excitable nature" will be fruitless without "an extensive knowledge of differences" among various cases (*Deronda* 57). No longer is it regarded as valid to assume a straightforward continuity or point-for-point correspondence between some impression and some idea or action. The possible outcomes are too numerous because the pressures on any organism come from every other organism in relation. Thus predicting behavior is nearly impossible, even when some "general certainties" are available: "Of what use, however, is a general certainty that an insect will not walk with his head hindmost, when what you need to know is the play of inward stimulus that sends him hither and thither in a network of possible paths?" (261). Without a complete history of the individual mind, especially its unique features, the general principles are nearly worthless. "There is a great deal of unmapped country within us which would have to be taken into account in an explanation of our gusts and storms," she observes (257). There is no doubt, however, that if the inner country could be mapped, the map would be helpful, and if one could know the history of a mind or of a consciousness, one would know how it might be likely to behave.

The psychological interest is much more overt in *Daniel Deronda* than in the earlier novels. No subtitle like *Middlemarch*'s "A Study of Provincial Life" would be possible here, unless "life" were replaced by "life of the mind." One very obvious signal of this interest is the explicitly psychological nature of some of the chapter epigraphs, such as this, to chapter 25: "How trace the why and wherefore in a mind reduced to the barrenness of a fastidious egoism, in which all direct desires are dulled, and have dwindled from motives into a vacillating expectation of motives: a mind made up of moods, where a fitful impulse springs here and there conspicuously rank among the general weediness? 'Tis a condition apt to befall a life too much at large, unmoulded by the pressure of obligation. . . . *'As you like' is a bad finger-post*" (258). This chapter concentrates on Henleigh Grandcourt, who lives strictly to please himself; part of his pleasure includes making others suffer. His is not the vibrating life of Maggie Tulliver but a deadened and deadening vacillation. As the epigraph states in general and as many of the chapters dramatize, where there are no connecting fibers to other lives and where there is no sense of obligations resulting from expectations aroused in others, the mental life must be barren and the mind itself shapeless. Elsewhere it is noted of Grandcourt that his sudden impulses "have a false air of daemonic strength because they seem inexplicable, though perhaps their secret lies merely in the want of regulated channels for the soul to move in—good and sufficient ducts of habit without which our nature easily turns to mere ooze and mud, and at any pressure yields nothing but a spurt or a puddle" (141).

Grandcourt provides a standard against which to measure the mental and moral development of Gwendolen Harleth, as she grows very slowly throughout the novel from a young woman whose guiding principle is "as you like" into one who acknowledges "the pressure of obligation" and is able to develop "ducts of habit" to better control her mind. Early in the novel the narrator asks, "Could there be a slenderer, more insignificant thread in human history than this consciousness of a girl, busy with her small inferences of the way in which she could make her life pleasant?—in a time, too, when ideas were with fresh vigour making armies of themselves" (109). As a thread in the total fabric of human existence this particular consciousness is insignificant, but as Eliot has demonstrated in *Middlemarch* and has stated in *The Mill on the Floss,* "there is nothing petty to the mind that has a large vision of relations." Hers is such a mind.

In portraying the development of Gwendolen's mind, Eliot uses the full range of metaphors available, those drawing on mind-as-entity as well as those which she has created. The following examples illustrate this range:

Every word that Klesmer had said seemed to have been branded into her memory, as most words are which bring with them a new set of impressions and make an epoch for us. [243]

In the dark seed-growths of consciousness a new wish was forming itself. [271]

As always happens with a deep interest, the comparatively rare occasions on which she could exchange any words with Deronda had a diffusive effect in her consciousness, magnifying their communication with each other, and therefore enlarging the place she imagined it to have in his mind. [545]

The first example effectively conveys the experience of a single moment or event being marked as significant because of its intensity, but the phrase "set of impressions" shows Eliot's insistence on multiple pressures and threads. The second example demonstrates the occasional sensation of ideas having a life of their own from their first inception. This idea of Gwendolen's has a close family resemblance to the ideas flying around in the brain of Caleb Williams, but it differs in being explicitly related to Gwendolen's consciousness: it will sooner or later manifest itself fully in her conscious awareness. Had Eliot written something as simple as "Gwendolen began to be aware of a vague wish . . ." she would have failed to convey the subtle sense that we do occasionally become fully aware of ideas whose existence we have sensed or intuited for some time previously, that is, ideas that have been part of our uncognised *sentient* experience. The third example conveys a similarly common experience: rarity and interest combine to give an idea a disproportionate place in our consciousness. The actual mental operation is similar to that of the second example in taking place below the level of conscious awareness, but it differs in that it seems to be governed by a mechanical rather than an organic law, the law of "diffusion." This word is an important part of the explanatory apparatus of Eliot's contemporaries, especially Bain. Diffusion as an image conveys on the one hand the relationship between the subjective substance or weight of an idea on the one hand and on the other the density of the associated neural connections in the brain as well as the density of the associations themselves.

These examples also comprise an interesting historical progression. The first evokes a Lockean metaphor; the second has more of an affinity with Reid's portrayal of mental growth; the third resembles the descriptions of neural activity and brain activity given by the psychologists contemporary with Eliot. This historical progression also corresponds to Gwendolen's developing maturity. In the first her mind is a mere passive recipient of impressions. In the second, her uncognized experience is nurturing a new idea, although there is a definite connection with consciousness. In the third, the phenomenon is strictly within Gwendolen's consciousness. The figurative passages thus provide a measure of her progress toward a state of active, involved life.

These metaphors, together with Gwendolen's selfishness and thoughtlessness, provide a fairly complete map of part of her mental territory. But there remains that unmapped country where her puzzling actions originate. This country Eliot does not try to explore; she simply presents the actions and notes the puzzles. The first such action is Gwendolen's fainting spell from a mental shock. Gwendolen "wondered at herself in these occasional experiences, which seemed like a brief remembered madness, an unexplained exception from her normal life" (56). These moments of terror Eliot characterizes as her "liability to fits of spiritual dread." More explicitly, "Solitude in any wide scene impressed her with an undefined feeling of immeasurable existence aloof from her, in the midst of which she was helplessly incapable of asserting herself" (57). The references to religious awe constitute no explanation, however, only a description; Jacob Korg is incorrect in saying that this and other "motivations" in Eliot's world are "clear and determinant" (87).

Calculating the sum represented by Gwendolen Harleth and thus explaining her behavior is made even less possible by her reactions to men. To her first suitor, she bursts out with a fierce "Pray don't make love to me! I hate it" (73). She has known that he loves her but has not foreseen such a reaction in herself; it is "all a sudden, new experience." Even stranger is what she tells her mother after the distraught young man leaves: "I can't love people. I hate them" (74). She experiences the same confusion, a bit less violently, when she recognizes that she does not know what will be her answer to Grandcourt's proposal: "This subjection to a possible self, a self not to be absolutely predicted about, caused her some astonishment and terror" (121).

The most dramatic of Gwendolen's outbreaks, however, is prepared for, with metaphorical language that helps explain the process. On her wedding day she feels a triumph and, beneath that, a "yeasty mingling of dimly understood facts with vague but deep impressions, and with images half real, half fantastic." These facts and impressions originate from her earlier meeting at the Whispering Stones with Lydia Glasher, Grandcourt's former mistress and the mother of four children by him. Hearing Lydia's story, Gwendolen feels "a sort of terror . . . as if some ghostly vision had come to her in a dream and said, 'I am a woman's life'" (137). Gwendolen at once determines she cannot have anything more to do with Grandcourt, but when her family loses their small fortune and she sees poverty for all and life as a governess for herself, she changes her mind. "Everything is to be as I like," she tells her mother (282). But inevitably any yeasty mixture will continue to work somewhere in the mind. Thus when the newlyweds travel to Grandcourt's other estate and Gwendolen receives not only the family diamonds but also a verbally poisoned letter from Lydia, she begins to realize the extent of what she has done in marrying him, the total impossibility of her now living the life she had desired. When Grandcourt enters the room after she has read the letter, the yeasty mixture finally comes to a head: "The sight of him brought a new nervous shock, and Gwendolen screamed again and again with hysterical violence" (331).

Gwendolen is probably the first respectable woman in English-language fiction to be described as reacting in this way to her husband, but because of the metaphorical preparation for the scene, her reaction can be understood. The hysteria is a surprise to Grandcourt, who sees only her surface, but it is no surprise to the reader, who has been made privy to her inner state, to the turmoil in her consciousness. Gwendolen had been able to repress the effect of the interview with Lydia Glasher—indeed, she had to do this before she could accept Grandcourt's proposal—but these written words "hung on her consciousness with the weight of a prophetic doom. . . . [They] stirred continually the vision of the scene at the Whispering Stones. That scene was now like an accusing apparition" (395). The immediate result of this experience is that Gwendolen becomes "conscious of an uneasy, transforming process—all the old nature shaken to its depths, its hopes spoiled, its pleasures perturbed, but still showing wholeness and strength in the will to reassert itself" (394). She has lost the trait that was once most notable in her, "the belief in her own power of dominating"; the narrator links this loss to the already displayed "large discourse of imaginative fears" which Grandcourt has taken advantage of. Together, the images Eliot creates show not the primitive tissue of Gwendolen's mind but enough close analysis of her experiences to make her comprehensible. What caused those irrational reactions in her is less important than the changes that begin in her as a result of her marriage and her dependence on Daniel Deronda. Thus near the end of the novel she is "for the first time being dislodged from her supremacy in her own world, and getting a sense that her horizon was but a dipping onward of an existence with which her own was revolving" (748).

In building up the history and texture of Gwendolen's consciousness, the repetition, development, and overall consistency of Eliot's images are as important as the actual language. She presents the development of Deronda's consciousness in the same way, by identifying some guiding feelings and traits and showing how these interact with new experiences to produce new awareness, sometimes beginning at the pre-conscious level but always developing into consciousness. One of the major aspects of Deronda's character is his concern to know his parentage, which Eliot spends all of chapter 16 developing. While Daniel may have considered the question before in a passing way, it became central in his consciousness when he learned learned from his tutor why Roman Catholic prelates are always spoken of as having so many "nephews." He immediately made the connection with his own state as the supposed nephew of his guardian, Sir Hugo, and the result was, "A new idea had entered his mind, and was beginning to change the aspect of his habitual feelings." It was only at this moment that "there had darted into his mind with the magic of quick comparison, the possibility that here was the secret of his own birth," that Sir Hugo was really his father.

The immediate result of this idea was "a new sense in relation to all the elements of his life." A longer-term result was a sensitivity to the possibility that others knew things about him that he did not, a sensitivity that "set up in him a pre-mature reserve which helped to intensify his inward experience." After that day there existed in him "a newly-roused set of feelings" that were "ready to cluster themselves" around any incident that his "imagination could connect with his suspicions" (153). This is like the image used to describe Gwendolen's consciousness—a "set of impressions" and a "diffusive effect in her consciousness." Deronda's new feelings exist as a set and can cluster themselves around incidents. Already early in the novel Deronda is highly developed in this way. As a student he did not pursue a standard course at the university because he could not consent to the "demand for excessive retention and dexterity without any insight into the principles which form the vital connections of knowledge" (164). Rather, he feels that he has to maintain his connections with the whole large web. The same is true about his hesitancy in choosing a career: because he senses "wide-sweeping connections with all life and history," he feels he should not "draw strongly at any thread in the hopelessly-entangled scheme of things" (172). As the novel develops, the wisdom of these choices becomes clear. He finds his true connections first in a spiritual kinship with the Jewish people and then in an actual kinship when he learns that he was born a Jew.

Daniel's life is an embodiment of Bain's statement that "the sum of all consciousnesses is the sum of all existences" (*Mental Science,* appendix 93). The life of an individual mind is its consciousness, and its consciousness is to be understood in the context of the overall web of human existence. *Daniel Deronda* is Eliot's fullest portrayal of the development of the contents of consciousness and its operations, the most complete working out of her generative metaphor of the sentient web.

VII
AFTERWORD: WILLIAM JAMES' LANGUAGE OF THE MIND

Describing the principle of association in chapter 14 of his *Principles of Psychology* (1890), William James attributes to Locke and Descartes the correlation between the "psychological law of association" and the "physical fact that nerve-currents propagate themselves easiest through those tracts of conduction which have been already most in use" (531). James continues with a quotation from the *Essay*, into which he inserts a revealing comment: "'Custom,'" says Locke, "'settles habits of thinking in the understanding, as well as of determining in the will, and of motions in the body; all which seem to be but *trains of motion in the animal spirits* [by this Locke meant identically what we understand by *neural processes*], which, once set a-going, continue in the same shape they have been used to, which, by often treading, are worn into a smooth path, and the motion in it becomes easy, and as it were natural'" (531). This tip of the hat from one great student of psychology to another across almost exactly two centuries provides a fitting point of departure for a concluding meditation on metaphors of mind. In these few pages I will not attempt anything like a substantial analysis of William James' work. Rather, I will sketch out the hypothesis that mind-as-a-living-being functions for James as a generative metaphor and is manifested in the surface metaphor stream-of-consciousness. I will begin by showing that James' phrase "neural processes," interpolated into the quotation from Locke, does not "mean" the same thing as "trains of motion in the animal spirits": the two phrases are surrounded by entirely different contexts of relations and are put to different uses within the theories of mind of the two writers.

In the section James quotes from, Locke goes on to say that while the "natural cause" of ideas is probably "animal spirits," he will not try to determine if that is the cause in fact—he wants rather to use the hypothesis as a help toward conceiving of "Intellectual Habits, and of the tying together of *Ideas*" (Locke 396). For this purpose the more important component of the phrase is "trains of motion," which renders in an accessible way how the ideas are drawn together. "Trains of motion" is fundamental to Locke's descriptive and explanatory enterprise. It draws on the mind-as-entity metaphor by implying a mind made of material substance and occupying definite space, and it suits the concept of ideas as corpuscular, able to be tied together. The mind-as-entity metaphor provides the context of relations for the phrase, and the phrase itself functions in Locke's theory as the metaphorical embodiment of what would otherwise remain a vague abstraction.

As I have shown, mind-as-entity serves a theory-constitutive function in the language of the psychologists of the eighteenth century. The *meaning* of "trains of motion in the animal spirits" is the use to which Locke puts the phrase and the context of relations in which it exists—its rhetorical and explanatory functions in his psychology. By these criteria, which James himself would have to approve as eminently pragmatic, the meaning of the phrase is coextensive with the core of Locke's theory of the formation of ideas. "Trains of motion" is the surface manifestation of the mind-as-entity metaphor that *constitutes* Locke's theory. In James' *Principles*, two phrases are likely candidates for carrying this kind of meaning, this set of functions and relations: "neural processes" and "stream of consciousness." The two fit together in a complementary way: fundamental to neural processes is the flux of nerve current, what Bain called "ebullitions," and this physical stream has as its subjectively experienced, psychological counterpart the flow of thoughts and sensations.

This complementarity, however, will only gradually become apparent to a reader. The impression conveyed by the early pages of *Principles* is that James is not departing very far from earlier nineteenth-century psychological tenets and approaches. His opening sentence, "Psychology is the Science of Mental Life, both of its phenomena and of their conditions" (15), does sound several new notes. These include the unapologetic use of the term "psychology" rather than "mental science," and the assertion that the conditions of mental life can be studied scientifically. But for some pages thereafter he uses language reminiscent of the mind-as-entity orientation. The following three passages are typical:

> Phenomena have absolutely no power to influence our ideas until they have first impressed our senses and our brain. [17]

> Our first conclusion, then, is that a certain amount of brain-physiology must be presupposed or included in Psychology. [18]

> On the whole, few recent formulations have done more real service of a rough sort in psychology that the Spencerian one that the essence of mental life and of bodily life are one, namely, "the adjustment of inner to outer relations." [19]

These passages show the mind as impressible by the external world. The impressing operation can be approached through brain-physiology, which registers the adjustment *of* inner *to* outer relations. When James introduces the concept of the active nature of mind, he makes an evolutionist point: "*The pursuance of future ends and the choice of means for their attainment are thus the mark and criterion of the presence of mentality* in a phenomenon" (21). This statement is phrased in such an abstract way that a reader could be excused for regarding it as emanating from the same materialistic perspective responsible for the mind-as-entity metaphor.

After his introductory chapter describing the scope of psychology, James turns to the functions of the brain; this organization recalls the texts of Bain, Morell, and others. Applying the latest advances in "brain physiology," he uses diagrams and analogies to explain the "Meynert scheme": "the whole general notion that the hemispheres are a supernumerary surface for the projection and association of sensations and movements natively coupled in the centres below" (38 n.4). This "scheme," which regards the process of projection and association as "like the great commutating switch-board at a central telephone station" (38), James considers substantially correct, although, as he will show, it "makes the lower centres too machine-like and the hemispheres not quite machine-like enough" (39). His summary of the evidence pertinent to the Meynert scheme takes "currents" as the single most important term, and consciousness seems to come along as an afterthought both in the scheme and in James' description: a "'motor' centre" can be regarded as "only the mouth of the funnel, as it were, through which the stream of innervation, starting from elsewhere, pours; consciousness accompanying the stream" (73). Similarly, "the brain is essentially a place of currents, which run in organized paths" (78).

Habits, the topic of James' fourth chapter, are also to be understood in a materialistic way. Given the isolation of the hemispheres from the external world, they can be impressed only by the blood and by the nervous currents, and "the whole plasticity of the brain sums itself up in two words when we call it an organ in which currents pouring in from the sense-organs make with extreme facility paths which do not easily disappear" (112). "A path once traversed by a nerve-current," he continues, becomes "a natural drainage-channel" (113). The drainage-channel terminology recurs near the end of *Principles* when he considers why a nerve current takes the path it does the first time: "Each discharge from a sensory cell in the forward direction ["towards the motor cells"] tends to drain the cells lying behind the discharging one of whatever tension they may possess. The drainage from the rearward cells is what for the first time makes the fibres pervious. The result is a new-formed 'path'" (1186). These mechanical metaphors of currents and channels frame *Principles* and also provide a unifying thread.

Nevertheless, despite the prominence of "neural processes,"

there are several good reasons for not regarding the phrase as holding the same meaning relationship to *Principles* as "trains of motion in the animal spirits" holds with respect to Locke's *Essay*. The first is a fact that historians of psychology have long recognized: although James began his teaching career with a post in physiology, had a laboratory, and kept himself up to date on new developments in the area, he was by inclination more committed to introspection than to experimentation, more committed to analyzing the contents of the mind than the structure of the brain. Edmund Boring, for instance, sees James as an ancestor of both behaviorism and Gestalt psychology, but an ancestor because of his emphasis on cognition rather than his notable experimental insights (514-16). The second reason is more important, especially for a consideration of James' language of the mind: the fundamental step of his method was a "plunge into the 'stream of consciousness'" made at the very beginning of the inquiry (Peters 687). The phrase "stream of consciousness" of course does not surface in *Principles* until chapter 9, "The Stream of Thought." But it pre-dates the book by at least six years, James having used it in his 1884 article "On Some Omissions of Introspective Psychology." In this article the phrase is much more prominent than in chapter 9. It comes early (on page 2), is in the first sentence of a short paragraph, and leads into James' distinction between the two components of mental life, the "resting-places" and the "places of flight." The phrase may be regarded as the leading point of James' vigorous criticism of the associationist "demand for atoms of feeling," which he labels "an illegitimate metaphor" ("Omissions" 11).

The straightforward structuring function of "stream of consciousness" in the 1884 article becomes diffused in *Principles*, but it is still visible. In chapter 9 itself, the diffusing effect results partly from a two-fold increase in length, partly from some unhelpful diagrams, partly from a toning down of the criticisms, and partly from more space given to brain processes. But the important concept of "*psychic overtone, suffusion*, or *fringe*" still occupies an important place, and the references to the brain serve the analysis of the stream of consciousness, as here: "Our earlier chapters have taught us to believe that, whilst we think, our brain changes, and that, like the aurora borealis, its whole internal equilibrium shifts with every pulse of change. . . . Every brain-state is partly determined by the nature of this entire past succession. Alter the latter in any part, and the brain-state must be somewhat different. Each present brain-state is a record in which the eye of Omniscience might read all the foregone history of its owner" (*Principles* 228). Thus, James does not always place the physical before the psychological subject; sometimes the structure of his sentences and of his larger units of discourse shows the influence or impression moving in the other direction. By this reading, it is not correct to say that "James, the evolutionary naturalist, had to maintain that mental states grow out of physical states, in spite of whatever difficulties this view entails" (Earle 243).

The significance of "stream of consciousness" can also be seen in the beginnings of several chapters and in sentences that refer both to the stream and to nerve currents. Variations on the phrase bolster coherence at the beginnings of chapters by reminding the reader of what has been established previously before introducing something new. In chapter 10, on conception, the first paragraph concludes thus: "'*The same matters can be thought of in successive portions of the mental stream, and some of these portions can know that they mean the same matters which the other portions meant.*' One might put it otherwise by saying that '*the mind can always intend, and know when it intends, to think of the Same*'" (434). Rhetorically considered, the end of a first paragraph is one of the most important positions in a chapter or an essay; readers expect the note sounded there to continue throughout, and indeed James fulfills this expectation in the pages that follow.

The second paragraph of chapter 14, on association, begins, "The manner in which trains of imagery and consideration follow each other . . . the restless flight of one idea before the next . . . all this magical, imponderable streaming has from time immemorial excited the admiration of all whose attention happened to be caught by its omnipresent mystery" (519). By using or echoing "stream of consciousness" to weave new chapters into the text, James gains more than surface coherence. Each new beginning recurs to and evokes the governing conceptions of *Principles*, thus helping to carry a reader through the 1,280 pages. Each functions as a resting-place for the reader to become prepared for the conceptual flight to follow. The references to consciousness streaming implicitly remind us that the governing conceptions have to do with the *phenomena* and *conditions* of Mental Life.

Similarly, by linking references to stream of consciousness with references to neural processes, James gives to the former a more substantive role. I have already quoted his statement, "In the first place, the brain is essentially a place of currents, which run in organized paths" (78). One might reply to this that the brain is many more things than "essentially a place of currents." But the restricted, functional definition makes sense if James is being guided by a conception of the mind as first and foremost a stream of consciousness. If this is so, any description of the brain will have to suit that conception. The hypothesis that James is being guided in this way is supported by his discussion of the case of consciousness helping the "instable brain to compass its proper ends," that is, the case of consciousness intending a particular end: "The nerve-currents, coursing through the cells and fibres, must be supposed strengthened by the fact of their awaking one consciousness and dampened by awaking another" (144).

James was by no means the first psychologist to use the metaphor of a stream to illustrate some aspect of mental life. Bain refers to "the great complex currents of each one's individual existence"; each individual's current "embraces all our actions, all our sensations, emotions, volitions, in the order of their occurrence" (*Senses*, 3d ed., 450). Thomas Brown varied the metaphorical vehicle somewhat, reminding his audience in his nineteenth lecture, "The mind, in that central brain in which it is supposed to reside, communicating with all these extreme branches, has been compared, by a very obvious, but a very beautiful similitude, to the parent Ocean, receiving from innumerable distance the waters of its filial streams" (*Lectures* 185). As early as 1792, in the first volume of his *Elements*, Dugald Stewart wrote, "By means of the Association of Ideas, a constant current of thoughts, if I may use the expression, is made to pass through the mind while we are awake" (2:266). But the continuation of this passage shows that Stewart's conception of this stream was entirely different from James': "So completely, however, is the mind in this particular subjected to physical laws, that it has been justly observed, we cannot by an effort of our will call up any one thought, and that the train of our ideas depends on causes which operate in a manner inexplicable by us" (2:266).

These current and fluid metaphors share one key feature—they are all isolated occurrences, either isolated in the sense of being singular utterances (as in the Brown and Stewart examples) or isolated from the writer's psychological theory (Bain's currents remain essentially physiological). The examples from James, however, conform to the program made explicit in the opening sentence of *Principles* and to the metaphor underlying that sentence: mind-as-a-living-being. James' description of how consciousness controls the brain is especially suggestive in this regard; it implies a mind with the power and the will to make an impact on the physical world rather than an entity that simply has its seat in the skull. This metaphor, I suggest, though never enunciated as such by James, serves a generative function in his psychology. It suits his reaction against earlier atomistic psychology and his stress on the nature of cerebral life as a current (rather than on the equally plausible figure of a field, for example). It motivates his conception of the stream of consciousness as the most important element of mental life. Mind-as-a-living-being is the metaphor toward which Lewes may have been groping with his stress on sentience, the metaphor which could have vivified the mechanical stimulus and response models of Carpenter and Morell. In light of this metaphor, James' psychology may be read as fulfilling Reid's call for a science of the mind in the language of the mind. James demonstrates how the fundamental term of subjective mental life—*stream of consciousness*—can be translated into a term useful in understanding neural processes—*currents*—and thus how the insights from physiology can be brought into psychology without dominating.

One final piece of evidence in favor of reading *Principles* as generated by the mind-as-a-living-being metaphor is its relation to the novels I have discussed. All of them represent in figurative language the psychological manifestation of physiological phenomena and the physiological manifestation of psychological phenomena. The attention paid to this part of life becomes more pronounced in the later writers; they begin to show the mind less as a relatively passive, relatively malleable substance and more as a living, thinking, willing being. The following examples, discussed in earlier chapters, can speak for themselves as a condensed history of the shift in fiction to a new metaphor of mind:

1. These things oppressed my mind. [Defoe]
2. It would be impossible to say . . . which of all [Emma's] unpleasant sensations was uppermost. [Austen]
3. [M]y soul began to expand, to exult. [Brontë]
4. [For Strether, a day in Paris] had really been the process of feeling the stirred life of connections long since individually dropped. [Henry James]

This new metaphorical conception led to representations that more vividly and expressively reflected the increasing emphasis on subjective experiences of all kinds, especially the experience of sometimes seeming to have a whole world within our heads that operates by laws very different from those of the external physical world.

While the metaphor helped generate such verbal devices as the stream of consciousness, the mindscape, and the sentient web, it did not lead to a new governing psychological theory. As Allan Buss suggests, the history of psychology may make the most sense when seen as an oscillation between two paradigms: (1) *Person Constructs Reality* and (2) *Reality Constructs Person* (59). The metaphorical shift I have described constitutes a shift from the second to the first, in which *reality* means external, physical reality either impressing itself on the passive mental substance or being reconstituted within the individual by an active mind and its associated sentient processes. The mind-as-a-living-being metaphor, as I have shown, could at best share the field with mind-as-entity; paradigm (2) has remained somewhat plausible and at times quite useful. The result: a psychology for which no single metaphor can serve a theory-constitutive function. Or it may be that a study of the twentieth century's language*s* of the mind will reveal such a metaphor, perhaps even one that fulfills the autonomy thesis while maintaining contact with our everyday folk-psychological language.

WORKS CITED

Aarsleff, Hans. *The Study of Language in England, 1780-1860.* 2d ed. Minneapolis: University of Minnesota Press, 1983.

Abercrombie, John. *Inquiries concerning the Intellectual Powers, and the Investigation of Truth.* Ed. John Abbott. Boston: Otis, Broaders, and Co., 1841.

Adam, Ian, ed. *This Particular Web: Essays on Middlemarch.* Toronto: University of Toronto Press, 1975.

Allott, Miriam, ed. *The Brontës.* London: Routledge and Kegan Paul, 1974.

Alter, Robert. *Partial Magic: The Novel as a Self-Conscious Genre.* Berkeley: University of California Press, 1975.

Anderson, Howard. "Associationism and Wit in *Tristram Shandy.*" *Philological Quarterly* 48 (1969). Rpt. *Laurence Sterne*, ed. Gerd Rohmann, 96-112. Darmstadt: Wissenschaftliche Buchgesellschaft, 1980.

Armstrong, Paul B. *The Phenomenology of Henry James.* Chapel Hill: University of North Carolina Press, 1983.

Austen, Jane. *Emma.* 1816. 3d ed. London: Oxford University Press, 1966. Vol. 4 of *The Novels of Jane Austen.*

———. *Northanger Abbey.* 3d ed. London: Oxford University Press, 1965. Vol. 5 of *The Novels of Jane Austen.*

———. *Persuasion.* Harmondsworth: Penguin, 1965.

Bain, Alexander. *Mind and Body: The Theories of Their Relation.* New York: D. Appleton, 1875.

———. *Senses and the Intellect.* 1st ed. and 2d ed. London: Longman, 1855, 1864. 3d ed. 1868. New York: D. Appleton, 1887.

Beer, Gillian. "Myth and the Single Consciousness: *Middlemarch* and *The Lifted Veil.*" In Adam, 91-115.

Bergmann, Merrie. "Metaphor and Formal Semantic Theory." *Poetics* 8 (1979): 213-30.

Berkeley, George. *Treatise concerning the Principles of Human Knowledge*. 1710. Vol. 1 of *The Works of George Berkeley*. Ed. Alexander Campbell Fraser. Oxford: Clarendon, 1901.

Bickerton, Derek. "Prolegomena to a Linguistic Theory of Metaphor." *Foundations of Language* 5 (1969): 34-52.

Black, Max. *Models and Metaphors: Studies in Language and Philosophy*. Ithaca: Cornell University Press, 1962.

———. "More about Metaphor." In Ortony, *Metaphor and Thought*, 19-43.

Bodenheimer, Rosemarie. "Looking at the Landscape in Jane Austen." *Studies in English Literature* 21 (1981): 605-23.

Booth, Wayne. "Metaphor as Rhetoric: The Problem of Evaluation." *Critical Inquiry* 5 (1978): 49-72.

Boring, Edmund. *A History of Experimental Psychology*. 2d ed. New York: Appleton-Century-Crofts, 1950.

Boyd, Richard. "Metaphor and Theory Change: What Is 'Metaphor' a Metaphor For?" In Ortony, *Metaphor and Thought*, 356-408.

Brontë, Charlotte. *Jane Eyre*. 1847. Harmondsworth: Penguin, 1966.

———. *The Professor*. 1846. New York: Harper Brothers, 1900.

———. *Shirley*. 1849. Harmondsworth: Penguin, 1974.

———. *Villette*. 1853. Oxford: Clarendon Press, 1984.

Brown, Charles Brockden. *Wieland; or, The Transformation*. 1798. Ed. Fred Lewis Pattee. 1926; rpt. New York: Hafner, 1958.

Brown, Thomas. *Lectures on the Philosophy of the Human Mind*. 1820. Vol. 1. Hallowell: Glazier, Master, and Co., 1833.

———. *Sketch of a System of the Philosophy of the Human Mind*. Edinburgh: Bell et al., 1820.

Buss, Allan R. "The Structure of Psychological Revolutions." *Journal of the History of the Behavioral Sciences* 14 (1978): 57-64.

Caldwell, James R. *John Keats' Fancy: The Effect on Keats of the Psychology of His Day*. Ithaca: Cornell University Press, 1945.

Caplan, Ruth B. *Psychiatry and Community in Nineteenth-Century America. The Recurring Concern with the Environment in the Prevention and Treatment of Mental Illness*. New York: Basic Books, 1969.

Carpenter, William B. *Principles of Human Physiology*. 5th ed. Philadelphia: Blanchard and Lea, 1856.

———. *Principles of Mental Physiology*. 4th ed. 1876. New York: D. Appleton and Co., 1887.

Carroll, David. "*Middlemarch* and the Externality of Fact." In Adam, 73-90.

Chase, Karen. *Eros and Psyche: The Representation of Personality in Charlotte Brontë, Charles Dickens, and George Eliot*. New York: Methuen, 1984.

Churchland, Paul M. *Matter and Consciousness: A Contemporary Introduction to the Philosophy of Mind*. Cambridge: M.I.T. Press, 1984.

Cohen, Murray. *Sensible Words: Linguistic Practice in England 1640-1785*. Baltimore: Johns Hopkins University Press, 1977.

Colby, Robert. "*Villette* and the Life of the Mind." *PMLA* 75 (1960): 410-19.

Coleridge, Samuel Taylor. *Biographia Literaria*. Ed. James Engell and W. Jackson Bate. Vol. 1. Princeton: Princeton University Press, 1983.

Collins, K. K. "George Henry Lewes Revised: George Eliot and the Moral Sense." *Victorian Studies* 21 (1978): 463-92.

Crusius, Timothy, and W. Ross Winterowd. "The Apprehension of Metaphor." *Language and Style* 14 (1981): 20-33.

Cummins, Robert. *The Nature of Psychological Explanation*. Cambridge: M.I.T. Press, 1983.

Danziger, Kurt. "Mid-Nineteenth-Century British Psycho-Physiology: A Neglected Chapter in the History of Psychology." In Woodward and Ash, 119-46.

Daston, Lorraine J. "The Theory of Will vs the Science of Mind." In Woodward and Ash, 88-115.

Davidson, Arnold E. "Locke, Hume, and Hobby-Horses in *Tristram Shandy*." *International Fiction Review* 8 (1981): 17-21.

Davidson, Donald. "What Metaphors Mean." *Critical Inquiry* 5 (1978): 31-47.

Day, W. G. "Tristram Shandy: Locke May Not Be the Key." In *Laurence Sterne: Riddles and Mysteries*, ed. Valerie G. Myer, 75-83. London: Totowa, 1984. 75-83.

Defoe, Daniel. *The Fortunes and Misfortunes of the Famous Moll Flanders*. London: Dent, 1930.

Dickens, Charles. *Bleak House*. 1852-53. New York: Norton, 1977.

———. *David Copperfield*. 1849-50. Oxford: Clarendon Press, 1981.

———. *Dealings with the Firm of Dombey and Son*. 1846-48. Oxford: Clarendon Press, 1974.

———. *Oliver Twist*. 1838. Oxford: Clarendon Press, 1966.

———. *Our Mutual Friend*. 1864-65. Harmondsworth: Penguin, 1971.

Earle, William James. "James, William." *Encyclopedia of Philosophy*, 4:240-49. New York: Macmillan, 1967.

Edel, Leon. *Stuff of Sleep and Dreams: Experiments in Literary Psychology*. New York: Harper and Row, 1982.

Eliot, George. *Adam Bede*. 1859. Harmondsworth: Penguin, 1980.

———. *Daniel Deronda*. 1876. Oxford: Clarendon Press, 1984.

———. *Middlemarch*. 1871-72. New York: Norton, 1977.

———. *The Mill on the Floss*. 1860. Oxford: Clarendon Press, 1980.

———. "The Natural History of German Life." 1856. In *Essays of George Eliot*, ed. Thomas Pinney, 266-99. London: Routledge and Kegan Paul, 1963.

Emerson, Ralph Waldo. "The Over-Soul." *The Collected Works of Ralph Waldo Emerson*, ed. Alfred R. Ferguson, Jean Ferguson Carr, Joseph Slater, 2:159-75. Cambridge: Belknap Press, 1979.

Figlio, Karl M. "Theories of Perception and the Physiology of Mind in the Late Eighteenth Century." *History of Science* 12 (1975): 177-212.

Flanagan, Owen J. *The Science of the Mind*. Cambridge: M.I.T. Press, 1984.

Ford, George H. *Dickens and His Readers: Aspects of Novel Criticism since 1836*. Princeton: Princeton University Press, 1955.

Gilbert, Sandra. "Plain Jane's Progress." *Signs: Journal of Women in Culture and Society* 2 (1977): 779-804.

Godwin, William. *The Adventures of Caleb Williams*. 1798. London: Oxford University Press, 1970.

Goldfarb, Russell M. *Sexual Repression and Victorian Literature*. Lewisburg: Bucknell University Press, 1970.

Goodman, Kenneth. *Language and Literacy: The Selected Writings of Kenneth S. Goodman*. Vol. 1: Process, Theory, Research. Ed. Frederick V. Gollasch. London: Routledge and Kegan Paul, 1982.

Gose, Elliot B. *Imagination Indulged: The Irrational in the Nineteenth-Century Novel*. Montreal: McGill-Queen's University Press, 1972.

Grice, H. Paul. "Logic and Conversation." *Syntax and Semantics*. Vol. 3: Speech Acts, 41-58. Ed. Peter Cole and Jerry L. Morgan. New York: Academic Press, 1975.

Griffin, Susan M. "The Selfish Eye: Strether's Principles of Psychology." *American Literature* 56 (1984): 396-409.

Hamilton, Sir William. *The Philosophy of Sir William Hamilton*. Ed. O. W. Wight "for the use of schools and colleges." 5th ed. New York: D. Appleton, 1859.

Hart, Francis Russell. "The Experience of Character in the English Gothic Novel." In *Experience in the Novel: Selected Papers from the En-*

glish Institute, ed. Roy Harvey Pearce, 83-105. New York: Columbia University Press, 1968.

Hartley, David. *Observations on Man, His Frame, His Duty, and His Expectations*. 1749. New York: Garland, 1971.

Harvey, W. J. "Idea and Image in the Novels of George Eliot." In *Critical Essays on George Eliot*, ed. Barbara Hardy, 151-98. London: Routledge and Kegan Paul, 1970.

Haven, Joseph. *Mental Philosophy; Including the Intellect, Sensibilities and Will*. 1857. Boston: Gould and Lincoln, 1864.

Heath, Peter. "Reid on Conceiving and Imagining." *Monist* 61 (1978): 220-28.

Heilman, Robert B. "Charlotte Brontë, Reason, and the Moon." *Nineteenth-Century Fiction* 14 (1960): 283-302.

———. "Tulip-Hood, Streaks, and Other Strange Bedfellows: Style in *Villette*." *Studies in the Novel* 14 (1982): 223-47.

Hobbes, Thomas. *Leviathan*. 1651. Harmondsworth: Penguin, 1968.

Hocks, Richard A. *Henry James and Pragmatistic Thought: A Study in the Relationship between the Philosophy of William James and the Literary Art of Henry James*. Chapel Hill: University of North Carolina Press, 1974.

Holder-Barell, Alexander. *The Development of Imagery and its Functional Significance in Henry James's Novels*. Basel: Francke Verlag Bern, 1959.

Hook, Andrew, and Judith Hook. "Introduction." *Shirley*, Charlotte Brontë. Harmondsworth: Penguin, 1974.

Hume, David. *A Treatise of Human Nature*. 1739-40. Ed. L. A. Selby-Bigge, 1888. 2d ed. rev. P. H. Nidditch. Oxford: Clarendon, 1978.

Hume, Robert D. "Gothic versus Romantic: A Revaluation of the Gothic Novel." *PMLA* 84 (1969): 282-90.

Jack, Ian. "Phrenology, Physiognomy, and Characterisation in the Novels of Charlotte Brontë." *Brontë Society Transactions* 15 (no. 5, 1970): 377-91.

Jacyna, L. S. "The Physiology of Mind, the Unity of Nature, and the Moral Order in Victorian Thought." *The British Journal for the History of Science* 14 (1981): 109-32.

James, Henry. *The Ambassadors*. 1903. New York: Norton, 1964.

———. *The American*. 1877. New York: Norton, 1978.

———. "The Art of Fiction." In *Henry James: The Future of the Novel. Essays on the Art of Fiction*, ed. Leon Edel, 3-27. New York: Vintage, 1956.

———. *The Portrait of a Lady*. Rev. ed. 1908. New York: Norton, 1975.

James, William. "On Some Omissions of Introspective Psychology." *Mind* 9 (1884): 1-26.

———. *The Principles of Psychology*. 1890. Cambridge: Harvard University Press, 1983.

Johnson, Mark, ed. *Philosophical Perspectives on Metaphor*. Minneapolis: University of Minnesota Press, 1981.

Johnson, Stuart. "Prelinguistic Consciousness in James's 'Is There a Life after Death?'" *Criticism* 26 (1984): 245-57.

Kaminsky, Alice R. "George Eliot, George Henry Lewes, and the Novel." *PMLA* 70 (1955): 997-1013.

Kintsch, Walter, and Teun A. van Dijk. *Strategies of Discourse Comprehension*. New York: Academic Press, 1983.

Knies, Earl A. *The Art of Charlotte Brontë*. Athens: Ohio University Press, 1969.

Korg, Jacob. "How George Eliot's People Think." In *George Eliot: A Centenary Tribute*, ed. Gordon S. Haight and Rosemary T. Van Arsdel, 82-89. London: Macmillan, 1982.

Kuhn, Thomas. *The Structure of Scientific Revolutions*. 2d ed. Chicago: University of Chicago Press, 1970.

Lakoff, George, and Mark Johnson. *Metaphors We Live By*. Chicago: University of Chicago Press, 1980.

Langbaum, Robert. *The Mysteries of Identity. A Theme in Modern Literature*. New York: Oxford University Press, 1977.

Leary, David. "Wundt and After: Psychology's Shifting Relations with the Natural Sciences, Social Sciences, and Philosophy." *Journal of the History of the Behavioral Sciences* 15 (1979): 231-41.

Levine, George. "Determinism and Responsibility in George Eliot." *PMLA* 77 (1962): 268-79. Rpt. in *A Century of George Eliot Criticism*, ed. Gordon S. Haight, 349-60. Boston: Houghton Mifflin, 1965.

Lewes, George Henry. "Mind as a Function of the Organism." In *Problems of Life and Mind*, 3d series, problem 2, 3-220. Boston: Houghton, Osgood, and Co. 1880.

———. *The Study of Psychology. Its Object, Scope, and Method*. In *Problems of Life and Mind*, 3d series, problem 1. Boston: Houghton, Osgood, and Co. 1879.

Locke, John. *An Essay concerning Human Understanding*. 4th ed. 1700. Ed. Peter H. Nidditch. Oxford: Clarendon Press, 1975.

Loewenberg, Ina. "Identifying Metaphors." In Johnson, *Philosophical Perspectives*, 154-81.

Loverso, Marco P. "Self-Knowledge and the Lockean 'Self' in the Sermons of Mr. Yorick: A Link with the Shandean World." *English Studies in Canada* 8 (1982): 138-53.

Lowry, Richard. *The Evolution of Psychological Theory, 1650 to the Present.* Chicago: Aldine Atherton, 1971.

Lyon, Judson S. "Romantic Psychology and the Inner Senses: Coleridge." *PMLA* 81 (1966): 246-60.

Mack, Dorothy. "Metaphoring as Speech Act: Some Happiness Conditions for Implicit Similes and Simple Metaphors." *Poetics* 4 (1975): 221-56.

MacLean, Kenneth. *John Locke and English Literature of the Eighteenth Century*. New Haven: Yale University Press, 1936.

Martin, Robert B. *The Accents of Persuasion: Charlotte Brontë's Novels*. New York: Norton, 1966.

Mason, Michael York. "*Middlemarch* and Science: Problems of Life and Mind." *Review of English Studies* 22 (1971): 151-69.

Masson, David. "Dickens and Thackeray." 1859. In *The Dickens Critics*, ed. George H. Ford and Lauriat Lane, 25-37. Ithaca: Cornell University Press, 1961.

Miall, David S. "Introduction." In Miall, xi-xix.

———, ed. *Metaphor: Problems and Perspectives*. Sussex: Harvester Press, 1982.

Mill, John Stuart. *A System of Logic, Ratiocinative and Inductive*. 1st ed. New York: Harper and Brothers, 1846. 3d ed. Vol. 1. London: Longmans, Green, Reader, and Dyer, 1872.

Miller, J. Hillis. "Three Problems of Fictional Form." In *Experience in the Novel: Selected Papers from the English Institute*, ed. Roy Harvey Pearce, 21-48. New York: Columbia University Press, 1968.

———. *Charles Dickens: The World of His Novels*. Cambridge: Harvard University Press, 1958.

Moglen, Helene. *The Philosophical Irony of Laurence Sterne*. Gainesville: University Presses of Florida, 1975.

Morell, John D. *Elements of Psychology*. London: William Pickering, 1853.

Morris, Charles W. *Six Theories of Mind*. Chicago: University of Chicago Press, 1932.

Nash, Harvey. "The Role of Metaphor in Psychological Theory." *Behavioral Science* 8 (1963): 336-45.

Ortony, Andrew, ed. *Metaphor and Thought*. Cambridge: Cambridge University Press, 1979.

———. "Some Psycholinguistic Aspects of Metaphor." In *Cognition and Figurative Language*, ed. Richard P. Honeck and Robert R. Hoffman, 72-84. Hillsdale: Lawrence Erlbaum, 1980.

Pepper, Stephen. *World Hypotheses: A Study in Evidence*. Berkeley: University of California Press, 1942.

Peters, R. S., ed. *Brett's History of Psychology*. 2d ed. Cambridge: M.I.T. Press, 1965. (An abridgement of Brett's *History of Psychology*, 3 vols., 1912-21.)

Poe, Edgar Allen. *The Narrative of Arthur Gordon Pym*. 1838. New York: Hill and Wang, 1960.

Putzell-Korab, Sara M. *The Evolving Consciousness: An Hegelian Reading of the Novels of George Eliot*. Salzburg: Institut für Anglistik und Amerikanistik, 1982.

Ray, Isaac. *Mental Hygiene*. 1863. In *Delicate Branch: The Vision of Moral Psychiatry*, ed. John C. Shershow, 116-48. Oceanside, New York: Dabor Science, 1977.

Reed, Sampson. *Observations on the Growth of the Mind with Remarks on Some Other Subjects*. 3d ed., 1838. Gainesville, Fla.: Scholars' Facsimiles, 1970.

Rees, Abraham, et al. "Philosophy, Mental, or the Philosophy of the Human Mind." *The Cyclopaedia; or, Universal Dictionary of Arts, Sciences, and Literature*. Vol. 27. London: Longman, 1819.

Reid, Thomas. *Essays on the Intellectual Powers of Man*. 1785. Cambridge: M.I.T. Press, 1969.

———. *An Inquiry into the Human Mind*. 1764. Chicago: University of Chicago Press, 1970.

Reinhart, Tanya. "On Understanding Poetic Metaphor." *Poetics* 5 (1976): 383-402.

Richards, I. A. *Coleridge on Imagination*. New York: Harcourt, Brace and Co., 1935.

———. *The Philosophy of Rhetoric*. New York: Oxford University Press, 1936.

Richardson, Samuel. *Pamela; Or, Virtue Rewarded*. 1740. Boston: Houghton Mifflin, 1971.

Richmond, Hugh M. "Personal Identity and Literary Personae: A Study in Literary Psychology." *PMLA* 90 (1975): 209-25.

Robinson, Daniel N. *An Intellectual History of Psychology*. New York: Macmillan, 1976.

———. *The Mind Unfolded: Essays on Psychology's Historic Texts*. Washington, D.C.: University Publications of America, 1978.

Romano, John. *Dickens and Reality*. New York: Columbia University Press, 1978.

Ryan, Judith. "The Vanishing Subject: Empirical Psychology and the Modern Novel." *PMLA* 95 (1980): 857-69.

Ryle, Gilbert. *The Concept of Mind*. New York: Barnes and Noble, 1949.

Schön, Donald A. "Generative Metaphor: A Perspective on Problem-Setting in Social Policy." In Ortony, *Metaphor and Thought*, 254-83.

Scull, Andrew. *Museums of Madness: The Social Organization of Insanity in Nineteenth-Century England*. London: Allen Lane, 1979.

Searle, John. "Metaphor." In Johnson, *Philosophical Perspectives*, 248-85.

See, Fred G. "Henry James and the Art of Possession." In *American Realism: New Essays*, ed. Eric J. Sundquist, 119-37. Baltimore: Johns Hopkins University Press, 1982.

Senseman, Wilfred M. "Charlotte Brontë's Use of Physiognomy and Phrenology." *Papers of the Michigan Academy of Science, Arts, and Letters* 38 (1952): 475-86.

Shuttleworth, Sally. "The Language of Science and Psychology in George Eliot's *Daniel Deronda*." *Victorian Science and Victorian Values*. Vol. 360 of the New York Academy of Sciences, 269-98. Ed. James Paradis and Thomas Postlewait. New York: New York Academy of Sciences, 1981. 269-98.

Smith, Michael K., Howard R. Pollio, and Marian K. Pitts. "Metaphor as Intellectual History: Conceptual Categories underlying Figurative Usage in American English from 1675-1975." *Linguistics* 19 (1981): 911-35.

Soskice, Janet M. *Metaphor and Religious Language*. London: Oxford University Press, 1985.

Spencer, Herbert. "The Physiology of Laughter." 1860. Vol. 14 of *The Works of Herbert Spencer*, 452-66. Osnabrück: Otto Zeller, 1966.

———. *The Principles of Psychology*. 1st ed. London: Longman and Company, 1855. 2d ed. 2 vols. New York: D. Appleton and Co., 1873.

Sterne, Laurence. *The Life and Opinions of Tristram Shandy, Gentleman*. 1759-67. Harmondsworth: Penguin, 1967.

Stewart, Dugald. *Elements of the Philosophy of the Human Mind*. Vols. 2-4 of *The Collected Works*. Ed. Sir William Hamilton. Edinburgh: Thomas Constable, 1854.

———. "On the Sublime." *Philosophical Essays*, 3d ed. Edinburgh: Archibald Constable, 1818.

Swearingen, James E. *Reflexivity in Tristram Shandy: An Essay in Phenomenological Criticism*. New Haven: Yale University Press, 1977.

Timko, Michael. "The Victorianism of Victorian Literature." *New Literary History* 6 (1975): 607-27.

Tourangeau, Roger. "Metaphor and Cognitive Structure." In Miall, 14-35.

Tuveson, Ernest. *The Imagination as a Means of Grace: Locke and the Aesthetics of Romanticism*. 1960. New York: Gordian Press, 1974.

———. "Locke and Sterne." In *Reason and the Imagination: Studies in the History of Ideas 1600-1800*, ed. J. A. Mazzeo, 255-77. New York: Columbia University Press, 1962.

Upham, Thomas C. *Elements of Intellectual Philosophy, Designed as a Text-Book*. 2d ed. Portland: Shirley and Hyde, 1828.

———. *Elements of Mental Philosophy, Abridged and Designed as a Text-Book for Academies and High Schools*. New York: Harper and Brothers, 1854.

Van Ghent, Dorothy. *The English Novel: Form and Function*. 1953. New York: Harper, 1961.

Veeder, William. "Image as Argument: Henry James and the Style of Criticism." M/MLA Seminar on Henry James, St. Louis, November 1985.

Watt, Ian. *The Rise of the Novel: Studies in Defoe, Richardson, and Fielding*. Berkeley: University of California Press, 1957.

Williams, Raymond. *Keywords: A Vocabulary of Culture and Society*. New York: Oxford University Press, 1976.

Wimsatt, William. *Philosophic Words: A Study of Style and Meaning in the Rambler and Dictionary of Samuel Johnson*. 1948. Hamden, Conn.: Archon Books, 1968.

Woodward, William R., and Mitchell G. Ash, eds. *The Problematic Science: Psychology in Nineteenth-Century Thought*. New York: Praeger Publishers, 1982.

Wordsworth, William. "Expostulation and Reply." In *Wordsworth: Poetical Works*, ed. Ernest de Selincourt, 377. London: Oxford University Press, 1966.

Yeazell, Ruth Bernard. *Language and Knowledge in the Late Novels of Henry James*. Chicago: University of Chicago Press, 1976.

Young, Robert M. "The Functions of the Brain: Gall to Ferrier." *Isis* 59 (1968): 251-68.

———. *Mind, Brain, and Adaptation in the Nineteenth Century: Cerebral*

Localization and Its Biological Context from Gall to Ferrier. Oxford: Clarendon Press, 1970.

———. "Psychology in Nineteenth-Century Evolutionary Debate." In *Historical Conceptions of Psychology*, ed. Mary Henle, Julian Jaynes, and John J. Sullivan, 180-204. New York: Springer, 1973.

INDEX